D0384267

Praise for

The Paradox of Choice

"*The Paradox of Choice* has a simple yet profoundly life-altering message for all Americans. Schwartz's eleven practical, simple steps to becoming less choosey will change much in your daily life. . . . Buy This Book Now!"

—PHILIP G. ZIMBARDO,
author of *Shyness: What It Is, What to Do About It*

"In this revolutionary and beautifully reasoned book, Barry Schwartz shows that there is vastly too much choice in the modern world. This promiscuous amount of choice renders the consumer helpless and dissatisfied. *The Paradox of Choice* is a *must* read for every thoughtful person."

—MARTIN E. P. SELIGMAN,
author of *Learned Optimism and Authentic Happiness*

"Today's world offers us more choices but, ironically, less satisfaction. This provocative and riveting book shows us steps we can take toward a more rewarding life."

—DAVID G. MYERS,
author of *Intuition: Its Powers and Perils*

"This book is valuable in two ways. It argues persuasively that most of us would often be better off with fewer options and that many of us try too hard to make the best choices. While making its case, the book also provides an engaging introduction to current psychological research on choice and on well-being."

—DANIEL KAHNEMAN,
2002 Nobel laureate in economic sciences,
Eugene Higgins Professor of Psychology and
Professor of Public Affairs at the Woodrow Wilson School
of Public and International Affairs, Princeton University

"Brilliant. . . . The case Schwartz makes for a correlation between our emotional state and what he calls the 'tyranny of choice' is compelling, the implications disturbing. . . . An insightful book."

—*Christian Science Monitor*

"Schwartz lays out a convincing argument. . . . [He] is a crisp, engaging writer with an excellent sense of pace."

—*Austin American-Statesman*

"Schwartz chronicles well how our choices have expanded, how our demands for perfection have increased and how we suffer as a result—from regret, missed opportunities and feelings of inadequacy. . . . Schwartz offers helpful suggestions of how we can manage our world of overwhelming choices."

—*St. Petersburg Times*

"*The Paradox of Choice* is genuine and useful. The book is well-reasoned and solidly researched."

—*New York Observer*

"Schwartz has clearly put his finger on a national mood."

—*The Christian Century*

"An insightful study that winningly argues its subtitle."

—*Philadelphia Inquirer*

"Schwartz has plenty of insightful things to say about the perils of everyday life."

—*Booklist*

"*The Paradox of Choice* is this year's 'must read' book."

—*Guardian* (London)

"With its clever analysis, buttressed by sage *New Yorker* cartoons, *The Paradox of Choice* is persuasive."

—*BusinessWeek*

The Paradox of Choice

Also by Barry Schwartz

The Battle for Human Nature:
Science, Morality, and Modern Life

The Costs of Living: How Market
Freedom Erodes the Best Things in Life

Psychology of Learning and Behavior

Behaviorism, Science,
and Human Nature

Learning and Memory

Practical Wisdom:
The Right Way to Do the Right Thing

Why We Work

The Paradox of Choice

Why More Is Less, Revised Edition

Barry Schwartz

An Imprint of HarperCollins Publishers

THE PARADOX OF CHOICE: WHY MORE IS LESS, REVISED EDITION.
Copyright © 2004, 2016 by Barry Schwartz. All rights reserved. Printed in the
United States of America. No part of this book may be used or reproduced in
any manner whatsoever without written permission except in the case of brief
quotations embodied in critical articles and reviews. For information address
HarperCollins Publishers Inc., 195 Broadway, New York, NY 10007.

HarperCollins books may be purchased for educational, business,
or sales promotional use. For information please e-mail the Special
Markets Department at SPsales@harpercollins.com.

FIRST EDITION

Library of Congress Cataloging-in-Publication Data has been applied for.

ISBN 978-0-06-244992-4

16 17 18 19 20   DIX/RRD   10 9 8 7 6 5 4 3 2 1

For Myrna, the best choice I ever made

Contents

Preface to the Second Edition
Barry Schwartz

A MERICANS SHARE A SET OF BELIEFS SO DEEPLY EMBEDDED IN OUR worldview that we may not realize we live by them. These beliefs take the form of a kind of syllogism:

The more freedom people have, the more well-being they will have.

The more choice people have, the more freedom they have.

Therefore, the more choice people have, the more well-being they have.

It is hard to quarrel with any of these statements. For most Americans, freedom is the highest good. The more freedom people have, the better off they are, and the better our society is. When the government tries to step in to restrict our freedom—by forcing us to wear seatbelts, or have health insurance—it has to work hard to justify these impositions.

If we are committed to enhancing freedom, how do we go about doing so? Freedom without choice is completely hollow. Giving citizens the freedom to watch TV whenever they want, but restricting viewing options to a single TV station, does not offer viewers much freedom at all. So the way to enhance freedom is to increase choice. Virtually any economist will tell you that adding options will make some people better off while making no one worse off. If you're happy alternating between cornflakes and oatmeal, you can ignore the dozens of other cereals on the shelves. If you're happy with ESPN and CNN, you can ignore the hundreds of other TV channels that are available. More options won't hurt you. But if you're not happy with cornflakes and oatmeal, you can choose from a range of other cereals. Thus, the conclusion of our syllogism: the more choice people have, the more well-being they will have. As the argument goes, allowing parents to choose where they send their children to school will not impinge on the well-being of parents who are happy with the standard public schools, but it will improve the lives of those who find the standard public schools lacking.

If you accept this syllogism about freedom, choice, and well-being, you can see the appeal of organizing life around a set of competitive markets—not just for cereal or television, but also for health insurance, education, and prescription drug plans. Rather than allowing governments to dictate our choices, the logic goes, we should let providers of goods and services compete against each other and allow citizens to choose among those competitors. The winners of the competition will be winners precisely *because* they are giving us what we want.

For many years, starting in the 1970s, I worried about society's enthusiastic embrace of the free market as the magic bullet that will enable people to get exactly what they want in life. I didn't believe the assumptions economists made about how people make decisions. The main virtue of the market, from my point of view, is that it caters to individual freedom of choice. But people are not perfect "rational choosers," as the economists assume. We all make bad decisions. at least some of the time. Moreover, I didn't think the most vital choices—such as where to send children to school, where to work, how to seek and pay for medical care, and how to participate in civic life, to name a few—are best addressed by markets. In some cases, markets should be restrained, not encouraged. The market has its place, but that place isn't every place.

In 1994, I wrote a book that made these arguments called *The Costs of Living: How Market Freedom Erodes the Best Things in Life.* It was in the course of writing the book that I started thinking seriously about the advantages and disadvantages presented by unlimited freedom of choice. There were a handful of philosophers who had seriously considered the possibility that, even though freedom of choice was good, there could be too much of a good thing. These voices were isolated, however, and most social scientists, policy makers, and ordinary citizens embraced the syllogism I mentioned above.

Then, in 1999, psychologists Sheena Iyengar and Mark Lepper published an article that changed my life. The article, which I discuss in detail in this book, reported three studies, each of which showed that presenting people with a wide array of options doesn't liberate them: it paralyzes them. If people overcome this paralysis and choose from the large set of options, they are less satisfied with their choice than they would have been if their options had been more limited. Around the same time the Iyengar and Lepper article was published, I was asked to write an article for a distinguished psychology journal on the value of individual autonomy, and I returned to my research on freedom and choice as it relates to autonomy. In the article, I suggested that it might not be true that, when presented with more options and thus more autonomy, people will be more satisfied with their choices. Shortly after writing the article, I went shopping for jeans. I hadn't bought jeans in a while and I was astonished by the number of options that faced me. With all this choice, I managed to find the best-fitting pair of jeans

I had ever owned. And yet, I felt dissatisfied. *The Paradox of Choice* started there.

Since *The Paradox of Choice* was published in 2005, I have had many opportunities to discuss the book. I've given perhaps a hundred lectures, I've participated in many radio and television interviews, and I've spoken with even more print journalists. I gave a talk at the annual TED conference that has now been viewed by about 8 million people. Reactions from audiences have been gratifyingly positive. Again and again, people tell me that I've put my finger on the source of some of their own difficulties, and many have their own version of my "shopping for jeans" experience.

Since then, I've also conducted some of my own research. With my colleagues Andrew Ward, Sonja Lyubomirsky, John Monterosso, Katherine White, and Darrin Lehman, I explored the possibility that large choice sets might not pose the same problem for everyone. If you are out to find the best—whether it's a TV show, a type of cereal, a home, a car, a job, or a romantic partner—then large choice sets pose a major problem, because the only way to know you have the best is by examining all the options. In contrast, if you are out to find something that is "good enough," large choice sets are less of a problem. Indeed, they may not be a problem at all. People looking for things that are "good enough" stop searching as soon as they find them. With my colleagues, I developed a scale, called the Maximizing Scale, which distinguishes these people from those who generally want the best. We found that people do differ in their aspirations when it comes to making choices: people who are out for the best—maximizers—have more trouble choosing and are less satisfied with their choices and with their lives in general, than people who are out for good enough—the people we call "satisficers." The distinction between maximizing and satisficing and the scale used to measure it are discussed in Chapter 4.

In 2005, I concluded that choice is not an unmitigated good, and that having very high standards can make the choice problem worse. In the decade or so since the book came out, there has been a good deal of research on both of these points. The research has convinced me that, while a surfeit of choices does pose legitimate problems, those problems do not present themselves to all people in all situations. Sometimes, for some people, the syllogism seems to be true: more choice is better than less choice. Whereas the distinction between maximizing and satisficing is also legitimate when examined against recent research, we do not yet fully understand the psychological dimensions that these two ideas encompass.

In this new edition of *The Paradox of Choice*, I have changed as little as possible. The structure of the book is the same as in the previous edition, as are the arguments I make in it about the costs and benefits of choice. I have updated some discussions to include research that was done after the book was published, and I have added references to even more recent research in the Notes at the end of the book. For the most part, however, for someone who has already read the book, the new edition will feel much more like rereading something familiar than encountering something new. Even with much more evidence in hand, the arguments I made in 2005 stand.

I do want to make it clear that while too much choice can present problems, these are very much problems for the affluent. It is pretty much true that the more money you have, the more options you have. In the U.S., wealth is a reliable proxy for freedom of choice. If you don't have any discretionary income, it really doesn't matter how many options are available because they are not available to you. This is also true of choices that don't involve money. If you work to near-exhaustion every day just to make ends meet, for example, you don't have the time or energy to make many lifestyle improvement decisions. Though the problems I write about in this book are legitimate, the majority of people in the world would happily replace their current problems with the problem of choice. I recognize that most people in the world have too little freedom and too little choice, and readers should note that, instead of grappling with this disparity, this book illustrates how attempts to introduce more choice into our lives might bring problems of their own.

Would we be better off if most decisions were made for us? No. Though I am suggesting that we would be better off if *some* decisions were made for us—it should be up to us to decide which ones. We have to "choose when to choose," as I put it in the book, and choose when to put ourselves in the hands of other people who care about our well-being and have the expertise to make good decisions on our behalf.

For example, consider a study Sheena Iyengar conducted with some colleagues. She measured the rate of participation in the voluntary 401(k) plans of more than 750,000 employees at almost one thousand companies. What she found was that, for every ten additional mutual funds offered by the employer, the rate of participation went *down* 2%. At many of these companies, by choosing not to participate, employees were not only creating serious repercussions for their retirement, they were also passing up employer-matching funds, which in some cases exceeded $5,000. I have no doubt that employers thought they were doing employees a favor by offering them so many different options. But they weren't. Most of the employees would have been better off with just a few, expertly selected, retirement funds from which to choose than they were with ten, or twenty, or even a hundred.

If you find the arguments in my book convincing, then you're faced with another question: how do we decide when and how to limit options? How do we decide which options to eliminate? For the most part, given the society we live in, it is up to us as individuals to decide when, where, and how to simplify our lives and reduce the options we face. As a society, we should be skeptical of policies that promise to improve our lives simply by giving us more options. We *may* be better off being able to choose where we invest our retirement money, where we send our kids to school, which health insurance or prescription drug plan we sign up for, and so on. But we may also be worse off with all these choices: we may lack the expertise to make them wisely, we make lack the time to develop that expertise, and we may already be so overburdened with decisions that adding more will render us unable to make any.

If you limit the number of choices you make and the number of options you consider, you're going to have more time available for what's important than do people who are plagued by one decision after another, always in search of the best. You could use that time wisely by spending more time with your children, your parents, your friends, your patients, your clients, your students. The real challenges in life are social. How do we properly balance honesty with kindness, courage with caution, encouragement with criticism, empathy with detachment, paternalism with respect for autonomy? We have to figure this balance out case by case, person by person, and the only way to do so is by developing our relationships with the people who matter to us most—by taking the time to listen to them, to imagine life through their eyes, and to allow ourselves to be changed, and even transformed, by them. In a hurried world that forces us to make decision after decision, each involving almost unlimited options, it's hard to find that time. Our effort to get the best car might interfere with our desire to be a good friend. Our effort to get the best job might intrude on our duty to be the best parent. If the time you save by following some of my suggestions in this book is redirected to improving your relationships with the important people in your life, you will not only increase your well-being, you will increase theirs as well. This would be a change that economists call "Pareto efficient"—a change that benefits everybody.

Acknowledgments

■

THE IDEAS IN THIS BOOK BEGAN TO DEVELOP WHEN I WAS INVITED BY Marty Seligman to contribute an article on "self-determination" to a special issue of the journal *American Psychologist*. It seemed obvious and undeniable that people prized and valued the opportunity to be self-determining. Yet, all was not right with freedom, autonomy, and self-determination; they did not seem to be unalloyed blessings. This book is my effort to explore and explain this "darker side" of freedom.

My thinking about this topic was clarified and advanced a great deal by an empirical research project (supported in part by funds from the Positive Psychology Network and Swarthmore College) I conducted in collaboration with colleagues Andrew Ward, John Monterosso, Darrin Lehman, Sonja Lyubomirsky, and Katherine White. I am deeply grateful to these colleagues (especially Ward, whose office is next door to mine and who thus must put up with almost daily discussions) for the role they played in the research and for the many illuminating conversations we had in the course of completing the project. Their insights are reflected throughout the book. I have also learned much from collaborators on related empirical projects: Dov Cohen, Jane Gillham, Jamin Halberstadt, Tim Kasser, Mary Frances Luce, and Ken Sheldon.

In the course of presenting some of my ideas at meetings and conferences, I have also learned much from conversations with many, especially Jon Haidt, Dacher Keltner, Jonathan Schooler, and Susan Sugarman.

On the book itself, Judy Dogin and Beth Gross read early drafts that were much longer, and much less fun to read, than this one. Thanks to them, the rest of the world's burden is eased. Rebecca Schwartz, Allison Dworkin, and Ted Dworkin forced me to confront the fact that many of the issues I write about look different to my children's generation than they do to mine. Though they may not agree with *all* of the final product, Becca, Allie, and Ted helped to shape it by changing my thinking and writing about several things. My editor at Ecco Press, Julia Serebrinsky, helped show me how to tame the manuscript. She also identified parts of the exposition that weren't as clear as I thought they were. And Bill Patrick did an extraordinary job of helping me improve both the organization of the book and the writing.

There would have been no book without the help of my agent, Tina Bennett. Aside from doing beautifully the kinds of businesslike things that agents do, Tina worked with me through several drafts of a proposal, in the course of which she helped shape the book into its final form. I am extraordinarily fortunate to have an agent who is at the same time a smart, wise, and sympathetic editor. Only Tina got to see the worst of my ideas.

Finally, I owe special thanks to my best editor, and best friend, Myrna Schwartz. Her convictions about the value and importance of the ideas in this book have been unflagging. By being simultaneously my most sympathetic and most demanding reader, Myrna has read insightfully through several drafts of the book, each time pointing out to me serious problems that needed to be fixed, but doing so with such love and enthusiasm that I was able to drag myself back to the keyboard to make another stab. Myrna has played this role on each of my major projects, and what I've learned, over more than three decades, is that she's almost always right. Sometimes, satisficers like me get lucky.

The Paradox of Choice

The Paradox of Choice: A Road Map

ABOUT TWENTY YEARS AGO, I WENT TO THE GAP TO BUY A PAIR OF jeans. I tend to wear my jeans until they're falling apart, so it had been quite a while since my last purchase. A nice young salesperson walked up to me and asked if she could help.

"I want a pair of jeans—32–28," I said.

"Do you want them slim fit, easy fit, relaxed fit, baggy, or extra baggy?" she replied. "Do you want them stonewashed, acid-washed, or distressed? Do you want them button-fly or zipper-fly? Do you want them faded or regular?"

I was stunned. A moment or two later I sputtered out something like, "I just want regular jeans. You know, the kind that used to be the only kind." It turned out she didn't know, but after consulting one of her older colleagues, she was able to figure out what "regular" jeans used to be, and she pointed me in the right direction.

The trouble was that with all these options available to me now, I was no longer sure that "regular" jeans were what I wanted. Perhaps the easy fit or the relaxed fit would be more comfortable. Having already demonstrated how out of touch I was with modern fashion, I persisted. I went back to her and asked what difference there was between regular jeans, relaxed fit, and easy fit. She referred me to a diagram that showed how the different cuts varied. It didn't help narrow the choice, so I decided to try them all. With a pair of jeans of each type under my arm, I entered the dressing room. I tried on all the pants and scrutinized myself in a mirror. I asked once again for further clarification. Whereas very little was riding on my decision, I was now convinced that one of these options had to be right for me, and I was determined to figure it out. But I couldn't. Finally, I chose the easy fit, because "relaxed fit" implied that I was getting soft in the middle and needed to cover it up.

The jeans I chose turned out just fine, but it occurred to me that day that buying a pair of pants should not be a daylong project. By creating all these options, the store undoubtedly had done a favor for customers with varied tastes and body types. However, by vastly expanding the range of choices, they had also created a new problem that needed to be solved. Before these options were available, a buyer like myself had to settle for an imperfect fit, but at least purchasing jeans was a five-minute affair. Now it was a complex decision in which I was forced to invest time, energy, and no small amount of self-doubt, anxiety, and dread.

Buying jeans is a trivial matter, but it suggests a much larger theme we will pursue throughout this book, which is this: When people have no choice, life is almost unbearable. As the number of available choices increases, as it has in our consumer culture, the autonomy, control, and liberation this variety brings are powerful and positive. But as the number of choices keeps growing, negative aspects of having a multitude of options begin to appear. As the number of choices grows further, the negatives escalate until we become overloaded. At this point, choice no longer liberates, but debilitates. It might even be said to tyrannize.

Tyrannize?

That's a dramatic claim, especially following an example about buying jeans. But our subject is by no means limited to how we go about selecting consumer goods.

This book is about the choices Americans face in almost all areas of life: education, career, friendship, sex, romance, parenting, religious observance. There is no denying that choice improves the quality of our lives. It enables us to control our destinies and to come close to getting exactly what we want out of any situation. Choice is essential to autonomy, which is absolutely fundamental to well-being. Healthy people want and need to direct their own lives.

On the other hand, the fact that *some* choice is good doesn't necessarily mean that *more* choice is better. As I will demonstrate, there is a cost to having an overload of choice. As a culture, we are enamored of freedom, self-determination, and variety, and we are reluctant to give up any of our options. But clinging tenaciously to all the choices available to us contributes to bad decisions, to anxiety, stress, and dissatisfaction—even to clinical depression.

Many years ago, the distinguished political philosopher Isaiah Berlin made an important distinction between "negative liberty" and "positive liberty." Negative liberty is "freedom from"—freedom from constraint, freedom from being told what to do by others. Positive liberty is "freedom to"—the availability of opportunities to be the author of your life and to make it meaningful and significant. Often, these two kinds of liberty will go together. If the constraints people want "freedom from" are rigid enough, they won't be able to attain "freedom to." But these two types of liberty need not always go together.

Nobel Prize–winning economist and philosopher Amartya Sen has also examined the nature and importance of freedom and autonomy and the conditions that promote it. In his book *Development as Freedom* he distinguishes the importance of choice, in and of itself, from the functional role it plays in our lives. He suggests that instead of being fetishistic about freedom of choice, we should ask ourselves whether it nourishes us or deprives us, whether it makes us mobile or hems us in, whether it enhances self-respect or diminishes it, and whether it enables us to participate in our communities or prevents us from doing so. Freedom is essential to self-respect, public participation, mobility, and nourishment, but not all choice enhances freedom. In particular, increased choice among goods and services may contribute little or nothing to the kind of freedom that counts. Indeed, it may impair freedom by taking time and energy we'd be better off devoting to other matters.

I believe that many modern Americans are feeling less and less satisfied even as their freedom of choice expands. This book is intended to explain why this is so and suggest what can be done about it.

Which is no small matter. The United States was founded on a commitment to individual freedom and autonomy, with freedom of choice as a core value. And yet it is my contention that we do ourselves no favor when we equate liberty too directly with choice, as if we necessarily increase freedom by increasing the number of options available.

Instead, I believe that we make the most of our freedoms by learning to make good choices about the things that matter, while at the same time unburdening ourselves from too much concern about the things that don't.

Following that thread, Part I discusses how the range of choices people face every day has increased in recent years. Part II discusses how we choose and shows how difficult and demanding it is to make wise choices. Choosing well is especially difficult for those determined to make only the best choices, individuals I refer to as "maximizers." Part III is about how and why choice can make us suffer. It asks whether increased opportunities for choice actually make people happier, and concludes that often they do not. It also identifies several psychological processes that explain why added options do not make people better off: adaptation, regret, missed opportunities, raised expectations, and feelings of inadequacy in comparison with others. It concludes with the suggestion that increased choice may actually contribute to the recent epidemic of clinical depression affecting much of the Western world. Finally, in Part IV, I offer a series of recommendations for taking advantage of what is positive, and avoiding what is negative, in our modern freedom of choice.

Throughout the book, you will learn about a wide range of research findings from psychologists, economists, market researchers, and decision scientists, all related to choice and decision making. There are important lessons to be learned from this research, some of them not so obvious, and others even counterintuitive. For example, I will argue that:

1. We would be better off if we embraced certain voluntary constraints on our freedom of choice, instead of rebelling against them.
2. We would be better off seeking what was "good enough" instead of seeking the best (have you ever heard a parent say, "I want only the 'good enough' for my kids"?).
3. We would be better off if we lowered our expectations about the results of decisions.
4. We would be better off if the decisions we made were nonreversible.
5. We would be better off if we paid less attention to what others around us were doing.

These conclusions fly in the face of the conventional wisdom that the more choices people have, the better off they are, that the

"Oh, Richard, the possibilities!"

A WORLD OF UNLIMITED CHOICE

© *The New Yorker Collection 2000 Jack Zeigler from cartoonbank.com. All Rights Reserved.*

best way to get good results is to have very high standards, and that it's always better to have a way to back out of a decision than not. What I hope to show is that the conventional wisdom is wrong, at least when it comes to what satisfies us in the decisions we make.

As I mentioned, we will examine choice overload as it affects a number of areas in human experience that are far from trivial. But to build the case for what I mean by "overload," we will start at the bottom of the hierarchy of needs and work our way up. We'll begin by doing some more shopping.

When We Choose

Part I

CHAPTER ONE

Let's Go Shopping

A Day at the Supermarket

A S I WAS PREPARING TO WRITE THE FIRST EDITION OF THIS BOOK, about a dozen years ago, I took a trip to the local supermarket. Scanning the shelves I found 85 different varieties and brands of crackers. As I read the packages, I discovered that some brands had sodium, others didn't. Some were fat-free, others weren't. They came in big boxes and small ones. They came in normal size and bite size. There were mundane saltines and exotic and expensive imports.

My neighborhood supermarket is not a particularly large store, and yet next to the crackers were 285 varieties of cookies. Among chocolate chip cookies, there were 21 options. Among Goldfish (I don't know whether to count them as cookies or crackers), there were 20 different varieties to choose from.

Across the aisle were juices—13 "sports drinks," 65 "box drinks" for kids, 85 other flavors and brands of juices, and 75 iced teas and adult drinks. I could get these tea drinks sweetened (sugar or artificial sweetener), lemoned, and flavored.

Next, in the snack aisle, there were 95 options in all—chips (taco and potato, ridged and flat, flavored and unflavored, salted and unsalted, high fat, low fat, no fat), pretzels, and the like, including a dozen varieties of Pringles. Nearby was seltzer, no doubt to wash down the snacks. Bottled water was displayed in at least 15 flavors.

In the pharmaceutical aisles, I found 61 varieties of suntan oil and sunblock, and 80 different pain relievers—aspirin, acetaminophen, ibuprofen; 350 milligrams or 500 milligrams; caplets, capsules, and tablets; coated or uncoated. There were 40 options for toothpaste, 150 lipsticks, 75 eyeliners, and 90 colors of nail polish from one brand alone. There were 116 kinds of skin cream, and 360 types of shampoo, conditioner, gel, and mousse. Next to them were 90 different cold remedies and decongestants. Finally, there was dental floss: waxed and unwaxed, flavored and unflavored, offered in a variety of thicknesses.

Returning to the food shelves, I could choose from among 230 soup offerings, including 29 different chicken soups. There were 16 varieties of instant mashed potatoes, 75 different instant gravies, 120 different pasta sauces. Among the 175 different salad dressings were 16 "Italian" dressings, and if none of them suited me, I could choose from 15 extra-virgin olive oils and 42 vinegars and make my own. There were 275 varieties of cereal, including 24 oatmeal options and 7 "Cheerios" options. Across the aisle were 64 different kinds of barbecue sauce and 175 types of tea bags.

Heading down the homestretch, I encountered 22 types of frozen waffles. And just before the checkout (paper or plastic; cash or credit or debit), there was a salad bar that offered 55 different items.

This brief tour of one modest store barely suggests the bounty that lies before today's middle-class consumer. I left out the fresh fruits and vegetables (organic, semi-organic, and regular old fertilized and pesticized), the fresh meats, fish, and poultry (free-range organic chicken or penned-up chicken, skin on or off, whole or in pieces, seasoned or unseasoned, stuffed or empty), the frozen foods, the paper goods, the cleaning products, and on and on and on.

© *The New Yorker Collection 1999 Roz Chast from cartoonbank.com. All Rights Reserved.*

A typical supermarket carries up to 50,000 items. That's a lot to choose from. And more than 20,000 *new* products hit the shelves every year, almost all of them doomed to failure.

Comparison shopping to get the best price adds still another dimension to the array of choices, so that if you were a truly careful shopper, you could spend the better part of a day just to select a box of crackers, as you worried about price, flavor, freshness, fat, sodium, and calories. But who has the time to do this? Perhaps that's the reason consumers tend to return to the products they usually buy, not even noticing 75% of the items competing for their attention and their dollars. Who but a professor doing research would even stop to consider that there are almost 300 different cookie options to choose among?

Supermarkets are unusual as repositories for what are called "nondurable goods," goods that are quickly used and replenished. So buying the wrong brand of cookies doesn't have significant emotional or financial consequences. But in most other settings, people are out to buy things that cost more money, and that are meant to last. And here, as the number of options increases, the psychological stakes rise accordingly.

Shopping for Gadgets

CONTINUING MY MISSION TO EXPLORE OUR RANGE OF CHOICES, I left the supermarket and stepped into my local consumer electronics store. Here I discovered:

- 45 different car stereo systems, with 50 different speaker sets to go with them.
- 42 different computers, most of which could be customized in various ways.

- 27 different printers to go with the computers.
- 110 different televisions, offering high definition, flat screen, varying screen sizes and features, and various levels of sound quality.
- 30 different VCRs and 50 different DVD players.
- 20 video cameras.
- 85 different telephones, not counting the cellular phones.
- 74 different stereo tuners, 55 CD players, 32 tape players (remember tapes?), and 50 sets of speakers. (Given that these components could be mixed and matched in every possible way, that provided the opportunity to create 6,512,000 different music systems.) And if you didn't have the budget or the stomach for configuring your own stereo system, there were 63 small, integrated systems to choose from.

Unlike supermarket products, those in the electronics store don't get used up so fast. If we make a mistake, we either have to live with it or return it and go through the difficult choice process all over again. Also, we really can't rely on habit to simplify our decision, because we don't buy stereo systems every couple of weeks and because technology changes so rapidly that chances are our last model won't exist when we go out to replace it. At these prices, choices begin to have serious consequences.

Shopping by Mail

MY WIFE AND I RECEIVE ABOUT 20 CATALOGS A WEEK IN THE MAIL. We get catalogs for clothes, luggage, housewares, furniture, kitchen appliances, gourmet food, athletic gear, computer equipment, linens, bathroom furnishings, and unusual gifts, plus a few that are hard to classify. These catalogs spread like a virus—once you're on the mailing list for one, dozens of others seem to follow. Buy one thing from a catalog and your name starts to spread from one mailing list to another. From one month alone, I have 25 clothing catalogs sitting on my desk. Opening just one of them, a summer catalog for women, we find

- 19 different styles of women's T-shirts, each available in 8 different colors,
- 10 different styles of shorts, each available in 8 colors,
- 8 different styles of chinos, available in 6 to 8 colors,
- 7 different styles of jeans, each available in 5 colors,
- dozens of different styles of blouses and pants, each available in multiple colors,
- 9 different styles of thongs, each available in 5 or 6 colors.

And then there are bathing suits—15 one-piece suits, and among two-piece suits:

- 7 different styles of tops, each in about 5 colors, combined with,
- 5 different styles of bottoms, each in about 5 colors (to give women a total of 875 different "make your own two-piece" possibilities).

Shopping Online

STILL GET ALL THOSE CATALOGS EVEN THOUGH ALMOST NO ONE looks at catalogs anymore. In the years since I wrote this book, the Internet as a purchasing alternative has just exploded. As I'm sure you are aware, no matter how big a brick-and-mortar store is, it can't include everything. When new products come in, old ones disappear. But the Internet is a store with infinite floor space. It is largely true nowadays that pretty much any version of any item manufactured anywhere on the planet is just a mouse click away. A quick look at Amazon revealed to me that we can choose among 400 different types of athletic shoes (not counting variations in color), 400 toothbrushes, 500 sweaters, and 20,000 pairs of jeans (for women; men have only about 12,500 options).

Shopping for Knowledge

THESE DAYS, A TYPICAL COLLEGE CATALOG HAS MORE IN COMMON with the one from J. Crew than you might think. Most liberal arts colleges and universities now embody a view that celebrates freedom of choice above all else, and the modern university is a kind of intellectual shopping mall.

A century ago, a college curriculum entailed a largely fixed course of study, with a principal goal of educating people in their ethical and civic traditions. Education was not just about learning a discipline—it was a way of raising citizens with common values and aspirations. Often the capstone of a college education was a course taught by the college president, a course that integrated the various fields of knowledge to which the students had been exposed. But more important, this course was intended to teach students how to use their college education to live a good and an ethical life, both as individuals and as members of society.

This is no longer the case. Now there is no fixed curriculum, and no single course is required of all students. There is no attempt to teach people how they should live, for who is to say what a good life is? When I went to college, fifty years ago, there were almost two years' worth of general education requirements that all students had to complete. We had *some* choices among courses that met those requirements, but they were rather narrow. Almost every department had a single, freshman-level introductory course that prepared the student for more advanced work in the department. You could be fairly certain, if you ran into a fellow student you didn't know, that the two of you would have at least a year's worth of courses in common to discuss.

Today, the modern institution of higher learning offers a wide array of different "goods" and allows, even encourages, students—the "customers"—to shop around until they find what they like. Individual customers are free to "purchase" whatever bundles of knowledge they want, and the university provides whatever its customers demand. In some rather prestigious institutions, this shopping-mall view has been carried to an extreme. In the first few weeks of classes, students sample the merchandise. They go to a class, stay ten minutes to see what the professor is like, then walk out, often in the middle of the professor's sentence, to try another class. Students come and go in and out of classes just as browsers go in and out of stores in a mall. "You've got ten minutes," the students seem to be saying, "to show me what you've got. So give it your best shot." Students even describe themselves in the early days of each semester as "shopping courses."

About thirty years ago, somewhat dismayed that their students no longer shared enough common intellectual experiences, the Harvard faculty revised its general education requirements to form a "core curriculum." Students now had to take at least one course in each of seven different broad areas of inquiry. Among those areas, there were a total of about 220 courses from which to choose. "Foreign Cultures" had 32, "Historical Study" had 44, "Literature and the Arts" had 58, "Moral Reasoning" had 15, as did "Social Analysis," Quantitative Reasoning" had 25, and "Science" had 44. What were the odds that two random students who bumped into each other would have courses in common?

In recent years, this core curriculum has been replaced by a general education requirement that offers students a selection of about 200 courses in different subject areas.

At the advanced end of the curriculum, Harvard offers about 40 majors. For students with interdisciplinary interests, these can be combined into an almost endless array of joint majors. And if that doesn't do the trick, students can create their own degree plan.

And Harvard is not unusual. Princeton offers its students a choice of 350 courses from which to satisfy its general education requirements. Stanford, which has a larger student body, offers even more. Even at my small school, Swarthmore College, with only 1,350 students, we offer about 120 courses to meet our version of the general education requirement, from which students must select nine. And though I have mentioned only extremely selective, private institutions, don't think that the range of choices they offer is peculiar to them. Thus, at Penn State, for example, liberal arts students can choose from over 40 majors and from hundreds of courses intended to meet general education requirements.

There are many benefits to these expanded educational opportunities. The traditional values and traditional bodies of knowledge transmitted from teachers to students in the past were constraining and often myopic. Until very recently, important ideas reflecting the values, insights, and challenges of people from different traditions and cultures had been systematically excluded from the curriculum. The tastes and interests of the idiosyncratic students had been stifled and frustrated. In the modern university, each individual student is free to pursue almost any interest, without having to be harnessed to what her intellectual ancestors thought was worth knowing. But this freedom may come at a price. Now students are required to make choices about education that may affect them for the rest of their lives. And they are forced to make these choices at a point in their intellectual development when they may lack the resources to make them intelligently.

Shopping for Entertainment

EFORE THE ADVENT OF CABLE, AMERICAN TELEVISION VIEWERS HAD the three networks from which to choose. In large cities, there were up to a half dozen additional local stations. When cable first came on the scene, its primary function was to provide better reception. Then new stations appeared, slowly at first, but more rapidly as time went on. Now there are 200 or more (my cable provider offers 270), not counting the on-demand movies we can obtain. If 200 options aren't enough, there are special subscription services that allow you to watch any football game being played by a major college anywhere in the country. And the advent of high-speed Internet service has brought with it the possibility of streaming, which makes the number of viewing options essentially infinite.

But what if, with all these choices, we find ourselves in the bind of wanting to watch two shows broadcast in the same time slot? Thanks to DVRs, that's no longer a problem. Watch one, and record one (or several) for later.

And programmable, electronic boxes like TiVo enable us, in effect, to create our own TV stations. We can program those devices to find exactly the kinds of shows we want and to cut out the commercials, the promos, the lead-ins, and whatever else we find annoying. And the boxes can "learn" what we like and then "suggest" to us programs that we may not have thought of. We can now watch whatever we want whenever we want to. We don't have to schedule our TV time. We don't have to look at the TV page in the newspaper. Indeed, there is no TV page in the newspaper. Middle of the night or early in the morning—no matter when that old movie is on, it's available to us exactly when we want it.

So the TV experience is now the very essence of choice without boundaries. With these boxes in everybody's home, it's a good bet that when folks gather around the watercooler to discuss last night's big TV events, no two of them will have watched the same shows. Like the college freshmen struggling in vain to find a shared intellectual experience, American TV viewers will be struggling to find a shared TV experience.

But Is Expanded Choice Good or Bad?

AMERICANS SPEND MORE TIME SHOPPING THAN THE MEMBERS OF any other society. Americans go to shopping centers about once a week, more often than they go to houses of worship, and Americans now have more shopping centers than high schools. In a survey, 93 percent of teenage girls surveyed said that shopping was their favorite activity. Mature women also say they like shopping, but working women say that shopping is a hassle, as do most men. When asked to rank the pleasure they get from various activities, grocery shopping ranks next to last, and other shopping fifth from the bottom. And the trend over recent years is downward. Apparently, people are shopping more now but enjoying it less.

There is something puzzling about these findings. It's not so odd, perhaps, that people spend more time shopping than they used to. With all the options available, picking what you want takes more effort. But why do people enjoy it less? And if they do enjoy it less, why do they keep doing it? If we don't like shopping at the supermarket, for example, we can just get it over with, and buy what we always buy, ignoring the alternatives. Shopping in the modern supermarket demands extra effort only if we're intent on scrutiniz-ing every possibility and getting the best thing. And for those of us who shop in this way, increasing options should be a good thing, not a bad one.

And this, indeed, is the standard line among social scientists who study choice. If we're rational, they tell us, added options can only make us better off as a society. Those of us who care will benefit, and those of us who don't care can always ignore the added options. This view seems logically compelling; but empirically, it isn't true.

A series of revolutionary studies, titled "When Choice Is Demo-tivating," provide the evidence. One study was set in a gourmet food store in an upscale community where the owners commonly set up sample tables of new items. When researchers set up a display fea-turing a line of exotic, high-quality jams, customers who came by could taste samples, and they were given a coupon for a dollar off if they bought a jar. In one condition of the study, 6 varieties of the jam were available for tasting. In another, 24 varieties were avail-able. In either case, the entire set of 24 varieties was available for purchase. The large array of jams attracted more people to the table than the small array, though in both cases people tasted about the same number of jams on average. When it came to buying, how-ever, a huge difference became evident. Thirty percent of the people exposed to the small array of jams actually bought a jar; only 3 per-cent of those exposed to the large array of jams did so.

In a second study, this time in the laboratory, college students were asked to evaluate a variety of gourmet chocolates, in the guise of a marketing survey. The students were then asked which chocolate—based on description and appearance—they would choose for themselves. Then they tasted and rated that chocolate. Finally, in a different room, the students were offered a small box of the chocolates in lieu of cash as payment for their participation. For one group of students, the initial array of chocolates numbered 6, and for the other, it numbered 30. The key results of this study were that the students faced with the small array were more satisfied with their tasting than those faced with the large array. In addition, they were four times as likely to choose chocolate rather than cash as compensation for their participation.

The authors of the study speculated about several explanations for these results. A large array of options may discourage consumers because it forces an increase in the effort that goes into making a decision. So consumers decide not to decide, and don't buy the product. Or if they do, the effort that the decision requires detracts from the enjoyment derived from the results. Also, a large array of options may diminish the attractiveness of what people *actually* choose, the reason being that thinking about the attractions of some of the unchosen options detracts from the pleasure derived from the chosen one. I will be examining these and other possible explanations throughout the book. But for now, the puzzle we began with remains: why can't people just ignore many or some of the options, and treat a 30-option array as if it were a 6-option array?

There are several possible answers. First, an industry of marketers and advertisers makes products difficult or impossible to ignore. They are in our faces all the time. Second, we have a tendency to look around at what others are doing and use them as a standard of comparison. If the person sitting next to me on an airplane is using an extremely light, compact laptop computer with a large, crystal-clear screen, the choices for me as a consumer have just been expanded, whether I want them to be or not. Third, we may suffer from what economist Fred Hirsch referred to as the "tyranny of small decisions." We say to ourselves, "Let's go to one more store" or "Let's look at one more website," and not "Let's go to all the stores" or "let's look at all the websites." It always seems easy to add just one more item to the array that is already being considered. So we go from 6 options to 30, one option at a time. By the time we're done with our search, we may look back in horror at all the alternatives we've considered and discarded along the way.

But what I think is most important is that people won't ignore alternatives if they don't realize that too many alternatives can create a problem. And our culture sanctifies freedom of choice so profoundly that the benefits of infinite options seem self-evident. When experiencing dissatisfaction or hassle on a shopping trip, consumers are likely to blame it on something else—surly salespeople, traffic jams, high prices, items out of stock—anything but the overwhelming array of options.

Nonetheless, certain indicators pop up occasionally that signal discontent with this trend. There are now several books and magazines devoted to what is called the "voluntary simplicity" movement. Its core idea is that we have too many choices, too many decisions, too little time to do what is really important.

We can imagine a point at which the options would be so copious that even the world's most ardent supporters of freedom of choice would begin to say, "enough already." Unfortunately, that point of revulsion seems to recede endlessly into the future.

In the next chapter, we'll explore some of the newer areas of choice that have been added to complicate our lives. The question is, does this increased complexity bring with it increased satisfaction?

CHAPTER TWO

New Choices

■

FILTERING OUT EXTRANEOUS INFORMATION IS ONE OF THE BASIC functions of consciousness. If everything available to our senses demanded our attention at all times, we wouldn't be able to get through the day. Much of human progress has involved reducing the time and energy, as well as the number of processes we have to engage in and think about, for each of us to obtain the necessities of life. We moved from foraging and subsistence agriculture to the development of crafts and trade. As cultures advanced, not every individual had to focus every bit of energy, every day, on filling his belly. One could specialize in a certain skill and then trade the products of that skill for other goods. Eons later, manufacturers and merchants made life simpler still. Individuals could simply purchase food and clothing and household items, often, until very recently, at the same general store. The variety of offerings was meager, but the time spent procuring them was minimal as well.

In the past few decades, though, that long process of simplifying and bundling economic offerings has been reversed. Increasingly, the trend moves back toward time-consuming foraging behavior, as each of us is forced to sift for ourselves through more and more options in almost every aspect of life.

Choosing Utilities

NOT THAT LONG AGO, ALL UTILITIES WERE REGULATED MONOPOLIES. Consumers didn't have to make decisions about who was going to provide telephone or electric service. Then came the breakup of "Ma Bell." What followed in its wake was a set of options that has grown, over time, into a dizzying array. We face many different possible long-distance providers, each offering many different possible plans. We now even face choice among local telephone service providers. And the cell phone revolution has given us the choice of cell phone service providers, multiplying options yet again. I get about two solicitations a week from companies that want to help me make my calls, texts, and web-surfs and we are all assaulted daily with broadcast, digital, and print advertising. Phone service has become a decision to weigh and contemplate.

The same thing has begun to happen with electric power. Companies are now competing for our business in many parts of the country. Again, we are forced to educate ourselves so that the decisions we make will be well informed.

I am not suggesting, by the way, that deregulation and competition in the telephone and power industries are bad things. Many experts suggest that in the case of phone service, deregulation brought improved service at lower prices. With electric power, the jury is still out. In some places, the introduction of choice and competition has gone smoothly. In other places, it has been rough, with spotty service and increased prices. But even if we assume that the kinks will be worked out eventually and competitive electric-power provision will benefit consumers, the fact remains that it's another choice we have to make.

In discussing the introduction of electric power competition in

New York, Edward A. Smeloff, a utility industry expert, said, "In the past we trusted that state regulators who were appointed by our elected officials were watching out for us, which may or may not have been true. The new model is, 'Figure it out for yourself.' " Is this good news or not? According to a survey conducted by Yankelovich Partners, a majority of people want more control over the details of their lives, but a majority of people also want to simplify their lives. There you have it—the paradox of our times.

As evidence of this conflicted desire, it turns out that many people, though happy about the availability of telephone choices or electric choices, don't really make them. They stick with what they already have without even investigating alternatives. Most folks don't even shop around for calling plans within their phone company. And in Philadelphia, with the arrival of electricity competition, only an estimated 15 percent of customers shopped for better deals. You might think that there's no harm in this, that customers are just making a sensible choice not to worry. But the problem is that state regulators aren't there anymore to make sure consumers don't get ripped off. In an era of deregulation, even if you keep what you've always had, you may end up paying substantially more for the same or worse service.

Choosing Health Insurance

HEALTH INSURANCE IS SERIOUS BUSINESS, AND THE CHOICES WE MAKE with respect to it can have devastating consequences. Not too long ago, only one kind of health insurance was available to most people, usually some local version of Blue Cross or a nonprofit health care provider like Kaiser Permanente. And these companies didn't offer a wide variety of plans to their subscribers. Nowadays, organizations present their employees with options—one or more HMOs or PPOs. And within these plans, there are more options—the level of deductible, the prescription drug plan, dental plan, vision plan, and so on. If consumers are buying their own insurance rather than choosing from what employers provide, even more options are available. Once again, I don't mean to suggest that we can't or don't benefit from these options. Perhaps many of us do. But it presents yet another thing to worry about, to master, or, perhaps, to get very wrong. With the coming of the Affordable Care Act, more commonly known as "Obamacare," the health insurance landscape changed. It included a "mandate" that people get health insurance. But an important part of the act was to make sure consumers had choices about *which* insurance. And in most states, they do.

In the presidential election of 2000, one of the points of contention between George W. Bush and Al Gore concerned the matter of choice in health insurance. Both candidates supported providing prescription drug coverage for senior citizens, but they differed dramatically in their views about how best to do that. Gore favored adding prescription drug coverage to Medicare. A panel of experts would determine what the coverage would be, and every senior citizen would have the same plan. Senior citizens would not have to gather information, or make decisions. Under the Bush plan, private insurers would come up with a variety of drug plans, and then seniors would choose the plan that best suited their needs. Bush had great confidence in the magic of the competitive market to generate high-quality, low-cost service. What we ended up with, in Medicare Part D, was a mixture. The senior prescription drug plan became part of Medicare, but private providers created the actual plans, and senior citizens found themselves with thirty, forty, sixty plans to choose from.

Perhaps confidence in the market is justified. But even if it is, it shifts the burden of making decisions from the government to the individual. And not only is the health insurance issue incredibly complicated (I think I've met only one person in my entire life who fully understands what his insurance covers and what it doesn't and what those statements that come from the insurance company really mean), but the stakes are astronomical. A bad decision about a prescription drug plan by a senior citizen can bring complete financial ruin, leading perhaps to choices between food and medicine, just the situation that prescription drug coverage is intended to prevent.

Choosing Retirement Plans

THE VARIETY OF PENSION PLANS OFFERED TO EMPLOYEES PRESENTS the same difficulty. Over the years, more and more employers have switched from what are called "defined benefit" pension plans, in which retirees get whatever their years of service and terminal salaries entitle them to, to "defined contribution" plans, in which employee and employer each contribute to some investment instrument. What the employee gets at retirement depends on the performance of the investment instrument.

With defined contribution plans came choice. Employers might offer a few plans, differing, perhaps, in how speculative the investments they made were, and employees would choose from among them. Typically, employees could allocate their retirement contributions among plans in pretty much any way they liked, and could change their allocations from year to year. What has happened in recent years is that choice among pension plans has exploded. So not only do employees have the opportunity to choose among relatively high- and low-risk investments, but they now have the opportunity to choose among several candidates in each category. For example, a relative of mine was a partner in a midsized accounting firm. The firm had offered its employees 14 different pension options, which could be combined in any way employees wanted. But several partners decided that this set of choices was inadequate, so they developed a retirement plan that had 156 options. Option number 156 was that employees who didn't like the other 155 could design their own.

This increase in retirement investment opportunities appears to be beneficial to employees. If you once had a choice between Fund A and Fund B, and now Fund C and Fund D are added, you can always decide to ignore the new choices. Funds C and D will appeal to some, and others won't be hurt by ignoring them. But the problem is that there are a lot of funds—well over 5,000—out there. Which one is just right for you? How do you decide which one to choose? When employers are establishing relations with just a few funds, they can rely on the judgments of financial experts to choose those funds in a way that benefits employees. That is, employers can, like the government, be looking over their employees' shoulders to protect them from really bad decisions. As the number of options increases, the work involved in employer oversight goes up.

Moreover, I think the adding of options brings with it a subtle shift in the responsibility that employers feel toward their employees. When the employer is providing only a few routes to retirement security, it seems important to take responsibility for the quality of those routes. But when the employer takes the trouble to provide many routes, then it seems reasonable to think that by providing options, the employer has done his or her part. Choosing wisely among those options becomes the employee's responsibility.

Just how well do people choose when it comes to their retirement? A study of people actually making decisions about where to put their retirement contributions found that when people are confronted with a large number of options, they typically adopt a strategy of dividing their contributions equally among the options—50–50 if there are two; 25–25–25–25, if there are four; and so on. What this means is that whether employees are making wise decisions depends entirely on the options that are being provided for them by their employers. So an employer might, for example, provide one conservative option and five more speculative ones, on the grounds that conservative investments are basically all alike, but that people should be able to choose their own risks. A typical employee, putting a sixth of her retirement in each fund, might have no idea that she has made an extremely high-risk decision, with 83 percent of her money tied to the perturbations of the stock market. And in addition to making bad decisions, psychologist Sheena Iyengar and colleagues (she did the "jam study" I discussed in the last chapter) have shown, when employees are offered many retirement investment options, the chances go up that they make no decision at all. In other words, instead of many options making it easier for employees to find something they like, it paralyzes them. "This is complicated. I'll decide next week." But it's just as complicated, and life is just as busy, next week.

You might think that if people can be so inattentive to something as important as retirement, they deserve what they get. The employer is doing right by them, but they aren't doing right by themselves. There is certainly something to be said for this view, but my point here is that the retirement decision is only one among very many important decisions. And most people may feel that they lack the expertise to make decisions about their money by themselves. Once again, new choices demand more extensive research and create more individual responsibility for failure.

Choosing Medical Care

S EVERAL WEEKS AGO MY WIFE WENT TO A NEW DOCTOR FOR HER annual physical. She had the checkup, and all was well. But as she walked home, she became increasingly upset at how perfunctory the whole exchange had been. No blood work. No breast exam. The doctor had listened to her heart, taken her blood pressure, arranged for a mammogram, and asked her if she had any complaints. That was about it. This didn't seem like an annual physical to my wife, so she called the office to see whether there had been some misunderstanding about the purpose of her visit. She described what had transpired to the office manager, who proceeded to tell her that this doctor's philosophy was to have her examinations guided by the desires of the patient. Aside from a few routine procedures, she had no standard protocol for physical exams. Each was a matter of negotiation between physician and patient. The office manager apologized that the doctor's approach had not been made clear to my wife, and suggested a follow-up conversation between my wife and the doctor about what checkups would be like in the future.

My wife was astonished. Going to the doctor—at least this doctor—was like going to the hairdresser. The client (patient) has to let the professional know what she wants out of each visit. The patient is in charge.

Responsibility for medical care has landed on the shoulders of patients with a resounding thud. I don't mean choice of doctors; we've always had that (if we aren't among the nation's poor), and with managed care, we surely have less of it than we had before. I mean choice about what the doctors *do*. The tenor of medical practice has shifted from one in which the all-knowing, paternalistic doctor tells the patient what must be done—or just does it—to one in which the doctor arrays the possibilities before the patient, along with the likely plusses and minuses of each, and the patient makes a choice. The attitude was well described by physician and *New Yorker* contributor Atul Gawande:

> Only a decade ago, doctors made the decisions; patients did what they were told. Doctors did not consult patients about their desires and priorities, and routinely withheld information—sometimes crucial information, such as what drugs they were on, what treatments they were being given, and what their diagnosis was. Patients were even forbidden to look at their own medical records; it wasn't their property, doctors said. They were regarded as children: too fragile and simpleminded to handle the truth, let alone make decisions. And they suffered for it.

They suffered because some doctors were arrogant and/or careless. Also, they suffered because sometimes choosing the right course of action was not just a medical decision, but a decision involving other factors in a patient's life—the patient's network of family and friends, for example. Under these circumstances, surely the patient should be the one making the decision.

According to Gawande, *The Silent World of Doctor and Patient*, by physician and ethicist Jay Katz (published in 1984), launched the transformation in medical practice that has brought us where we are today. And Gawande has no doubt that giving patients more responsibility for what their doctors do has greatly improved the quality of medical care they receive. But he also suggests that the shift in responsibility has gone too far:

The new orthodoxy about patient autonomy has a hard time acknowledging an awkward truth: patients frequently don't want the freedom that we've given them. That is, they're glad to have their autonomy respected, but the exercise of that autonomy means being able to relinquish it.

Gawande goes on to describe a family medical emergency in which his own newborn daughter, Hunter, stopped breathing. After some vigorous shaking started the little girl breathing again, Gawande and his wife rushed her to the hospital. His daughter's breathing continued to be extremely labored, and the doctors on duty asked Gawande whether he wanted his daughter intubated. This was a decision that he wanted the doctors—people he had never met before—to make for him:

> The uncertainties were savage, and I could not bear the possibility of making the wrong call. Even if I made what I was sure was the right choice for her, I could not live with the guilt if something went wrong . . . I needed Hunter's physicians to bear the responsibility: they could live with the consequences, good or bad.

Gawande reports that research has shown that patients commonly prefer to have others make their decisions for them. Though as many as 65 percent of people surveyed say that if they were to get cancer, they would want to choose their own treatment, in fact, among people who *do* get cancer, only 12 percent actually want to do so. What patients really seem to want from their doctors, Gawande believes, is competence and kindness. Kindness of course includes respect for autonomy, but it does not treat autonomy as an inviolable end in itself.

When it comes to medical treatment, patients see choice as both a blessing and a burden. And the burden falls primarily on women, who are typically the guardians not only of their own health, but that of their husbands and children. "It is an overwhelming task for women, and consumers in general, to be able to sort through the information they find and make decisions," says Amy Allina, program director of the National Women's Health Network. And what makes it overwhelming is not only that the decision is ours, but that the number of sources of information from which we are to make the decisions has exploded. It's not just a matter of listening to your doctor lay out the options and making a choice. We now have encyclopedic lay-people's guides to health, "better health" magazines, and, most dramatic of all, the Internet. So now the prospect of a medical decision has become everyone's worst nightmare of a term paper assignment, with stakes infinitely higher than a grade in a course.

And beyond the sources of information about mainstream medical practices to which we can now turn, there is an increasing array of nontraditional practices—herbs, vitamins, diets, acupuncture, copper bracelets, and so on. In 1997, Americans spent about $27 billion on nontraditional remedies, most of them unproven. Every day, these practices become less and less fringy, more and more regarded as reasonable options to be considered. The combination of decision autonomy and a proliferation of treatment possibilities places an incredible burden on every person in a high-stakes area of decision making that did not exist twenty years ago.

The latest indication of the shift in responsibility for medical decisions from doctor to patient is the widespread advertising of prescription drugs that exploded onto the scene after various federal restrictions on such ads were lifted in 1997. Ask yourself what is the point of advertising prescription drugs (antidepressant, anti-inflammatory, antiallergy, diet, ulcer, sexual performance enhancement—you name it) on prime-time television. We can't just go to the drugstore and buy them. The doctor must prescribe them. So why are drug companies investing big money to reach us, the consumers, directly? Clearly they hope and expect we will notice their products and demand that our doctors write the prescriptions. The doctors are now merely instruments for the execution of our decisions.

Choosing Beauty

W HAT DO YOU WANT TO LOOK LIKE? THANKS TO THE OPTIONS modern surgery provides, we can now transform our bodies and our facial features. In 2014, over 15 million cosmetic surgical procedures were done on Americans—210,000 liposuctions, 285,000 breast augmentations, 207,000 eyelid surgeries, 128,000 face-lifts, 217,000 nose jobs, 6.7 million Botox injections. Though it is mostly (92 percent) women who avail themselves of these procedures, men do it too. "We think of it like getting your nails done or going to a spa," says a spokesman for the American Society of Plastic Surgeons. Another says that going under the knife is no different "from putting a nice sweater on, or combing your hair, or doing your nails, or having a little tan." In other words, cosmetic surgery is slowly shifting from being a procedure that people gossip about to being a commonplace tool for self-improvement. To the extent that this is true, fundamental aspects of appearance become a matter of choice. How people look is yet another thing that they are now responsible for deciding for themselves. As journalist Wendy Kaminer puts it, "Beauty used to be a gift bestowed upon the few for the rest of us to admire. Today it's an achievement, and homeliness is not just misfortune but a failure."

Choosing How to Work

THROUGHOUT ITS HISTORY, THE UNITED STATES HAS TAKEN PRIDE in the social mobility afforded to its citizens, and justly so. Some two-thirds of American high-school graduates attend college. A degree then opens up a wide variety of employment opportunities. What kind of work Americans choose to do is remarkably unconstrained either by what their parents did before them or by what kind of work is available where they grew up. I know that employment prospects and possibilities are not equally available to *everyone* in America. Family finances and national economic trends impose serious constraints on many. But not *as* many as in the past.

After people choose a career path, new choices face them. The telecommunications revolution has created enormous flexibility about when and where many people can work. Companies are slowly, if reluctantly, accepting the idea that many people can do their jobs productively from home, spared interruptions and unnecessary oversight. The number of people who do at least some "tele-working" grew almost 80 percent between 2005 and 2012. And once people are in the position to be able to work at any time from any place, they face decisions every minute of every day about whether or not to be working. E-mail is just a mouse click away. Should we check it before we go to bed? Should we bring our laptop along on our vacation? Should we dial into the office voice-mail system with our cell phone and check for messages while waiting between courses at the restaurant? For people in many occupations, there are few obstacles standing in the way of working all the time. And this means that whether or not we work has become a matter of hour-by-hour, minute-by-minute choice.

And who do we work for? Here, too, it seems that every day we face a choice. The average American thirty-two-year-old has already worked for nine different companies. In an article several years ago about the increasingly peripatetic American work force, *U.S. News & World Report* estimated that 17 million Americans would *voluntarily* leave their jobs in 1999 to take other employment. People switch jobs to get big raises and to pursue opportunities for advancement. They switch jobs because they want to live in a different city. They switch jobs because they're bored. Indeed, job-switching has become so natural that individuals who have worked for the same employer for five years are regarded with suspicion. No longer are they seen as loyal; instead, their desirability or ambition is called into question—at least when times are good and jobs are plentiful. When times are harder, as they are right now, there will obviously be much less job switching than there was in 1999. But people will still be looking.

When should you start looking for a new job? The answer seems to be that you start looking the day you begin your current job. Think for a moment about what this means to each of us as decision makers. It means that the questions "Where should I work?" and "What kind of work should I do?" are never resolved. Nothing is ever settled. The antennae for new and better opportunities are always active. The old Microsoft ad that asked us "Where do you want to go today?" is not just about web surfing.

This kind of job mobility offers many opportunities. Being able to move around, changing employers and even careers, opens doors to challenging and fulfilling options. But it comes at a price, and the price is the daily burden of gathering information and making decisions. People can never relax and enjoy what they have already achieved. At all times, they have to stay alert for the next big chance.

Even how we dress for work has taken on a new element of

choice, and with it, new anxieties. The practice of having a "dress-down day" or "casual day," which began to emerge a generation or so ago, was intended to make life easier for employees, to enable them to save money and feel more relaxed at the office. The effect, however, was just the reverse. In addition to the normal workplace wardrobe, employees had to create a "workplace casual" wardrobe. It couldn't really be the sweats and T-shirts you wore around the house on the weekend. It had to be a selection of clothing that sustained a certain image—relaxed, but also meticulous and serious. All of a sudden, the range of wardrobe possibilities was expanded, and a decision-making problem emerged. It was no longer a question of the blue suit or the brown one, the red tie or the yellow one. The question now was: What is casual? A *New Yorker* piece about this phenomenon identified at least six different kinds of casual: active casual, rugged casual, sporty casual, dressy casual, smart casual, and business casual. As writer John Seabrook put it, "This may be the most depressing thing about the casual movement: no clothing is casual anymore." So we got the freedom to make an individual choice about how to dress on a given day, but for many, that choice entailed more complications than it was worth.

Choosing How to Love

HAVE A FORMER STUDENT (LET'S CALL HIM JOSEPH) WITH WHOM I'VE remained close since he graduated from college in the early nineties. He went on to earn a PhD and currently works as a researcher at a major university. A few years ago, Joseph and a fellow graduate student (let's call her Jane) fell in love. "This is it," Joseph assured me; there was no doubt in anyone's mind.

With his career on track and a life partner selected, it might appear that Joseph had made the big decisions. Yet, in the course of their courtship, Joseph and Jane had to make a series of tough choices. First, they had to decide whether to live together. This decision involved weighing the virtues of independence against the virtues of interdependence, and measuring various practical advantages (convenience, financial savings) of living together against possible parental disapproval. A short time later they had to decide when (and how) to get married. Should they wait until their respective careers were more settled or not? Should they have a religious ceremony, and if so, would it be his religion or hers? Then, having decided to marry, Joseph and Jane had to decide if they should merge their finances or keep them separate, and if separate, how they should handle joint expenses.

With marital decisions settled, they next had to face the dilemma of children. Should they have them? Yes, they easily decided. However, the question of timing led to another series of choices involving ticking biological clocks, the demands of finishing PhDs, and uncertainty about future employment circumstances. They also had to resolve the question of religion. Were they going to give their kids a religious upbringing, and if so, in whose religion?

Next came a series of career-related choices. Should they each look for the best possible job and be open to the possibility that they might have to live apart for some time? If not, whose career should get priority? In looking for jobs, should they restrict their search to be near his (West Coast) family or her (East Coast) family, or should they ignore geography completely and just look for the best jobs they could find in the same city, wherever it was? Facing and resolving each of these decisions, all with potentially significant consequences, was difficult for Joseph and his Jane. They thought that they had already made the hard decisions when they fell in love and made a mutual commitment. Shouldn't that be enough?

A range of life choices has been available to Americans for quite some time. But in the past, the "default" options were so powerful and dominant that few perceived themselves to be making choices. Whom we married was a matter of choice, but we knew that we would do it as soon as we could and have children, because that was something all people did. The anomalous few who departed from this pattern were seen as social renegades, subjects of gossip and speculation. These days, it's hard to figure out what kind of romantic choice would warrant such attention. Wherever we look, we see almost every imaginable arrangement of intimate relations. Though unorthodox romantic choices are still greeted with opprobrium or much worse in many parts of the world and in some parts of the United States, it seems clear that the general trend is toward ever greater tolerance of romantic diversity. Even on network television—hardly the vanguard of social evolution—there are people who are married, unmarried, remarried, heterosexual and homosexual, childless families and families with lots of kids, all trying each week to make us laugh. Today, all romantic possibilities are on the table; all choices are real. Which is another explosion of freedom, but which is also another set of choices to occupy our attention and fuel our anxieties. Comedian Aziz Ansari has recently published a very funny and very perceptive book about dating in the Internet age. *Modern Romance*, a mixture of wry observation, focus-group interviews, and empirical surveys, depicts both the benefits and the pitfalls of a world in which the set of possible romantic partners is virtually infinite. The benefits are obvious. The pitfalls are less obvious. How do you know when to commit when someone better might come along the next time you visit Tinder or Match.com? A term for this commitment anxiety has come into common usage and has even made it into the *Oxford English Dictionary*: "FOMO" (fear of missing out).

Choosing How to Pray

E VEN THOUGH MOST AMERICANS SEEM TO LEAD THOROUGHLY SECU-
lar lives, the nation as a whole professes to be deeply religious.
According to a decade-old Gallup poll, 96 percent of Americans
believe in "God, or a universal spirit," and 87 percent claim that
religion is at least fairly important in their own lives. Though only
a small fraction of this 90+ percent of Americans participates regularly in religious activities as part of communities of faith, there
is no doubt that we are a nation of believers. But believers in what?

Whereas most of us inherit the religious affiliations of our parents, we are remarkably free to choose exactly the "flavor" of that
affiliation that suits us. We are unwilling to regard religious teachings as *commandments*, about which we have no choice, rather than
suggestions, about which we are the ultimate arbiters. We look upon
participation in a religious community as an opportunity to choose
just the form of community that gives us what we want out of religion. Some of us may be seeking emotional fulfillment. Some may
be seeking social connection. Some may be seeking ethical guidance
and assistance with specific problems in our lives. Religious institutions then become a kind of market for comfort, tranquility, spiri-
tuality, and ethical reflection, and we "religion consumers" shop in
that market until we find what we like.

It may seem odd to talk about religious institutions in these kinds
of shopping-mall terms, but I think such descriptions reflect what
many people want and expect from their religious activities and
affiliations. This is not surprising, given the dominance of individual
choice and personal satisfaction as values in our culture. Even when
people join communities of faith and expect to participate in the life
of those communities and embrace (at least some of) the practices of

those communities, they simultaneously expect the communities to be responsive to *their* needs, *their* tastes, and *their* desires.

Sociologist Alan Wolfe documented this change in people's orientation to religious institutions and teachings in the book *Moral Freedom: The Search for Virtue in a World of Choice.* Wolfe conducted in-depth interviews with a wide variety of people scattered throughout the United States, and what he found was near unanimity that it was up to each person, as an individual, to pick her or his own values and make her or his own moral choices.

For people who have experienced religion more as a source of oppression than of comfort, guidance, and support, freedom of choice in this area is surely a blessing. They can elect the denomination that is most compatible with their view of life, then select the particular institution that they feel best embodies that view. They can pick and choose from among the practices and teachings those that seem to suit them best, including, paradoxically, the choice of conservative denominations that are attractive in part because they limit the choices people face in other parts of their lives. On the positive side, an individual can experience a personal form of participation consistent with his or her lifestyle, values, and goals. The negative is the burden of deciding which institution to join, and which practices to observe.

Choosing Who to Be

WE HAVE ANOTHER KIND OF FREEDOM OF CHOICE IN MODERN society that is surely unprecedented. We can choose our identities. Each person comes into the world with baggage from his ancestral past—race, ethnicity, nationality, religion, social and economic class. All this baggage tells the world a lot about who we are. Or, at least, it used to. It needn't anymore. Now greater possi-

"We're thinking maybe it's time you started getting some religious instruction. There's Catholic, Protestant, and Jewish—any of those sound good to you?"

© *The New Yorker Collection 2000 Robert Weber from cartoonbank.com. All Rights Reserved.*

bilities exist for transcending inherited social and economic class. Some of us manage to cast off the religion into which we were born. We can choose to repudiate or embrace our ethnic heritage. We can celebrate or suppress our nationality. And even race—that great sore of American history—has become more fluid. As multiracial marriages become more common, the offspring of those marriages display a variety of hues and physical features that make racial identification from the *outside* more difficult. And, as society becomes more tolerant, it permits racial identification from the *inside* to be more flexible. Furthermore, because most of us possess multiple identities, we can highlight different ones in different contexts. The young New York immigrant woman from Mexico sitting in a college class in contemporary literature can ask herself, as class discussion of a novel begins, whether she's going to express her identity as the Latina, the Mexican, the woman, the immigrant, or the teenager as class discussion unfolds. I can be an American who happens to be Jewish on my job, and a Jew who happens to be American in my synagogue. Identity is much less a thing people "inherit" than it used to be.

Amartya Sen has pointed out that people have always had the power to choose identity. It has always been possible to say no to aspects of an identity that are thrust upon us, even if the consequences are severe. But as with marriage, choice of identity has been moving from a state in which the default option was extremely powerful and the fact of choice had little psychological reality to a state in which choice is very real and salient. As with all the issues I've been discussing in this chapter, this change in the status of personal identity is both good and bad news: good news because it liberates us, and bad news because it burdens us with the responsibility of choice.

What It Means to Choose

NOVELIST AND EXISTENTIALIST PHILOSOPHER ALBERT CAMUS POSED the question, "Should I kill myself, or have a cup of coffee?" His point was that everything in life is choice. Every second of every day, we are choosing, and there are always alternatives. Existence, at least human existence, is defined by the choices people make. If that's true, then what can it mean to suggest, as I have in these first two chapters, that we face more choices and more decisions today than ever before?

Think about what you do when you wake up in the morning. You get out of bed. You stagger to the bathroom. You brush your teeth. You take a shower. We can break things down still further. You remove the toothbrush from its holder. You open the toothpaste tube. You squeeze toothpaste onto the brush. And so on.

Each and every part of this boring morning ritual is a matter of choice. You don't have to brush your teeth; you don't have to take a shower. When you dress, you don't have to wear underwear. So even before your eyes are more than half open—long before you've had your first cup of coffee—you've made a dozen choices or more. But they don't count, really, as choices. You could have done otherwise, but you never gave it a thought. So deeply ingrained, so habitual, so automatic, are these morning activities that you don't really contemplate the alternatives. So though it is logically true that you could have done otherwise, there is little psychological reality to this freedom of choice. On the weekend, perhaps, things are different. You might lie in bed asking whether you'll bother to shower now or wait till later. You might consider passing up your morning shave as well. But during the week, you're an automaton.

This is a very good thing. The burden of having every activity be a matter of deliberate and conscious choice would be too much for any of us to bear. The transformation of choice in modern life is that choice in many facets of life has gone from implicit and often psychologically unreal to explicit and psychologically very real. So we now face a demand to make choices that is unparalleled in human history.

We probably would be deeply resentful if someone tried to take our freedom of choice away in any part of life that we really cared about and really knew something about. If it were up to us to choose whether or not to have choice, we would opt for choice almost every time. But it is the *cumulative* effect of these added choices that I think is causing substantial distress. As I mentioned in Chapter 1, we are trapped in what Fred Hirsch called "the tyranny of small decisions." In any given domain, we say a resounding "yes" to choice, but we never cast a vote on the whole package of choices. Nonetheless, by voting yes in every particular situation, we are in effect voting yes on the package—with the consequence that we're left feeling barely able to manage.

In the pages that follow, we will begin to look at some of the ways we can ease that burden and, thereby, lessen the stress and dissatisfaction that comes with it.

How We Choose

Part II

CHAPTER THREE

Deciding and Choosing

■

CHOOSING WELL IS DIFFICULT, AND MOST DECISIONS HAVE SEVERAL DIFferent dimensions. When leasing an apartment, you consider location, spaciousness, condition, safety, and rent. When buying a car, you look at safety, reliability, fuel economy, style, and price. When choosing a job, it is salary, location, opportunity for advancement, potential colleagues, as well as the nature of the work itself, that factor into your deliberations.

Most good decisions will involve these steps:

1. Figure out your goal or goals.
2. Evaluate the importance of each goal.
3. Array the options.
4. Evaluate how likely each of the options is to meet your goals.
5. Pick the winning option.
6. Later use the consequences of your choice to modify your goals, the importance you assign them, and the way you evaluate future possibilities.

For example, after renting an apartment you might discover that easy access to shopping and public transportation turned out to be more important, and spaciousness less important, than you thought when you signed the lease. Next time around, you'll weight these factors differently.

Even with a limited number of options, going through this process can be hard work. As the number of options increases, the effort required to make a good decision escalates as well, which is one of the reasons that choice can be transformed from a blessing into a burden. It is also one of the reasons that we don't always manage the decision-making task effectively.

Knowing Your Goals

THE PROCESS OF GOAL-SETTING AND DECISION MAKING BEGINS WITH the question: "What do I want?" On the surface, this looks as if it should be easy to answer. The welter of information out there in the world notwithstanding, "What do I want?" is addressed largely through internal dialogue.

But knowing what we want means, in essence, being able to anticipate accurately how one choice or another will make us feel, and that is no simple task.

Whenever you eat a meal in a restaurant, or listen to a piece of music, or go to a movie, you either like the experience or you don't. The way that the meal or the music or the movie makes you feel in the moment—either good or bad—could be called *experienced utility*. But before you actually *have* the experience, you have to choose it. You have to pick a restaurant, a CD, or a movie, and you make these choices based upon how you *expect* the experiences to make you feel. So choices are based upon *expected utility*. And once you have had experience with particular restaurants, CDs, or movies, future choices will be based upon what you remember about these past experiences, in other words, on their *remembered utility*. To say that we know what we want, therefore, means that these three utilities align, with expected utility being matched by experienced utility, and experienced utility faithfully reflected in remembered utility. The trouble is, though, that these three utilities rarely line up so nicely.

Nobel Prize–winning psychologist Daniel Kahneman and his colleagues have shown that what we remember about the pleasurable quality of our past experiences is almost entirely determined by two things: how the experiences felt when they were at their peak (best or worst), and how they felt when they ended. This "peak-end" rule of Kahneman's is what we use to summarize the experience, and then we rely on that summary later to remind ourselves of how the experience felt. The summaries in turn influence our decisions about whether to have that experience again, and factors such as the proportion of pleasure to displeasure during the course of the experience, or how long the experience lasted, have almost no influence on our memory of it.

Here's an example. Participants in a laboratory study were asked to listen to a pair of very loud, unpleasant noises played through headphones. One noise lasted for eight seconds. The other lasted sixteen. The first eight seconds of the second noise were identical to the first noise, whereas the second eight seconds, while still loud and unpleasant, were not *as* loud. Later, the participants were told that they would have to listen to one of the noises again, but that they could choose which one. Clearly the second noise is worse—the unpleasantness lasted twice as long. Nonetheless, the overwhelming majority of people chose the second to be repeated. Why? Because whereas both noises were unpleasant and had the same aversive peak, the second had a less unpleasant end, and so was remembered as less annoying than the first.

Here's another, quite remarkable example of the peak-end rule in operation. Men undergoing diagnostic colonoscopy exams were asked to report how they felt moment by moment while having the exam, and how they felt when it was over. This was in the days prior to the use of general anaesthetic during the procedure, so most people found these exams, in which a tube with a tiny camera on the end is inserted up the rectum and then moved around to allow the inspection of the gastrointestinal system, quite unpleasant—so much so that patients avoided getting regular tests, much to their peril. In the test, one group of patients had a standard colonoscopy. A second group had a standard colonoscopy plus. The "plus" was that after the actual examination was over, the doctor left the instrument in place for a short time. This was still unpleasant, but much less so because the scope wasn't moving. (Note that both groups of patients were having the colonoscopies for legitimate medical reasons; they were not subjecting themselves to these procedures just for the sake of the experiment.) So the second group experienced the same moment-by-moment discomfort as the first group, with the addition of somewhat lesser discomfort for twenty seconds more. And that is what they reported, moment-by-moment, *as they were having the procedure*. But a short time after it was over, the second group rated their experience as *less* unpleasant than did the first. Whereas both groups had the same peak experience, the second group had a milder end experience.

And it made a difference. It turned out that, over a five-year period after this exam, patients in the second group were more likely to comply with calls for follow-up colonoscopies than patients in the first group. Because they remembered their experiences as less unpleasant, they were less inclined to avoid them in the future.

In the same way, we evaluate positive experiences on the basis of how good they feel at their best, and how good they feel at the end. Thus, you might, in retrospect, remember a one-week vacation that had some great moments and finished with a bang as more pleasurable than a three-week vacation that also had some great moments, but finished only with a whimper. The two extra weeks of relaxing in the sun or seeing the sights or eating great food make little difference, because they recede from awareness over time.

So how well do we know what we want? It's doubtful that we would truly prefer intense pain followed by mild pain over experiencing intense pain alone. It's unlikely that a great one-week vacation is truly better than a great-single-week-followed-by-a-pretty-good-two-weeks vacation. But that's what people say they prefer. The discrepancy between logic and memory suggests that we don't always know what we want.

Another illustration of our lack of self-knowledge comes from a study in which researchers asked a group of college students to choose a series of snacks. Each week they had a three-hour seminar with one break that allowed participants to stretch their legs, use the bathroom, clear their heads, and have something to eat. When the professor asked the students to pick a snack for each of the next three weeks, the students picked a variety, thinking they'd get tired of the same snack each week. In contrast, another group in the same study got to choose their snack every week, and these students, choosing for one week at a time, tended to choose the same thing each week.

These two sets of participants were faced with different tasks. The students who were choosing one snack at a time simply had to ask themselves what they felt like eating at the moment. Those who were choosing for three weeks had to *predict* what they would feel like eating two or three weeks from the moment of choice. And they got the prediction wrong, no doubt thinking that their low enthusiasm for pretzels after having just eaten a bag was how they would feel about pretzels a week later.

People who do their grocery shopping once a week succumb to the same erroneous prediction. Instead of buying several packages of their favorite X or Y, they buy a variety of Xs and Ys, failing to predict accurately that when the time comes to eat X or Y, they would almost certainly prefer their favorite. In a laboratory simulation of this grocery shopping situation, participants were given eight categories of basic foods and asked to imagine doing their shopping for the day and buying one item in each category. Having done this, they were asked to imagine doing it again, the next day, and so on, for several days. In contrast, another group of people were asked to imagine going shopping to buy three days' worth of food, and thus selecting three things in each category. People in this latter group made more varied selections within each category than people in the former group, predicting, inaccurately, that they would want something different on day two from what they had eaten on day one.

So it seems that neither our predictions about how we *will* feel after an experience nor our memories of how we *did* feel during the experience are very accurate reflections of how we actually *do* feel while the experience is occurring. And yet it is memories of the past and expectations for the future that govern our choices.

In a world of expanding, confusing, and conflicting options, we can see that this difficulty in targeting our goals accurately—step one on the path to a wise decision—sets us up for disappointment with the choices we actually make.

Gathering Information

HOWEVER WELL OR POORLY WE DETERMINE OUR GOALS BEFORE making a decision, having set them, we then go through the task of gathering information to evaluate the options. To do this, we review our past experience as well as the experience and expertise of others. We talk to friends. We read consumer, investment, or lifestyle magazines. We get recommendations from salespeople. And increasingly, we use the Internet. But more than anything else, we get information from advertising. Even in pre-Internet days, the average American saw three thousand ads a day. As advertising professor James Twitchell puts it, "Ads are what we know about the world around us."

So we don't have to do our choosing alone and unaided. Once we figure out what we want, we can use various resources to help evaluate the options. But we need to know that the information is reliable, and we need to have enough time to get through all the information that's available. Three thousand ads a day breaks down to about two hundred per waking hour, more than three per waking minute, and that is an overwhelming amount to sift through and evaluate.

Quality and Quantity of Information

TO ACCOMMODATE THE EVER-INCREASING NUMBER OF ADS, YOUR favorite sitcom has about four fewer program minutes than it did a generation ago. On top of that, the advent of cable TV and its many channels has brought with it the "infomercial," a show that is an ad masquerading as entertainment. Newspapers and magazines contain hundreds of pages of which just a small fraction are devoted to content. Movie producers now "place" branded products in their films for high fees. Increasingly, sports stadiums are named for a sponsoring company, often at a fee of several million dollars a year. Every race car is tattooed with brand names, as are many athletes' uniforms. Even public television now has ads, disguised as public service announcements, at the start and end of almost every show.

Unfortunately, providing consumers with useful decision-making information is not the point of all this advertising. The point of advertising is to sell brands. According to James Twitchell, the key insight that has shaped modern advertising came to cigarette manufacturers in the 1930s. In the course of market research, they discovered that smokers who taste-tested various cigarette brands without knowing which was which couldn't tell them apart. So, if the manufacturer wanted to sell more of his particular brand, he was either going to have to make it distinctive or make consumers *think* it was distinctive, which was considerably easier. With that was born the practice of selling a product by associating it with a glamorous lifestyle.

We probably like to think that we're too smart to be seduced by such "branding," but we aren't. If you ask test participants in a study to explain their preferences in music or art, they'll come up with some account based on the qualities of the pieces themselves. Yet several studies have demonstrated that "familiarity breeds liking." If you play snippets of music for people or show them slides of paintings and vary the number of times they hear or see the music and the art, on the whole people will rate the familiar things more positively than the unfamiliar ones. The people doing the ratings don't know that they like one bit of music more than another *because* it's more familiar. Nonetheless, when products are essentially equivalent, people go with what's familiar, even if it's only familiar because they know its name from advertising.

If people want *real* information, they have to go beyond advertising to disinterested sources such as *Consumer Reports*. Its publisher, Consumers Union, is an independent, nonprofit organization whose mission is to help consumers. It does not allow any of its reports or ratings to be used in advertising, nor does the magazine contain any commercial advertising. When it was launched about seventy-five years ago, *Consumer Reports* offered comparisons among things like Grade A milk and Grade B milk. Today it offers comparisons among 220 new car models, 250 breakfast cereals, 400 VCRs, 40 household soaps, 500 health insurance policies, 350 mutual funds, and even 35 showerheads. And this barely scratches the surface. For every type of product that *Consumer Reports* evaluates, there are many that it passes over. And new models appear with such frequency that the evaluations are at least slightly out of date by the time they are published. The same limitation is true, of course, of other, more specialized guides—travel guides, college guides, and the like.

The Internet can give us information that is absolutely up-to-the-minute, but as a resource, it is democratic to a fault—everyone with a computer and smartphone can express their opinion, whether they know anything or not. The avalanche of electronic information we now face is such that in order to solve the problem of choosing from among 200 brands of cereal or 5,000 mutual funds, we must first solve the problem of choosing from 10,000 websites offering to make us informed consumers. If you want to experience this problem for yourself, pick some prescription drug that is now being marketed directly to you, then do a web search to find out what you can about the drug that goes beyond what the ads tell you. I just tried it for Prilosec, one of the largest-selling medications in existence, which is heavily advertised by its manufacturer. I got more than 900,000 hits!

And there is good evidence that the absence of filters on the Internet can lead people astray. The RAND Corporation conducted an assessment of the quality of websites providing medical information and found that "with rare exceptions, they're all doing an equally poor job." Important information was omitted, and sometimes the information presented was misleading or inaccurate.

Moreover, surveys indicate that these websites actually influence the health-related decisions of 70 percent of the people who consult them.

Evaluating the Information

EVEN IF WE CAN ACCURATELY DETERMINE WHAT WE WANT AND THEN find good information, in a quantity we can handle, do we really know how to analyze, sift, weigh, and evaluate it to arrive at the right conclusions and make the right choices? Not always. Spearheaded by psychologists Daniel Kahneman and Amos Tversky, researchers have spent the last thirty years studying how people make decisions. Their work documents the variety of rules of thumb we use that often lead us astray as we try to make wise decisions.

Availability

IMAGINE THAT YOU'RE IN THE MARKET FOR A NEW CAR AND THAT you care about only two things: safety and reliability. You dutifully check out *Consumer Reports*, which rates Volvo highest for safety and reliability, so you resolve to buy a Volvo. That evening, you're at a cocktail party and you mention your decision to a friend. "You're not going to buy a Volvo," she says. "My friend Jane bought one about six months ago, and she's had nothing but trouble. First there was an oil leak; then she had trouble starting it; then the CD player started malfunctioning. She's had it in the shop maybe five times in the six months she's owned it."

. You might feel lucky to have had this conversation before making a terrible mistake, but actually, maybe you're not so fortunate. *Consumer Reports* makes its judgments about the reliability of cars by soliciting input from its thousands and thousands of readers. It compiles this input into an estimate of reliability for each make and model of car. So when *Consumer Reports* says that a car is reliable, it is basing its conclusion on the experience of thousands of people with thousands of cars. This doesn't mean that every single Volvo driver will have the same story to tell. But on average, the reports of Volvo owners are more positive about reliability than the reports of the owners of other cars. Now along comes this friend to tell you about one particular Volvo owner and one particular Volvo. How much weight should you give this story? Should it undo conclusions based on the thousands of cases assessed by *Consumer Reports?* Of course not. Logically, it should have almost no influence on your decision.

Unfortunately, most people give substantial weight to this kind of anecdotal "evidence," perhaps so much so that it will cancel out the positive recommendation found in *Consumer Reports.* Most of us give weight to these kinds of stories because they are extremely vivid and based on a personal, detailed, face-to-face account.

Kahneman and Tversky discovered and reported on people's tendency to give undue weight to some types of information in contrast to others. They called it the *availability heuristic.* This needs a little explaining. A *heuristic* is a rule of thumb, a mental shortcut. The availability heuristic works like this: suppose someone asked you a silly question like "What's more common in English, words that begin with the letter *t* or words that have *t* as the third letter?" How would you answer this question? What you probably would do is try to call to mind words that start with *t* and words that have *t* as the third letter. You would then discover that you had a much easier time generating words that start with *t*. So words starting with *t* would be more "available" to you than words that have *t* as the third letter. You would then reason roughly as follows: "In general, the more often we encounter something, the easier it is for us to recall it in the future. Because I had an easier time recalling words that start with *t* than recalling words with *t* as the third letter, I must have encountered them more often in the past. So there must be more words in English that start with *t* than have it as the third letter." But your conclusion would be wrong.

The availability heuristic says that we assume that the more available some piece of information is to memory, the more frequently we must have encountered it in the past. This heuristic is partly true. In general, the frequency of experience does affect its availability to memory. But frequency of experience is not the *only* thing that affects availability to memory. Salience or vividness matters as well. Because starting letters of words are much more salient than third letters, they are much more useful as cues for retrieving words from memory. So it's the *salience* of starting letters that makes *t*-words come easily to mind, while people mistakenly think it's the *frequency* of starting letters that makes them come easily to mind. In addition to affecting the ease with which we retrieve information from memory, salience or vividness will influence the weight we give any particular piece of information.

There are many examples of the availability heuristic in operation. When college students who are deciding what courses to take next semester are presented with summaries of course evaluations from several hundred students that point in one direction, and a videotaped interview with a single student that points in the other direction, they are more influenced by the vivid interview than by the summary judgments of hundreds. Vivid interviews with people have profound effects on judgment even when people are told, in advance of seeing the interviews, that the subjects of the interview are atypical. Thus seeing an interview of an especially vicious (or humane) prison guard or an especially industrious (or slothful) welfare recipient shifts people's opinions of prison guards or welfare recipients in general. When spouses are asked (separately) a series of questions about what's good and bad about their marriage, each spouse holds him or herself more responsible than his or her partner, for both the good *and* the bad. People's natural egocentrism makes it much easier to bring their own actions to mind than those of their partner. Because our own actions are more available to us from memory, we assume they are more frequent.

Now consider the availability heuristic in the context of advertising, whose main objective is to make products appear salient and vivid. Does a particular carmaker give safety a high priority in the manufacture of its cars? When you see film footage of a crash test in which a $50,000 car is driven into a wall, it's hard to believe the car company doesn't care about safety, no matter what the crash-test statistics say.

How we assess risk offers another example of how our judgments can be distorted by availability. In one study, researchers asked respondents to estimate the number of deaths per year that occur as a result of various diseases, car accidents, natural disasters, electrocutions, and homicides—forty different types of misfortune in all. The researchers then compared people's answers to actual death rates, with striking results. Respondents judged accidents of all types to cause as many deaths as diseases of all types, when in fact disease causes sixteen times more deaths than accidents. Death by homicide was thought to be as frequent as death from stroke, when in fact eleven times more people die of strokes than from homicides. In general, dramatic, vivid causes of death (accident, homicide, tornado, flood, fire) were overestimated, whereas more mundane causes of death (diabetes, asthma, stroke, tuberculosis) were underestimated.

Where did these estimates come from? The authors of the study looked at two newspapers, published on opposite sides of the United States, and they counted the number of stories involving various causes of death. What they found was that the frequency of news-paper coverage and the respondents' estimates of the frequency of death were almost perfectly correlated. People mistook the perva-siveness of newspaper stories about homicides, accidents, or fires—vivid, salient, and easily available to memory—as a sign of the frequency of the events these stories profiled. This distortion causes us to miscalculate dramatically the various risks we face in life, and thus contributes to some very bad choices.

What often saves us from our faulty decision-making process is that different people experience different vivid or salient events, and thus have different events available to memory. You may have just read that Kias are actually very safe and you are all set to buy one. You mention this to me, but I've just read a story about a Kia being crushed by an SUV in an accident. So I tell you about my vivid memory, and that convinces you to revise your opinion. We are all susceptible to making errors, but we're not each susceptible to mak-ing the *same* errors, because our experiences are different. As long as we include social interactions in our information gathering, and as long as our sources of information are diverse, we can probably steer clear of the worst pitfalls.

The benefits of multi-individual information assessment is nicely illustrated by a demonstration that financial analyst Paul Johnson has done over the years. He asks students to predict who will win the Academy Award in several different categories. He tabulates the pre-dictions and comes up with group predictions—the nominees cho-sen by the most people for each category. What he finds, again and again, is that the group predictions are better than the predictions of any individual. In 1998, for example, the group picked eleven out of twelve winners, while the average individual in the group picked only five out of twelve, and even the best individual picked only nine.

But while diversity of individual experience can limit our propensity to choose in error, how much can we count on diversity of experience? As the number of choices we face continues to escalate and the amount of information we need escalates with it, we may find ourselves increasingly relying on secondhand information rather than on personal experience. Moreover, as telecommunications becomes ever more global, each of us, no matter where we are, may end up relying on the *same* secondhand information. National news sources such as CNN or *USA Today* tell everyone in the country, and now even the world, the same story, which makes it less likely that an individual's biased understanding of the evidence will be corrected by his friends and neighbors. Those friends and neighbors will have the same biased understanding, derived from the same source. When you hear the same story everywhere you look and listen, you assume it must be true. And the more people believe it's true, the more likely they are to repeat it, and thus the more likely you are to hear it. This is how inaccurate information can create a bandwagon effect, leading quickly to a broad, but mistaken, consensus.

Anchoring

SENSITIVITY TO AVAILABILITY IS NOT OUR ONLY ACHILLES' HEEL when it comes to making informed choices. How do you determine how much to spend on a suit? One way is to compare the price of one suit to another, which means using the other items as anchors, or standards. In a store that displays suits costing over $1,500, an $800 pinstripe may seem like a good buy. But in a store in which most of the suits cost less than $500, that same $800 suit might seem like an extravagance. So which is it, a good buy or a self-indulgence? Unless you're on a strict budget, there are no abso-lutes. In this kind of evaluation, any particular item will always be at the mercy of the context in which it is found.

One high-end catalog seller of mostly kitchen equipment and gourmet foods offered an automatic bread maker for $279. Some-time later, the catalog began to offer a larger capacity, deluxe ver-sion for $429. They didn't sell too many of these expensive bread makers, but sales of the less expensive one almost doubled! With the expensive bread maker serving as an anchor, the $279 machine had become a bargain.

Anchoring is why department stores seem to have some of their merchandise on sale most of the time, to give the impression that customers are getting a bargain. The original ticket price becomes an anchor against which the sale price is compared.

A more finely tuned example of the importance of the context of comparison comes from a study of supermarket shoppers done in the 1970s, shortly after unit pricing started appearing on the shelves just beneath the various items. When unit price informa-tion appeared on shelf tags, shoppers saved an average of 1 per-cent on their grocery bills. They did so mostly by purchasing the larger-sized packages of whatever brand they bought. However, when unit prices appeared on lists comparing different brands, shoppers saved an average of 3 percent on their bills. They did so now mostly by purchasing not larger sizes, but cheaper brands. To understand the difference, think about how most supermarket shelves are arranged. Different-sized packages of the same brand are typically adjacent to each other. In this case, what the shopper gets to see, side by side, is the "small," "large," and "family" sizes of the same item along with their respective unit prices. This makes it easy to compare unit prices within the same brand. To compare unit prices across brands might require walking from one end of the aisle to the other. The multibrand list of unit prices makes it easier for shoppers to do cross-brand comparisons. And when such comparisons are easy to make, shoppers follow through and act on the information.

When we see outdoor gas grills on the market for $8,000, it seems quite reasonable to buy one for $1,200. When a wristwatch that is no more accurate than one you can buy for $50 sells for $20,000, it seems reasonable to buy one for $2,000. Even if companies sell almost none of their highest-priced models, they can reap enormous benefits from producing such models because they help induce people to buy their cheaper (but still extremely expensive) ones. Alas, there seems to be little we can do to avoid being influenced by the alternatives that anchor our comparison processes.

Frames and Accounts

AND CONTEXT THAT INFLUENCES CHOICE CAN ALSO BE CREATED BY language.

Imagine two gas stations at opposite corners of a busy intersection. One offers a discount for cash transactions and has a big sign that says:

DISCOUNT FOR PAYING CASH!
CASH—$1.85 per GALLON
CREDIT—$1.95 per GALLON

The other, imposing a surcharge for credit, has a small sign, just above the pumps, that says:

Cash—$1.85 per Gallon
Credit—$1.95 per Gallon

The sign is small, and doesn't call attention to itself, because people don't like surcharges.

Beyond the difference in presentation, though, there is no difference in the price structure at these two gas stations. A discount for paying cash is, effectively, the same as a surcharge for using credit. Nonetheless, fuel-hungry consumers will have very different subjective responses to the two different propositions.

Daniel Kahneman and Amos Tversky call this effect *framing*. What determines whether a given price represents a discount or a surcharge? Consumers certainly can't tell from the price itself. In addition to the current price, potential buyers would need to know the standard or "reference" price. If the reference price of gas is $1.95, then those who pay cash are getting a discount. If the reference price is $1.85, then those who use credit are paying a surcharge. What the two gas station proprietors are offering is two different assumptions about the reference price of gas.

The effects of framing become even more powerful when the stakes are higher:

> Imagine that you are a physician working in an Asian village, and six hundred people have come down with a life-threatening disease. Two possible treatments exist. If you choose treatment A, you will save exactly two hundred people. If you choose treatment B, there is a one-third chance that you will save all six hundred people, and a two-thirds chance that you will save no one. Which treatment do you choose, A or B?

The vast majority of respondents faced with this choice choose treatment A. They prefer saving a definite number of lives for sure to the risk that they will save no one. But now consider this slightly different problem:

> You are a physician working in an Asian village, and six hundred people have come down with a life-threatening disease. Two possible treatments exist. If you choose treatment C, exactly four hundred people will die. If you choose treatment D, there is a one-third chance that no one will die, and a two-thirds chance that everyone will die. Which treatment do you choose, C or D?

Now the overwhelming majority of respondents choose treatment D. They would rather risk losing everyone than settle for the death of four hundred.

It seems to be a fairly general principle that when making choices among alternatives that involve a certain amount of risk or uncertainty, we prefer a small, sure gain to a larger, uncertain one. Most of us, for example, will choose a sure $100 over a coin flip (a fifty-fifty chance) that determines whether we win $200 or nothing. When the possibilities involve losses, however, we will risk a large loss to avoid a smaller one. For example, we will choose a coin flip that determines whether we lose $200 or nothing over a sure loss of $100.

But the fact of the matter is that the dilemma facing the physician in each of the two cases above is actually the same.

If there are six hundred sick people, saving two hundred (choice A in the first problem) means losing four hundred (choice C in the second problem). A two-thirds chance of saving no one (choice B in the first problem) means a two-thirds chance of losing everyone (choice D in the second problem). And yet, based on one presentation, people chose risk, and based on the other, certainty. Just as in the matter of discounts and surcharges, it is the framing of the choice that affects our perception of it, and in turn affects what we choose.

Now let's look at another pair of questions:

Imagine that you have decided to see a concert where admission is $20 a ticket. As you enter the concert hall, you discover that you have lost a $20 bill. Would you still pay $20 for a ticket to the concert?

Almost 90 percent of respondents say yes. In contrast:

Imagine that you have decided to see a concert and already purchased a $20 ticket. As you enter the concert hall, you discover that you have lost the ticket. The seat was not marked and the ticket cannot be recovered. Would you pay $20 for another ticket?

In this situation, less than 50 percent of respondents say yes. What is the difference between these two cases? From the perspective of the "bottom line," they appear the same; both involve a choice between seeing a concert and being $40 poorer or not seeing it and being $20 poorer. Yet obviously we don't seem to see them as the same, because so many respondents choose differently in the two cases. Kahneman and Tversky, influenced by the pioneering work of economist Richard Thaler, suggest that the difference between the two cases has to do with the way in which we frame our "psychological accounts." Suppose that in a person's psychological ledger there is a "cost of the concert" account. In the first case, the cost of the concert is $20 charged to that account. But the lost $20 bill is charged to some other account, perhaps "miscellaneous." But in the second case, the cost of the concert is $40; the cost of the lost ticket, plus the cost of the replacement ticket, both charged to the same account.

The range of possible frames or accounting systems we might use is enormous. For example, an evening at a concert could be just one entry in a much larger account, say a "meeting a potential mate" account, because you're going out in the hope of meeting someone who shares your interests. Or it could be part of a "getting culture" account, in which case it would be one entry among others that might include subscribing to public television, buying certain books and magazines, and the like. It could be part of a "ways to spend a Friday night" account, in which case it would join entries like hanging out at a bar, going to a basketball game, or staying home and dozing in front of the television. How much this night at a concert is worth will depend on which account it is a part of. Forty dollars may be a lot to spend for a way to fill Friday evening, but not much to spend to find a mate. In sum, just how well this $40 night at the concert satisfies you will depend on how you do your accounting. People often talk jokingly about how "creative" accountants can make a corporate balance sheet look as good or as bad as they want it to look. Well, the point here is that we are all creative accountants when it comes to keeping our own psychological balance sheet.

Frames and Prospects

KAHNEMAN AND TVERSKY USED THEIR RESEARCH ON FRAMING and its effects to construct a general explanation of how we go about evaluating options and making decisions. They called it *prospect theory*.

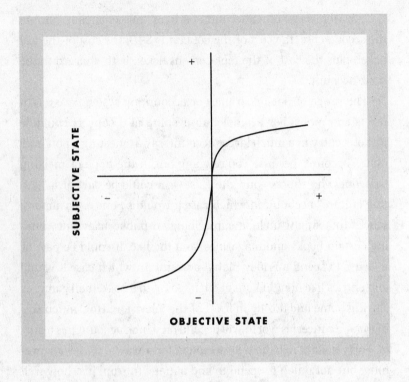

If you look at the diagram above, you see objective states of affairs along the horizontal axis—positive to the right of the vertical axis, and negative to the left of it. These might be gains or losses of money, gains or losses of status on the job, gains or losses in your golf handicap, and so on. Along the vertical axis are subjective or psychological responses to these changes in states of the affairs. How good do people feel when they win $1,000 at the racetrack? How bad do people feel when their golf handicap goes up three strokes? If psychological responses to changes were perfectly faithful reflections of those changes, the curve relating the objective to the subjective would be a straight line that went right through the 0-point, or origin, of the graph. But as you can see, that is not the case.

To figure out why prospect theory gives us this curve rather than a straight line, let's look at the two halves of the graph separately. The top, right portion of the graph depicts responses to positive events. The thing to notice about this curve is that its steepness decreases as it moves further to the right. Thus, an objective gain of, say, $100 may give 10 units of subjective satisfaction, but a gain of $200 won't give 20 units of satisfaction. It will give, say, 18 units. As the magnitude of the gain increases, the amount of additional satisfaction people get out of each additional unit decreases. The shape of this curve conforms to what economists have long talked about as the "law of diminishing marginal utility." As the rich get richer, each additional unit of wealth satisfies them less.

With the graph of prospect theory in view, think about this question: would you rather have $100 for sure or have me flip a coin and give you $200 if it comes up heads and nothing if it comes up tails? Most people asked this question go for the sure $100. Let's see why. A sure $100 and a fifty-fifty chance for $200 are in some sense equivalent. The fact that the payoff for the risky choice is double the payoff for the sure thing exactly compensates for the fact that the chances you'll get the payoff are halved. But if you look at the graph, you'll see that psychologically, you won't feel twice as good with $200 in your pocket as you will with $100 in your pocket. You'll feel about 1.7 times as good. So to make the gamble psychologically worthwhile to you, I'd have to offer you something like $240 for a heads. Thus, Kahneman and Tversky point out, people tend to avoid taking risks—they are "risk averse"—when they are deciding among potential gains, potential positive outcomes.

Now let's look at the other side of the graph, which depicts response to losses. It too is a curve, not a straight line. So suppose I asked you this question: would you rather lose $100 for sure or have me flip a coin so that you lose $200 if it comes up heads and you lose nothing if it comes up tails? As in the last example, double the amount is compensated for by half the chances. If you don't like risks in the first problem, you probably won't like them in the second either. This suggests you'll take the sure loss of $100. But chances are you didn't, and the graph tells us why. Notice that the curve falls steeply at the beginning and then gradually levels off. This reflects what might be called the "decreasing marginal *disutility* of losses." Losing the first $100 hurts worse than losing the second $100. So although losing $200 may be twice as bad objectively as losing $100, it is not twice as bad subjectively. What that means is that taking the risk to perhaps avoid losing anything is a pretty good deal. Thus, as Kahneman and Tversky again point out, people embrace risk—they are "risk seeking"—in the domain of potential losses.

There is another feature of the graph worth noting: the loss portion of the graph is much steeper than the gain portion. Losing $100 produces a feeling of negativity that is more intense than the feelings of elation produced by a gain. Some studies have estimated that losses have more than twice the psychological impact as equivalent gains. The fact is, we all hate to lose, which Kahneman and Tversky refer to as *loss aversion*.

The last and crucial element to the graph is the location of the neutral point. This is the dividing line between what counts as a gain and what counts as a loss, and here, too, subjectivity rules. When there is a difference in price between cash and credit at the gas station, is it a discount for cash or a surcharge for credit? If you think it's a discount for cash, then you're setting your neutral point at the credit-card price and paying cash is a gain. If you think it's a surcharge, then you're setting your neutral point at the cash price, and using your credit card is a loss. So fairly subtle manipulations of wording can affect what the neutral point is and whether we are thinking in terms of gains or losses. And these manipulations will in turn have profound effects on the decisions we make—effects that we really don't want them to have, since in an important sense, discounts and surcharges are just two ways of saying the same thing.

In the same way, we give disproportionate weight to whether yogurt is said to be 5 percent fat or 95 percent fat free. People seem to think that yogurt that is 95 percent fat free is a more healthful product than yogurt that has 5 percent fat, not realizing, apparently, that yogurt with 5 percent fat *is* 95 percent fat free.

Or suppose you are one of a large group of participants in a study and for your time and trouble, you are given either a coffee mug or a nice pen. The two gifts are of roughly equal value and randomly distributed—half of the people in the room get one, while the other half get the other. You and your fellow participants are then given the opportunity to trade. Considering the random distribution, you would think that about half the people in the group would have gotten the object they preferred and that the other half would be happy to swap. But in fact, there are very few trades. This phenomenon is called the *endowment effect*. Once something is given to you, it's yours. Once it becomes part of your endowment, even after a very few minutes, giving it up will entail a loss. And, as prospect theory tells us, because losses are more bad than gains are good, the mug or pen with which you have been "endowed" is worth more to you than it is to a potential trading partner. And "losing" (giving up) the pen will hurt worse than "gaining" (trading for) the mug will give pleasure. Thus, you won't make the trade.

The endowment effect helps explain why companies can afford to offer money-back guarantees on their products. Once people own them, the products are worth more to their owners than the mere cash value, because giving up the products would entail a loss. Most interestingly, people seem to be utterly unaware that the endowment effect is operating, even as it distorts their judgment. In one study, participants were given a mug to examine and asked to write down the price they would demand for selling it if they owned it. A few minutes later, they were actually given the mug, along with the opportunity to sell it. When they owned the mug, they demanded 30 percent more to sell it than they had said they would only a few minutes earlier!

One study compared the way in which the endowment effect influences people to make car-buying decisions under two conditions. In one condition, they were offered the car loaded with options, and their task was to eliminate the options they didn't want. In the second condition, they were offered the car devoid of options, and their task was to add the ones they wanted. People in the first condition ended up with many more options than people in the second. This is because when options are already attached to the car being considered, they become part of the endowment and passing them up entails a feeling of loss. When the options are not already attached, they are not part of the endowment and choosing them is perceived as a gain. But because losses hurt more than gains satisfy, people judging, say, a $400 stereo upgrade that is part of the car's endowment may decide that giving it up (a loss) will hurt worse than its $400 price. In contrast, when the upgrade is not part of the car's endowment, they may decide that choosing it (a gain) won't produce $400 worth of good feeling. So the endowment effect is operating even before people actually close the deal on their new car. Perhaps the most dramatic example of the endowment effect that I know of was reported by decision researchers Ziv Carmon and Dan Ariely. It concerned tickets to see the Duke University men's basketball team play in the national championships. Tickets were in extremely high demand among Duke students, with some of them camping out on a line for a week just to get entered into a lottery that would determine who got tickets and who didn't. Since the lottery results were random, presumably those who won the right to buy tickets and those who did not were equally desirous of the tickets. So Carmon and Ariely asked the unlucky losers how much they would pay for a ticket: $175 was the answer. And then they asked the lucky winners how much they would have to be paid to give up a ticket: $2,400 was the answer! For the winners, giving up a ticket they had won the right to purchase would be a loss of their "endowment," an endowment that had inflated the value of the ticket by a factor of fifteen.

Aversion to losses also leads people to be sensitive to what are called "sunk costs." Imagine having a $50 ticket to a basketball game being played an hour's drive away. Just before the game there's a big snowstorm—do you still want to go? Economists would tell us that the way to assess a situation like this is to think about the future, not the past. The $50 is already spent; it's "sunk" and can't be recovered. What matters is whether you'll feel better safe and warm at home, watching the game on TV, or slogging through the snow on treacherous roads to see the game in person. That's *all* that should matter. But it isn't all that matters. To stay home is to incur a loss of $50, and people hate losses, so they drag themselves out to the game.

Economist Richard Thaler provides another example of sunk costs that I suspect many people can identify with. You buy a pair of shoes that turn out to be really uncomfortable. What will you do about them? Thaler suggests:

> The more expensive they were, the more often you'll try to
>   wear them.
> Eventually, you'll stop wearing them, but you won't get
>   rid of them. And the more you paid for them, the longer
>   they'll sit in the back of your closet.

At some point, after the shoes have been fully "depreciated"
psychologically, you will finally throw them away.

Is there anyone who does not have some item of clothing sitting
unused (and never to be used) in a drawer or on a shelf?

Information Gathering in a World with Too Many Options

N THIS CHAPTER WE'VE SEEN SOME OF THE MISTAKES PEOPLE CAN
make predicting what they want, gathering information about
alternatives, and evaluating that information. The evidence clearly
demonstrates that people are susceptible to error even when choosing among a handful of alternatives to which they can devote their
full attention. Susceptibility to error can only get worse as the
number and complexity of decisions increase, which in general
describe the conditions of daily life. Nobody has the time or cognitive resources to be completely thorough and accurate with every
decision, and as more decisions are required and more options are
available, the challenge of doing the decision making correctly
becomes ever more difficult to meet.

With many decisions, the consequences of error may be trivial—a
small price to pay for the wealth of choices available to us. But with
some, the consequences of error may be quite severe. We may make
bad investments because we are not well informed enough about the
tax consequences of investing in the various possibilities. We may
choose the wrong health plan because we don't have time to read
all the fine print. We may go to the wrong school, choose the wrong
courses, embark on the wrong career, all because of the way in
which the options were presented to us. As we find more and more
important decisions on our plates, we may be forced to make many

of those decisions with inadequate reflection. And in these cases, the stakes can be high.

Even with relatively unimportant decisions, mistakes can take a toll. When you put a lot of time and effort into choosing a restaurant or a place to go on vacation or a new item of clothing, you want that effort to be rewarded with a satisfying result. As options increase, the effort involved in making decisions increases, so mistakes hurt even more. Thus the growth of options and opportunities for choice has three, related, unfortunate effects.

It means that decisions require more effort.
It makes mistakes more likely.
It makes the psychological consequences of mistakes more
    severe.

Finally, the very wealth of options before us may turn us from choosers into pickers. A chooser is someone who thinks actively about the possibilities before making a decision. A chooser reflects on what's important to him or her in life, what's important about this particular decision, and what the short- and long-range consequences of the decision may be. A chooser makes decisions in a way that reflects awareness of what a given choice means about him or her as a person. Finally, a chooser is thoughtful enough to conclude that perhaps none of the available alternatives are satisfactory, and that if he or she wants the right alternative, he or she may have to create it.

A picker does none of these things. With a world of choices rushing by like a music video, all a picker can do is grab this or that and hope for the best. Obviously, this is not such a big deal when what's being picked is breakfast cereals. But decisions don't always come at us with signs indicating their relative importance prominently attached. Unfortunately, the proliferation of choice in our lives robs us of the opportunity to decide for ourselves just how important any given decision is.

In the next chapter we will look more closely at how we make our decisions, and at the varying prices we pay for them.

CHAPTER FOUR

When Only the Best Will Do

CHOOSING WISELY BEGINS WITH DEVELOPING A CLEAR UNDER-standing of your goals. And the first choice you must make is between the goal of choosing the absolute best and the goal of choosing something that is good enough.

If you seek and accept only the best, you are a *maximizer*.

Imagine going shopping for a sweater. You go to a couple of department stores or boutiques, and after an hour or so, you find a sweater that you like. The color is striking, the fit is flattering, and the wool feels soft against your skin. The sweater costs $89. You're all set to take it to the salesperson when you think about the store down the street that has a reputation for low prices. You take the sweater back to its display table, hide it under a pile of other sweaters of a different size (so that no one will buy it out from under you), and leave to check out the other store.

Maximizers need to be assured that every purchase or decision was the best that could be made. Yet how can anyone truly know that any given option is absolutely the best possible? The only way to know is to check out all the alternatives. A maximizer can't be certain that she has found the best sweater unless she's looked at all the sweaters. She can't know that she is getting the best price unless she's checked out all the prices. As a decision strategy, maximizing creates a daunting task, which becomes all the more daunting as the number of options increases.

The alternative to maximizing is to be a *satisficer*. To satisfice is to settle for something that is good enough and not worry about the possibility that there might be something better. A satisficer has criteria and standards. She searches until she finds an item that meets those standards, and at that point, she stops. As soon as she finds a sweater that meets her standard of fit, quality, and price in the very first store she enters, she buys it—end of story. She is not concerned about better sweaters or better bargains just around the corner.

Of course no one is an absolute maximizer. Truly checking out all the sweaters in all the stores would mean that buying a single sweater could take a lifetime. The key point is that maximizers *aspire* to achieve that goal. Thus, they spend a great deal of time and effort on the search, reading labels, checking out consumer magazines, and trying new products. Worse, after making a selection, they are nagged by the options they haven't had time to investigate. In the end, they are likely to get less satisfaction out of the exquisite choices they make than will satisficers. When reality requires maximizers to compromise—to end a search and decide on something—apprehension about what might have been takes over.

To a maximizer, satisficers appear to be willing to settle for mediocrity, but that is not the case. A satisficer may be just as discriminating as a maximizer. The difference between the two types is that the satisficer is content with the merely excellent as opposed to the absolute best.

I believe that the goal of maximizing is a source of great dissatisfaction, that it can make people miserable—especially in a world that insists on providing an overwhelming number of choices, both trivial and not so trivial.

When Nobel Prize–winning economist and psychologist Herbert Simon initially introduced the idea of "satisficing" in the 1950s, he suggested that when all the costs (in time, money, and anguish) involved in getting information about all the options are factored in, satisficing *is*, in fact, the maximizing strategy. In other words, the best people can do, all things considered, is to satisfice. The perceptiveness of Simon's observation is at the heart of many of the strategies I will offer for fighting back against the tyranny of overwhelming choices.

Distinguishing Maximizers from Satisficers

WE ALL KNOW PEOPLE WHO DO THEIR CHOOSING QUICKLY AND decisively and people for whom almost every decision is a major project. A few years ago, several colleagues and I attempted to develop a set of questions that would diagnose people's propensity to maximize or satisfice. We came up with a thirteen-item survey.

We asked those taking the survey whether they agreed with each item. The more they agreed, the more they were maximizers. Try it for yourself. Write a number from 1 (completely disagree) to 7 (completely agree) next to each question. Now add up these thirteen numbers. Your score can range from a low of 13 to a high of 91. If your total is 65 or higher, you are clearly on the maximizing end of the scale. If your score is 40 or lower, you are on the satisficing end of the scale.

We gave this survey to several thousand people. The high score was 75, the low 25, and the average about 50. Perhaps surprisingly, there were no differences between men and women.

Let's go through the items on the scale, imagining what a maximizer would say to himself as he answered the questions.

MAXIMIZATION SCALE

1. Whenever I'm faced with a choice, I try to imagine what all the other possibilities are, even ones that aren't present at the moment.

2. No matter how satisfied I am with my job, it's only right for me to be on the lookout for better opportunities.

3. When I am in the car listening to the radio, I often check other stations to see if something better is playing, even if I am relatively satisfied with what I'm listening to.

4. When I watch TV, I channel surf, often scanning through the available options even while attempting to watch one program.

5. I treat relationships like clothing: I expect to try a lot on before finding the perfect fit.

6. I often find it difficult to shop for a gift for a friend.

7. Renting videos is really difficult. I'm always struggling to pick the best one.

8. When shopping, I have a hard time finding clothing that I really love.

9. I'm a big fan of lists that attempt to rank things (the best movies, the best singers, the best athletes, the best novels, etc.).

10. I find that writing is very difficult, even if it's just writing a letter to a friend, because it's so hard to word things just right. I often do several drafts of even simple things.

11. No matter what I do, I have the highest standards for myself.
12. I never settle for second best.
13. I often fantasize about living in ways that are quite different from my actual life.

(Courtesy of American Psychological Association)

1. **Whenever I'm faced with a choice, I try to imagine what all the other possibilities are, even ones that aren't present at the moment.** The maximizer would agree. How can you tell you have the "best" without considering all the alternatives? What about the sweaters that might be available in other stores?

2. **No matter how satisfied I am with my job, it's only right for me to be on the lookout for better opportunities.** A "good" job is probably not the "best" job. A maximizer is always concerned that there is something better out there and acts accordingly.

3. **When I am in the car listening to the radio, I often check other stations to see if something better is playing, even if I am relatively satisfied with what I'm listening to.** Yes, the maximizer likes this song, but the idea is to get to listen to the *best* song, not to settle for one that is good enough. Of course, nowadays, people probably don't listen to the radio much in their cars. They just plug their hand-crafted digital playlists into the car's sound system. But how hard was it for them to create those digital playlists?

4. **When I watch TV, I channel surf, often scanning through the available options even while attempting to watch one program.** Again, a maximizer seeks not just a good TV show, but the best one.

With all these stations available, there might be a better show on somewhere.

5. **I treat relationships like clothing: I expect to try a lot on before finding the perfect fit.** For a maximer, somewhere out there is the perfect lover, the perfect friend. Even though there is nothing wrong with your current relationship, who knows what's possible if you keep your eyes open. Journalist and psychologist Lori Gottlieb published an account of her (and other women's) travails as looking for "Mr. Perfect" that captures the pitfalls of being a maximizer when it comes to romance. She called her book *Marry Him: The Case for Settling for Mr. Good Enough*. The title says it all.

6. **I often find it difficult to shop for a gift for a friend.** Maximizers find it difficult because somewhere out there is the "perfect" gift.

7. **Renting videos is really difficult. I'm always struggling to pick the best one.** There are thousands of possibilities in the video store. There must be one that's just right for my current mood and the people I'll be watching with. I'll just pick out the best of the current releases and then scour the rest of the store to see if there's a classic that would be even better. As with car radios, people don't go to video stores anymore, but deciding what video to stream poses the same problem. Indeed, it may pose a worse problem, since the list of what you can stream is endless whereas even the most impressive video store couldn't stock everything.

8. **When shopping, I have a hard time finding clothing that I really love.** The only way a maximizer can "really love" a clothing item is by knowing that there isn't a better alternative out there somewhere.

9. **I'm a big fan of lists that attempt to rank things (the best movies, the best singers, the best athletes, the best novels, etc.).** People concerned with finding the best will be much more interested in ranking things than people happy with "good enough." (If you read

the novel or saw the movie *High Fidelity*, you've seen how this tendency can get wildly out of hand.)

10. **I find that writing is very difficult, even if it's just writing a letter to a friend, because it's so hard to word things just right. I often do several drafts of even simple things.** Maximizers can edit themselves into writer's block.

11. **No matter what I do, I have the highest standards for myself.** Maximizers want *everything* they do to be just right, which can lead to unhealthy self-criticism.

12. **I never settle for second best.** Here, self-editing and self-criticism can lead to inertia.

13. **I often fantasize about living in ways that are quite different from my actual life.** Maximizers spend more time than satisficers thinking about "roads not traveled." Whole shelves of psychological self-help books testify to the dangers of this "shoulda, woulda, coulda" thinking.

In another study, we asked respondents several questions that would reveal their maximizing tendencies in action. Not surprisingly, we found that

1. Maximizers engage in more product comparisons than satisficers, both before and after they make purchasing decisions.
2. Maximizers take longer than satisficers to decide on a purchase.
3. Maximizers spend more time than satisficers comparing their purchasing decisions to the decisions of others.
4. Maximizers are more likely to experience regret after a purchase.

EXAMPLE OF A MAXIMIZER

© *The New Yorker Collection 2000 Leo Cullum from cartoonbank.com. All Rights Reserved.*

5. Maximizers are more likely to spend time thinking about hypothetical alternatives to the purchases they've made.

6. Maximizers generally feel less positive about their purchasing decisions.

And when the questioning was broadened to include other experiences, we found something much more compelling:

1. Maximizers savor positive events less than satisficers and do not cope as well (by their own admission) with negative events.
2. After something bad happens to them, maximizers' sense of well-being takes longer to recover.
3. Maximizers tend to brood or ruminate more than satisficers.

The Price of Maximizing

THE PROBLEMS CREATED BY BEING AWASH WITH CHOICE SHOULD be much worse for maximizers than they are for satisficers. If you're a satisficer, the number of available options need not have a significant impact on your decision making. When you examine an object and it's good enough to meet your standards, you look no further; thus, the countless other available choices become irrelevant. But if you're a maximizer, every option has the potential to snare you into endless tangles of anxiety, regret, and second-guessing.

Does it follow that maximizers are less happy than satisficers? We tested this idea by having the same people who filled out the Maximization Scale fill out a variety of other questionnaires that have been shown over the years to be reliable indicators of well-being. One questionnaire measured happiness. A sample item from that questionnaire asked people to rate themselves on a scale that went from "not a very happy person" to "a very happy person." Another questionnaire measured optimism. A sample item asked people how much they agreed that "in uncertain times, I usually expect the best." Another questionnaire was the Satisfaction with Life Scale.

A sample item asked people how much they agreed that "the conditions of my life are excellent." A final questionnaire measured depression, and asked people how sad they felt, how much satisfaction they got out of various activities, how much interest they had in other people, and what they thought of their appearance, among other things.

Our expectation was confirmed: people with high maximization scores experienced less satisfaction with life, were less happy, were less optimistic, and were more depressed than people with low maximization scores. In fact, people with extreme maximization scores—scores of 65 or more out of 91—had depression scores that placed them in the borderline clinical depression range.

But I need to emphasize one important caveat: What these studies show is that being a maximizer is *correlated* with being unhappy. They do not show that being a maximizer *causes* unhappiness, because correlation does not necessarily indicate cause and effect. Nonetheless, I believe that being a maximizer does play a causal role in people's unhappiness, and I believe that learning how to satisfice is an important step not only in coping with a world of choice but in simply enjoying life.

Maximizing and Regret

MAXIMIZERS ARE MUCH MORE SUSCEPTIBLE THAN SATISFICERS TO all forms of regret, especially that known as "buyer's remorse." If you're a satisficer and you choose something that's good enough to meet your standards, you are less likely to care if something better is just around the corner. But if you're a maximizer, such a discovery can be a source of real pain. "If only I had gone to one more store." "If only I had read *Consumer Reports*." "If only I had listened to Jack's advice." You can generate *if only*'s indefinitely, and each one you generate will diminish the satisfaction you get from the choice you actually made.

It's hard to go through life regretting every decision you make because it might not have been the best possible decision. And it's easy to see that if you experience regret on a regular basis, it will rob you of at least some of the satisfaction that your good decisions warrant. What is even worse is that you can actually experience regret in *anticipation* of making a decision. You imagine how you'll feel if you discover that there was a better option available. And that leap of imagination may be all it takes to plunge you into a mire of uncertainty—even misery—over every looming decision.

I will have much more to say about regret in Chapter 7, but for now, let's take a look at another scale we developed in conjunction with our Maximization Scale to measure regret.

To score yourself on this scale, just put a number from 1 ("Disagree Completely") to 7 ("Agree Completely") next to each question. Then subtract from 8 the number you put next to the first question, and add the result to the other numbers. The higher your score, the more susceptible you are to regret.

Our findings with the Regret Scale have been dramatic. Almost everyone who scores high on the Maximization Scale also scores high on regret.

Imagine that you had to choose between two possible investments. Before choosing, you identify a target rate of return, say 8 percent. Then, you make your choice and you find out how each of the investments does over the course of a year. Suppose you choose Investment A and find out that it has earned 10 percent. Are you pleased? Now, suppose you find out that Investment B, the one you didn't choose, earned 12 percent. Are you still pleased? In a

REGRET SCALE

1. Once I make a decision, I don't look back.
2. Whenever I make a choice, I'm curious about what would have happened if I had chosen differently.
3. If I make a choice and it turns out well, I still feel like something of a failure if I find out that another choice would have turned out better.
4. Whenever I make a choice, I try to get information about how the other alternatives turned out.
5. When I think about how I'm doing in life, I often assess opportunities I have passed up.

(Courtesy of American Psychological Association)

study just like this, Wen-Hsien Huang and Marcel Zeelenberg found that as long as the chosen investment exceeded the target rate of return, people were happy with it. Unless they were maximizers. When maximizers found out that the option they didn't choose did better than the one they did choose, they were unhappy, even when the option they did choose exceeded their target.

Maximizing and the Quality of Decisions

OUR STUDIES SHOW THAT MAXIMIZERS PAY A SIGNIFICANT PRICE IN terms of personal well-being. But does their quest for perfection lead, at least, to better decisions? Since maximizers have higher standards than satisficers, one would think that they end up with better things. The "best" apartment is better than a "good enough" apartment. The "best" job is better than the "good enough" job. And the "best" romantic partner is better than the "good enough" romantic partner. How could it be otherwise?

The answer is complicated. Whereas maximizers might do better *objectively* than satisficers, they tend to do worse *subjectively*. Imagine a maximizer who succeeds in buying a sweater after an extensive search—a better sweater than any but the luckiest satisficer would end up with. How does he feel about the sweater? Is he frustrated at how much time and work went into buying it? Is he imagining unexamined alternatives that might be better? Is he asking himself whether friends of his might have gotten better deals? Is he scrutinizing every person he passes in the street to see if they're wearing sweaters that look finer? The maximizer might be plagued by any or all of these doubts and concerns while the satisficer marches on in warmth and comfort.

To illustrate this point consider a study in which Sheena Iyengar, Rachel Wells, and I followed college students for the better part of their senior year as they searched for jobs. They had all filled out the Maximization Scale at the start of the study. We found that people who scored high on the scale sought more options, did more research on job possibilities, compared themselves to their peers more, and spent more time on the process than people who scored low on our scale. They also got better jobs. Maximizers landed jobs with starting salaries that were 20 percent higher than the jobs that satisficers got. But (and it's a big but) maximizers were more pessimistic, anxious, stressed, worried, tired, depressed, regretful, and disappointed than satisficers were. And they were less optimistic, content, excited, and happy. In other words, maximizers did better than satisficers, but felt worse about how they did.

So we have to ask ourselves what counts when we assess the

quality of a decision. Is it *objective results* or *subjective experiences*? What matters to us most of the time, I think, is how we feel about the decisions we make. When economists theorize about how consumers operate in the market, they assume that people seek to maximize their preferences, or their satisfaction. What becomes clear about "satisfaction" or "preferences" as they are experienced in real life is that they are subjective, not objective. Getting the best objective result may not be worth much if we feel disappointed with it anyway.

But while this subjective satisfaction scale may work for trivial decisions, when it comes to important life issues—education, for instance—isn't objective quality all that matters? No, I don't think so. I have interacted with college students for many years as a professor, and in my experience, students who think they're in the right place get far more out of a particular school than students who don't. Conviction that they have found a good fit makes students more confident, more open to experience, and more attentive to opportunities. So while objective experience clearly matters, subjective experience has a great deal to do with the quality of that objective experience.

Which is not to say that students who are satisfied with bad colleges will get a good education, or that patients who are satisfied with incompetent doctors will not suffer in the end. But remember, I'm not saying that satisficers do not have standards. Satisficers may have very high standards. It's just that they allow themselves to be satisfied once experiences meet those standards.

Following Herbert Simon's reasoning, some might argue that my description of maximizers is actually a description of people who don't truly understand what it means to "maximize." A real maximizer would figure in the costs (in time and money and stress) of gathering and assessing information. An exhaustive search of the possibilities, which entails enormous "information costs," is not the way to maximize one's investment. The true maximizer would determine just how much information seeking was the amount needed to lead to a very good decision. The maximizer would figure out when information seeking had reached the point of diminishing returns. And at that point, the maximizer would stop the search and choose the best option encountered thus far.

But maximizing is not a measure of efficiency. It is a state of mind. If your goal is to get the best, then you will not be comfortable with compromises dictated by the constraints imposed by reality. You will not experience the kind of satisfaction with your choices that satisficers will. In every area of life, you will always be open to the possibility that you might find something better if you just keep looking.

Maximizing and Perfectionism

WHEN WE GO BEYOND CONSUMPTION AND INTO THE REALMS OF performance, it's important to distinguish between what we mean by "maximizers" and what describes "perfectionists." We have given some of the respondents who filled out our Maximization Scale a scale to measure perfectionism, and we have found that, while responses on the two scales are correlated, maximizing and perfectionism are not interchangeable.

A perfectionist is not satisfied doing a "good enough" job if he or she can do better. A musician keeps practicing and practicing a piece even after she has reached a level of performance that virtually everyone in the audience will regard as flawless. A top student keeps revising a paper long past the point where it is good enough to get an A. Tiger Woods works tirelessly on his game long after he has attained excellence that no one had previously thought possible. When it comes to achievement, being a perfectionist has clear advantages.

Thus perfectionists, like maximizers, seek to achieve the best. But I think there is an important difference between them. While maximizers and perfectionists both have very high standards, I think that perfectionists have very high standards that they don't expect to meet, whereas maximizers have very high standards that they *do* expect to meet.

Which may explain why we found that those who score high on perfectionism, unlike maximizers, are not depressed, regretful, or unhappy. Perfectionists may not be as happy with the results of their actions as they should be, but they seem to be happier with the results of their actions than maximizers are with the results of theirs.

When Do Maximizers Maximize?

I AM NOT A MAXIMIZER. WHEN I ANSWERED THE QUESTIONNAIRE ON maximizing, I scored less than 20. I hate to shop and when I have to, I can't wait to get it over with. I stick to the brands I know and do my best to ignore new choices on the market. I pay scant attention to my investments. I don't worry about whether I'm getting the best rates from my cell phone provider. I stick to old versions of computer software for as long as I can. And in my work, while I do adhere to very high standards, I don't expect to attain perfection. When I think a paper I'm writing or a class I'm preparing is good enough, I go on to something else. Perhaps if I spent some more time looking for better deals, I'd have more money. If I spent more time on my work, perhaps I'd be a better teacher. But I accept these "losses."

Nonetheless, like practically everyone else, I have my own select areas in which I tend to maximize. When I go into one of those fancy stores that sell elegantly prepared takeout foods or to a social gathering that offers a buffet that looks like it was prepared for *Gourmet* magazine, I look at the wide variety of delicious foods, and I want them all. I can imagine what they all taste like, and I want to experience each one. So I find myself reluctant to make a decision. As a maximizer in this regard, I experience many of the problems I've been talking about in this chapter. When I finally make a choice, I think about the items I've passed up. I second-guess myself, and I often regret my decision, not because it turns out badly, but because I suspect that a different decision might have turned out better. In restaurants, I have difficulty ordering, and then I look at food being brought out to other diners, and not infrequently conclude that they ordered more wisely than I did. All of which clearly diminishes the satisfaction I get from the choices I actually make.

You may not be a picky eater, but you may spend months looking for the right sound system. You may not care about clothes, but you will put your heart and soul into buying the best possible car you can afford. There are people who care desperately about maximizing their returns on investments even if they don't want to spend their money on anything in particular. The truth is that maximizing and satisficing orientations tend to be "domain specific." Nobody is a maximizer in every decision, and probably everybody is in some. Perhaps what distinguishes maximizers from satisficers is the range and number of decisions in which an individual operates as one or the other.

This is good news, because what it means is that most of us have the capacity to be satisficers. The task, then, for someone who feels overwhelmed by choices, is to apply the satisficing strategy more often, letting go of the expectation that "the best" is attainable.

Maximizing and the Choice Problem

FOR A MAXIMIZER, THE OVERLOAD OF CHOICE I DISCUSSED IN CHAPters 1 and 2 is a nightmare. But for a satisficer, it does not have to be such a burden. In fact, the more options there are, the more likely it is that the satisficer will find one that meets his or her standards. Adding options doesn't necessarily add much work for the satisficer, because the satisficer feels no compulsion to check out all the possibilities before deciding.

A friend of mine has two daughters who provide a case in point. When the older girl entered adolescence, my friend and his wife experienced the usual parent-versus-adolescent struggles for control. Often, the battles with their daughter were about buying clothes. Their daughter was style conscious and had expensive tastes, and her ideas about what she absolutely "needed" differed from her parents'. Then my friend and his wife had an idea. They negotiated a clothing allowance with their daughter, allocating funds for a reasonable number of reasonably priced items in the various categories of clothes. They gave her a lump sum, and she could then decide for herself how to spend it. It worked like a charm. Arguments about clothing stopped, and my friends were able to spend the rest of their daughter's adolescence fighting with her about more important things.

The couple were so pleased with the results of their strategy that they did the same thing with their younger daughter. However, the two girls are very different people. The older one is a satisficer, while the younger one is a maximizer (at least with regard to clothing). What this meant was that the older girl could take her clothing allowance, buy things she liked, often on impulse, and never worry about alternatives that she was passing up. This was not so easy for the younger daughter. Each shopping trip was accompanied by anguish about whether purchasing this or that item was really the best thing to do with her money. Would she regret having purchased this item two months later, when the seasons and styles changed? This was too much to ask of a twelve-year-old. Giving her all this freedom was not doing her an unalloyed favor. I suspect that she isn't sorry that she had this freedom to make her own decisions, but her "clothing liberation" provided her with much worry and little joy.

Why Would Anyone Maximize?

THE DRAWBACKS OF MAXIMIZING ARE SO PROFOUND AND THE BENE-fits so tenuous that we may well ask why anyone would pursue such a strategy. The first explanation is that many maximizers may not be aware of this tendency in themselves. They might be aware that they have trouble making decisions and that they fear they will regret decisions and that they often derive little lasting satisfaction from the decisions they have made, but all with no conscious awareness of what is at the root of the problem.

The second explanation is our concern with status. People have undoubtedly cared about status for as long as they have lived in groups, but status concern has taken on a new form in our time. In an era of global telecommunications and global awareness, only "the best" assures success in a competition against everybody else. With increased affluence, increased materialism, modern marketing techniques, and a stunning amount of choice thrown into the mix, it seems inevitable that concern for status would explode into a kind of arms race of exquisiteness. The only way to *be* the best is to have the best.

There's another dimension to the modern concern for status,

identified forty years ago by economist Fred Hirsch. He wrote about goods that were inherently scarce or whose value depended in part on their scarcity. Parcels of land on the ocean cannot be increased. Spots in the entering class at Harvard cannot be expanded. Access to the very best medical facilities cannot be made more plentiful. Suburban housing *can* be made more plentiful, but only by putting houses closer together or building farther away from the city, thereby negating much that makes them desirable. Technological innovation may enable us to feed more and more people with an acre of land, but it won't enable us to provide more and more people with an acre of land, near where they work, to live on. Hirsch suggested that the more affluent a society becomes, and the more basic material needs are met, the more people care about goods that are inherently scarce. And if you're in competition for inherently scarce goods, "good enough" is never good enough; only the best—only maximization—will do. You don't get into Harvard by being a very good student. You get in by being better than all the other very good students.

So it is possible that some people are aware of the negative side of being maximizers, but that they feel compelled by circumstance to be maximizers nonetheless. They might prefer a world in which there was less pressure on them to get and do the best, but that's not the world they inhabit.

Does Choice Create Maximizers?

WHAT I WANT TO EXPLORE FINALLY IS WHETHER THE PROLIFERA- tion of choices might *make* someone a maximizer. My experience buying jeans suggests that this is a possibility. As I indicated earlier, prior to that bewildering shopping trip, I didn't care very much about which jeans I bought. I especially didn't care very much about subtleties of fit. Then I found out that there were several different varieties, each designed to produce a different fit, available to me. Suddenly, I cared. I hadn't been turned into a "denim maximizer" by the availability of options, but I had certainly been nudged in that direction. My standards for buying jeans had been altered—forever.

Throughout this chapter, I have been talking about maximizing and the number of options people face as if the two were independent of each other. The world offers a wide range of options, and something (presently unknown) creates maximizers, and then the two combine to make people unhappy with their decisions. But it is certainly possible that choice and maximizing are not independent of each other. It is possible that a wide array of options can turn people into maximizers. If this is true, then the proliferation of options not only makes people who are maximizers miserable, but it may also make people who are satisficers into maximizers.

At present, the potential causal role that the availability of choice has in making people into maximizers is pure speculation. If the speculation is correct, we ought to find that in cultures in which choice is less ubiquitous and extensive than it is in the United States, there should be fewer maximizers. This would be important to know, because it would suggest that a way to reduce maximizing tendencies is by reducing the options that people confront in various aspects of their lives. As we'll see in the next chapter, there is good reason to take this speculation seriously. Studies comparing the well-being of people living in different cultures have shown that substantial differences between cultures in the consumption opportunities they make available to people have very small effects on people's satisfaction with their lives.

Why We Suffer

Part III

CHAPTER FIVE

Choice and Happiness

F REEDOM AND AUTONOMY ARE CRITICAL TO OUR WELL-BEING, AND choice is critical to freedom and autonomy. Nonetheless, though modern Americans have more choice than any group of people ever has had before, and thus, presumably, more freedom and auton-omy, we don't seem to be benefiting from it psychologically.

The Point of Choice

C HOICE HAS A CLEAR AND POWERFUL *INSTRUMENTAL* VALUE: IT enables people to get what they need and want in life. Whereas many needs are universal (food, shelter, medical care, social sup-port, education, and so on), much of what we need to flourish is highly individualized. We may need food, but we don't need Chil-ean sea bass. We may need shelter, but we don't all need a screen-ing room, an indoor basketball court, and a six-car garage. These Malibu-mogul appurtenances would mean very little to someone who prefers reading by the woodstove in a cottage in Vermont. Choice is what enables each person to pursue precisely those objects and activities that best satisfy his or her own preferences within the limits of his or her financial resources. You can be a vegan and I can be a carnivore. You can listen to hip-hop and I can listen to NPR.

You can stay single and I can marry. Any time choice is restricted in some way, there is bound to be someone, somewhere, who is deprived of the opportunity to pursue something of personal value.

Over two centuries ago Adam Smith observed that individual freedom of choice ensures the most efficient production and distribution of society's goods. A competitive market, unhindered by the government and filled with entrepreneurs eager to pinpoint consumers' needs and desires, will be exquisitely responsive to them. Supple, alert, unfettered by rules and constraints, producers of goods and providers of services will deliver to consumers exactly what they want.

As important as the instrumental value of choice may be, choice reflects another value that might be even more important. Freedom to choose has what might be called *expressive* value. Choice is what enables us to tell the world who we are and what we care about. This is true of something as superficial as the way we dress. The clothes we choose are a deliberate expression of taste, intended to send a message. "I'm a serious person," or "I'm a sensible person," or "I'm rich." Or maybe even "I wear what I want and I don't care what you think about it." To express yourself, you need an adequate range of choices.

The same is true of almost every aspect of our lives as choosers. The food we eat, the cars we drive, the houses we live in, the music we listen to, the books we read, the hobbies we pursue, the charities we contribute to, the demonstrations we attend—each of these choices has an expressive function, regardless of its practical importance. And some choices may have *only* an expressive function. Take voting, for example. Many voters understand that, the 2000 presidential election notwithstanding, a single vote almost never has instrumental significance. One vote is so unlikely to make a difference that it's hardly worth the inconvenience of walking across the street to the polling place. Yet people do vote, presumably at least in part because of what it says about who they are. Voters take citizenship seriously, they do their duty, and they do not take political freedom for granted. An illustration of the expressive function of voting is the story of two American political scientists who were in Europe on election day. They took a three-hour drive together to cast their absentee ballots, knowing they supported opposing candidates and that their votes would cancel each other out.

Every choice we make is a testament to our autonomy, to our sense of self-determination. Almost every social, moral, or political philosopher in the Western tradition since Plato has placed a premium on such autonomy. And each new expansion of choice gives us another opportunity to assert our autonomy, and thus display our character.

But choices have expressive functions only to the extent that we can make them freely. For example, consider the marital vow to stay together "for better for worse, . . . till death us do part." If you have no way to get out of a marriage, marital commitment is not a statement about you; it's a statement about society. If divorce is legal, but the social and religious sanctions against it are so powerful that anyone who leaves a marriage becomes a pariah, your marital commitment again says more about society than it does about you. But if you live in a society that is almost completely permissive about divorce, honoring your marital vows *does* reflect on you.

The value of autonomy is built into the fabric of our legal and moral system. Autonomy is what gives us the license to hold one another morally (and legally) responsible for our actions. It's the reason we praise individuals for their achievements and also blame them for their failures. There's not a single aspect of our collective social life that would be recognizable if we abandoned our commitment to autonomy.

But beyond our political, moral, and social reliance on the idea of autonomy, we now know that it also has a profound influence on our psychological well-being. In the 1960s, psychologist Martin Seligman and his collaborators performed an experiment that involved teaching three different groups of animals to jump over a little hurdle from one side of a box to the other to escape or avoid mildly painful electric shock. One of the groups was given the task with no prior exposure to such experiments. A second group had already learned to make a different response, in a different setting, to escape from shock. Seligman and his coworkers expected, and found, that this second group would learn a bit more quickly than the first, reasoning that some of what they had learned in the first experiment might transfer to the second. The third group of animals, also in a different setting, had been given a series of shocks that could not be escaped by any response.

Remarkably, this third group failed to learn at all. Indeed, many of them essentially had no chance to learn because they didn't even *try* to escape from the shocks. These animals became quite passive, lying down and taking the shocks until the researchers mercifully ended the experiment.

Seligman and his colleagues suggested that the animals in this third group had learned from being exposed to inescapable shocks that nothing they did made a difference; that they were essentially helpless when it came to controlling their fate. Like the second group, they had also transferred to the hurdle-jumping situation lessons they had learned before—in this case, *learned helplessness.*

Seligman's discovery of learned helplessness has had a monumental impact in many different areas of psychology. Hundreds of studies leave no doubt that we can learn that we don't have control.

And when we do learn this, the consequences can be dire. Learned helplessness can affect future motivation to try. It can affect future ability to detect that you do have control in new situations. It can suppress the activity of the body's immune system, thereby making helpless organisms vulnerable to a wide variety of diseases. And it can, under the right circumstances, lead to profound, clinical depression. So it is not an exaggeration to say that our most fundamental sense of well-being crucially depends on our having the ability to exert control over our environment and recognizing that we do.

Now think about the relation between helplessness and choice. If we have choices in a particular situation, then we should be able to exert control over that situation, and thus we should be protected from helplessness. Only in situations where there is no choice should vulnerability to helplessness appear. Quite apart from the *instrumental* benefits of choice—that it enables people to get what they want—and the *expressive* benefits of choice—that it enables people to say who they are—choice enables people to be actively and effectively engaged in the world, with profound *psychological* benefits.

At first glance, this may suggest that opportunities for choice should be expanded wherever possible. And because modern American society has done so, feelings of helplessness should now be rare. In 1966, and again in 1986, however, pollster Louis Harris asked respondents whether they agreed with a series of statements like "I feel left out of things going on around me" and "What I think doesn't matter anymore." In 1966, only 9 percent of people felt left out of things going on around them; in 1986, it was 37 percent. In 1966, 36 percent agreed that what they thought didn't matter; in 1986, 60 percent agreed.

There are two possible explanations for this apparent paradox. The first is that, as the experience of choice and control gets broader and deeper, *expectations* about choice and control may rise to match that experience. As one barrier to autonomy after another gets knocked down, those that remain are, perhaps, more disturbing. Like the mechanical rabbit at the dog-racing track that speeds along just ahead of the dogs no matter how fast they run, aspirations and expectations about control speed ahead of their realization, no matter how liberating the realization becomes.

The second explanation is simply that more choice may not always mean more control. Perhaps there comes a point at which opportunities become so numerous that we feel overwhelmed. Instead of feeling in control, we feel unable to cope. Having the opportunity to choose is no blessing if we feel we do not have the wherewithal to choose wisely. Remember the survey that asked people whether they would want to choose their mode of treatment if they got cancer? The majority of respondents to that question said yes. But when the same question was asked of people who actually had cancer, the overwhelming majority said no. What looks attractive in prospect doesn't always look so good in practice. In making a choice that could mean the difference between life and death, figuring out which choice to make becomes a grave burden.

So there is no doubt that choice is good for us, for a host of reasons. The mistake we have made, both as scientists and as citizens, is to assume that since *some* choice is good, *more* choice is better. What the too-much-choice effect tells us is that more and more choice does not make our lives better and better.

Is there an optimum number of options that we can have that will allow us to derive the benefits of choice without paying the price? Perhaps surprisingly, there has been little research directly on this topic. In one study, the experimenters set out a table with a variety of pens, which students could buy for $1 a pen. Some times there were only a few options; other times there were as many as 20. What the researchers found is that maximum pen purchasing occurred when people had about 8–10 options. When there were fewer, people didn't find any they liked; when there were more, people were overwhelmed and paralyzed. So does this mean that, say, ten options is the optimum number, in all domains of decision making? Most unlikely. In some domains, people may want more, whereas in others, they want fewer. In a given domain, some people may want lots of options whereas others want few. In addition, there is evidence that when people know exactly what they want, there is no such thing as too much choice. Large choice sets enable people to find exactly what they want—no problem—whereas small choice sets often do not.

To derive the benefits and avoid the burdens of choice, we must learn to be selective in exercising our choices. We must decide, individually, when choice really matters and focus our energies there, even if it means letting many other opportunities pass us by. The choice of when to be a chooser may be the most important choice we have to make.

Measuring Happiness

RESEARCHERS ALL OVER THE WORLD HAVE BEEN TRYING TO MEA-sure happiness for decades, partly to determine what makes people happy and partly to gauge social progress. Typically, studies of happiness take the form of questionnaires, and measures of happiness—or "subjective well-being," as it is often called—are derived from answers to lists of questions. Here is an example:

SATISFACTION WITH LIFE SCALE

1. In most ways, my life is close to ideal.
2. The conditions of my life are excellent.
3. I am satisfied with my life.
4. So far, I have gotten the important things I want in life.
5. If I could live my life over, I would change almost nothing.

(Courtesy of Lawrence Erlbaum Associates)

This is the Satisfaction with Life Scale. Respondents indicate the extent to which they agree with each statement on a 7-point scale, and the sum of those judgments is a measure of subjective well-being.

More recently, researchers have combined these questionnaire responses with other measures of happiness. Study participants walk around with little handheld computers, and periodically, the computers beep at them. In response to the beep, the participants are supposed to answer a series of questions displayed on the computer screen. The benefit of this technique—known as the "experience sampling method"—is that rather than relying on people to be able to look back accurately on how they've been feeling over a period of months, the computer asks them to assess how they're feeling at that very moment. Their answers to the questions over the course of the study—days, weeks, or even months—are then aggregated. Results using this technique have shown a rather consistent relation between respondents' answers to questions in the moment and their answers to questions on surveys like the Satisfaction with Life Scale. So there is some reason for confidence that studies using surveys really are telling us how people feel about their lives.

And one of the things these surveys tell us is that, not surprisingly, people in rich countries are happier than people in poor countries. Obviously, money matters. But what these surveys also reveal is that money doesn't matter as much as you might think. Once a society's level of per capita wealth crosses a threshold from poverty to adequate subsistence, further increases in national wealth have smaller effects on happiness. You find as many happy people in Poland as in Japan, for example, even though the average Japanese is almost ten times richer than the average Pole. And Poles are happier than Hungarians (and Icelanders happier than Americans) despite similar levels of wealth.

If, instead of looking at happiness across nations at a given time, we look within a nation at different times, we find a similar story. In the period from roughly 1960 to 2000, the per capita income of Americans (adjusted for inflation) more than doubled. The percentage of homes with dishwashers increased from 9 percent to 50 percent. The percentage of homes with clothes dryers increased from 20 percent to 70 percent. The percentage of homes with air-conditioning increased from 15 percent to 73 percent. Does this mean we had more happy people in 2000 than in 1960? Not at all. Even more striking, in Japan, where per capita wealth has increased by a factor of five in a forty-year period, there was no measurable increase in the level of individual happiness.

But if money doesn't do it for people, what does? What seems to be the most important factor in providing happiness is close social relations. People who are married, who have good friends, and who are close to their families are happier than those who are not. People who participate in religious communities are happier than those who do not. Being connected to others seems to be much more important to subjective well-being than being rich. But a word of caution is in order. We know with certainty that there is a relation between being able to connect socially and being happy. It is less clear, however, which is the cause and which is the effect. Miserable people are surely less likely than happy people to have close friends, devoted family, and enduring marriages. So it is at least possible that happiness comes first and close relations come second. What seems likely to me is that the causality works both ways: happy people attract others to them, and being with others makes people happy.

In the context of this discussion of choice and autonomy, it is also important to note that, in many ways, social ties actually *decrease* freedom, choice, and autonomy. Marriage, for example, is a commitment to a particular other person that curtails freedom of choice of sexual and even emotional partners. And serious friendship imposes a lasting hold on you. To be someone's friend is to undertake weighty responsibilities and obligations that at times may limit your own freedom. The same is true, obviously, of family. And to a large extent, the same is true of involvement with religious institutions. Most religious institutions call on their members to live their lives in a certain way and to take responsibility for the well-being of their fellow congregants. So, counterintuitive as it may appear, what seems to contribute most to happiness binds us rather than liberates us. How can this notion be reconciled with the popular belief that freedom of choice leads to fulfillment?

Two books have explored this incongruity. One, by psychologist David Myers, is called *The American Paradox: Spiritual Hunger in an Age of Plenty*. The other, by political scientist Robert Lane, is called *The Loss of Happiness in Market Democracies*. Both books point out how the growth of material affluence has not brought with it much of an increase in subjective well-being. But they go further. Both

SIPRESS

"The country grandpa came from was a stinking hellhole of unspeakable poverty where everyone was always happy."

MONEY AND HAPPINESS

© *The New Yorker Collection 2000 David Sipress from cartoonbank.com. All Rights Reserved.*

books argue that we are actually experiencing a fairly significant *decrease* in well-being. As Myers graphically puts it, between 1960 and 2000 in the United States, the divorce rate doubled, the teen suicide rate tripled, the recorded violent crime rate quadrupled, the prison population quintupled, the percentage of babies born to unmarried parents sextupled, and the rate of cohabitation without marriage (which actually is a pretty good predictor of eventual divorce) increased sevenfold. This is clearly not a mark of improved well-being. And as Lane points out, the rate of serious clinical depression more than tripled over the last three generations, and increased by perhaps a factor of ten from 1900 to 2000. All of which contributes to, and is exacerbated by, a massive increase in levels of stress, stress that in turn contributes to hypertension and heart disease, lowers immune responsiveness, and causes anxiety and dissatisfaction. But, as Lane put it very simply, in addition to the other factors contributing to our modern malaise:

> There are too many life choices . . . without concern for the resulting overload . . . and the lack of constraint by custom . . . that is, demands to discover or create an identity rather than to accept a given identity.

The rise in the frequency of depression is especially telling. While I will discuss depression at greater length in Chapter 10, I want to point out an important paradox. Earlier in the chapter I discussed Martin Seligman's work on learned helplessness and its relation to depression. That work strongly suggests that the more control people have, the less helpless, and thus the less depressed, they will be. I have also suggested that in modern societies we have more choice, and thus more control, than people have ever had before. Put these two pieces of information together, and it might lead you to expect that depression is going the way of polio, with autonomy and choice as the psychological vaccines. Instead, we are experiencing depression in epidemic numbers. Is Seligman's theory about helplessness and depression wrong? I don't think so; there is much evidence that strongly supports it. Then can it be that freedom of choice is not all it's cracked up to be?

Lane writes that we are paying for increased affluence and increased freedom with a substantial decrease in the quality and quantity of social relations. We earn more and spend more, but we spend less time with others. More than a quarter of Americans report being lonely, and loneliness seems to come not from being alone, but from lack of intimacy. We spend less time visiting with neighbors. We spend less time visiting with our parents, and much less time visiting with other relatives. And once again, this phenomenon adds to our burden of choice. As Lane writes: "What was once given by neighborhood and work now must be achieved; people have had to make their own friends . . . and actively cultivate their own family connections." In other words, our social fabric is no longer a birthright but has become a series of deliberate and demanding choices.

The Time Problem

BEING SOCIALLY CONNECTED TAKES TIME. FIRST, IT TAKES TIME TO *form* close connections. To form a real friendship with someone, or to develop a romantic attachment, we have to get to know the other person quite deeply. Only in Hollywood do such attachments come instantly and effortlessly. And close attachment, not acquaintanceship, is what people most want and need. Second, when we establish these deep connections, we have to devote time to maintaining them. When family, friends, fellow congregants need us, we have to be there. When disagreements or conflicts arise, we have to stay in the game and work them out. And the needs of friends and family don't arise on a convenient schedule, to be penciled into our day planner or our cell phone. They come when they come, and we have to be ready to respond.

Who has this kind of time? Who has the flexibility and breathing room in life's regularly scheduled activities to be there when needed without paying a heavy price in stress and distraction? Not me. Time is the ultimate scarce resource, and for some reason, even as one "time-saving" bit of technology after another comes our way, the burdens on our time seem to increase. Again, it is my contention that a major contributor to this time burden is the vastly greater number of choices we find ourselves preparing for, making, reevaluating, and perhaps regretting. Should you book a table at your favorite Italian place or that new bistro? Should you rent the cottage on the lake or take the plunge and go to Tuscany? Time to refinance again? Stick with your Internet provider or go with a new one? Move some stocks? Change your health insurance? Get a better rate on your credit card? Try that new herbal remedy? Time spent dealing with choice is time taken away from being a good friend, a good spouse, a good parent, and a good congregant.

Freedom or Commitment

STABLISHING AND MAINTAINING MEANINGFUL SOCIAL RELATIONS requires a willingness to be bound or constrained by them, even when dissatisfied. Once people make commitments to others, options close. Economist and historian Albert Hirschman, in his book *Exit, Voice, and Loyalty*, suggested that people have two general classes of responses available when they are unhappy. They can *exit* the situation, or they can protest and give *voice* to their concerns. In the marketplace, exit is the characteristic response to dissatisfaction. If a restaurant no longer pleases us, we go to another. If our once favorite breakfast cereal gets too expensive, we switch to a different brand. If our favorite vacation spot gets too crowded, we find a new one. One of the principal virtues of free-market choice is that it gives people the opportunity to express their displeasure by exit.

Social relations are different. We don't dismiss lovers, friends, or communities the way we dismiss restaurants, cereals, or vacation spots. Treating people in this way is unseemly at best and reprehensible at worst. Instead, we usually give *voice* to our displeasure, hoping to influence our lover, friend, or community. And even when these efforts fail, we feel bound to keep trying. Exit, or abandonment, is the response of last resort.

Most people find it extremely challenging to balance the conflicting impulses of freedom of choice on the one hand and loyalty and commitment on the other. Each person is expected to figure out this balance individually. Those who value freedom of choice and movement will tend to stay away from entangling relationships; those who value stability and loyalty will seek them. Many will cobble together some mixture of these two modes of social engagement. If we fail in establishing exactly the kinds of social relations we want, we will feel that we have only ourselves to blame. And many times we will fail.

Social institutions could ease the burden on individuals by establishing constraints that, while open to transformation, could not be violated willy-nilly by each person as he chooses. With clearer "rules of the game" for us to live by—constraints that specify how much of life each of us should devote to ourselves and what our obligations to family, friends, and community should be—much of the onus for making these decisions would be lifted.

But the price of accepting constraints imposed by social institutions is a restriction on individual freedom. Is it a price worth paying? A society that allows us to answer this question individually has already given us an answer, for by giving people the choice, it has opted for freedom. And a society that does not allow us to answer this question individually has also given an answer, opting for constraints. But if unrestricted freedom can impede the individual's pursuit of what he or she values most, then it may be that some restrictions make everyone better off. And if "constraint" sometimes affords a kind of liberation while "freedom" affords a kind of enslavement, then people would be wise to seek out some measure of appropriate constraint.

Second-Order Decisions

A WAY OF EASING THE BURDEN THAT FREEDOM OF CHOICE IMPOSES is to make decisions about when to make decisions. These are what Cass Sunstein and Edna Ullmann-Margalit call *second-order decisions*. One kind of second-order decision is the decision to follow a *rule*. If buckling your seat belt is a rule, you will always buckle up, and the issue of whether it's worth the trouble for a one-mile trip to the market just won't arise. If you adopt the rule that you will never cheat on your partner, you will eliminate countless painful and tempting decisions that might confront you later on. Having the discipline to live by the rules you make for yourself is, of course, another matter, but one thing's for sure: following rules eliminates troublesome choices in your daily life, each time you get into a car or each time you go to a cocktail party.

Presumptions are less stringent than rules. Presumptions are like the default settings on computer applications. When I set my word processor to use "Times 12" as the default font, I don't have to think about it. When, once in a while, I'm doing something special, such as preparing an overhead to be projected in a large auditorium, I can deviate from the default. But 99.9 percent of the time, my decision is made for me.

Standards are even less rigorous than rules or presumptions. When we establish a standard, we are essentially dividing the world of options into two categories: options that meet the standard and options that don't. Then, when we have to make a choice, we need only investigate the options within category number one. As we saw in the last chapter, it's a lot easier to decide whether something is good enough (to satisfice) than it is to decide whether something is the best (to maximize). This is especially true if we combine standards with *routines*, or habits. Deciding that once we find something that meets our standards we'll stick with it essentially takes away that area of decision making. Friendships often sustain themselves on a combination of standards and routines. We are drawn to people who meet our standards (of intelligence, kindness, character, loyalty, wit), and then we stick with them. We don't make a choice, every day, about whether to maintain the friendship; we just do. We don't ask ourselves whether we would get more out of a friendship with Mary than we do out of our friendship with Jane. There are countless "Marys" out there, and if we did ask ourselves this kind of question, we'd be continually choosing whether to maintain our friendships.

So by using rules, presumptions, standards, and routines to constrain ourselves and limit the decisions we face, we can make life more manageable, which gives us more time to devote ourselves to other people and to the decisions that we can't or don't want to avoid. While each second-order decision has a price—each involves passing up opportunities for something better—we could not get through a day without them.

At the turn of the twentieth century, biologist Jacob von Uexkull, observing how evolution shaped organisms so that their perceptual and behavioral abilities were precisely attuned to their survival, remarked that "security is more important than wealth." In other words, a squirrel in the wild doesn't have the "wealth" of experience and of choice that people do when they decide to take a walk in the forest. What the squirrel *does* have is the "security" that it will notice what matters most and know how to do what it needs to do to survive, because biology supplies the needed constraints on choice. It helps organisms recognize food, mates, predators, and other dangers, and it supplies them with a small set of activities appropriate for obtaining what they truly need. For people, such constraints have to come from culture. Some cultures have constraints in oppressive abundance, while our consumer culture has strived for decades to jettison as many constraints as possible. As I have argued from the outset, oppression can exist at either extreme of the continuum.

Wanting and Liking

IVEN THE HIGH VALUE WE PLACE ON AUTONOMY AND FREEDOM OF choice, you would think that having it would make us happier. Usually, the things we want are the things we like, the things that give us pleasure.

But powerful evidence has appeared that "wanting" and "liking" are served by fundamentally different brain systems—systems that often do, but certainly need not, work together. Drug addicts desperately "want" their drugs (such is the nature of addiction), even after they reach a point in their addiction where ingesting the drugs provides very little pleasure. And stimulation of certain areas of the brain can get rats to "want" food, though they show no evidence that they "enjoy" it even as they eat it. So wanting and liking can, under some circumstances, be dissociated, just as there is often a disconnect between our anticipated preferences and the options we actually choose.

Remember that 65 percent of people who didn't have cancer said that if they got it, they would prefer to choose their treatment. Of those who actually had cancer, 88 percent said they would prefer *not* to choose. Apparently we always think we want choice, but when we actually get it, we may not like it. Meanwhile, the need to choose in ever more aspects of life causes us more distress than we realize.

CHAPTER SIX

Missed Opportunities

I T'S FEBRUARY. IT'S FREEZING COLD. THE STREETS ARE LINED WITH soot-covered snow. As Angela commutes to and from work in the dark, what gets her through the end of another long winter is thinking about next summer's vacation.

She is considering two very different possibilities: touring in northern California or a week at a beach house on Cape Cod. How does she decide what to do? She might begin by considering what matters to her most when she goes on vacation. She appreciates the splendor of nature, so of course her destination has to be beautiful. She loves to spend time outdoors, but she hates heat and humidity, so the weather has to be just right. She loves long stretches of isolated coastline, but she also likes good food and a bustling nightlife, people-watching and window-shopping. Then again, she hates crowds. She likes to be physically active, but, sometimes she also likes to spend an afternoon just lounging in a comfortable chair and reading.

So now what? Two tasks remain. Angela has to assess the importance of these various features of vacation destinations. For example, is good weather more important than bustling nightlife? Then, she has to see how northern California and Cape Cod stack up. If one of these options is better than the other in every respect that Angela cares about, her decision will be easy. But more likely, she'll discover that each option has strengths that the other one lacks, so she'll end up having to make trade-offs. Nonetheless, if she lists the things that matter to her, determines how much they matter, and evaluates how each possibility measures up, Angela will be able to make a choice.

Now, let's say that a friend complicates Angela's life by suggesting she consider a lovely little cottage in Vermont. There are mountains for hiking, lakes for swimming, an arts festival, good restaurants, warm dry days, and crisp, cool nights. In addition, the town is near Burlington, where the nightlife is energetic. Finally, Angela's friend points out to her that since Angela has several good friends who own vacation houses in the area, she'll be able to spend time with them. Spending time with friends is something she didn't consider when choosing between California and Cape Cod. Now she needs to add it to her list of attractive features. Furthermore, she may want to reevaluate some of the scores she gave the first two places. She may knock Cape Cod's weather down a point or two because in contrast with the cool, clear Vermont alternative, it's not that great.

But this possibility of being near friends gets Angela thinking. Her kids live far away, and she misses them. If being with friends is nice, being with family is nicer. Maybe there's someplace close to where her kids live that's beautiful, has nice restaurants, good weather, and things to do at night. Or maybe there's someplace that they would be interested in going to with her. New possibilities get entertained and another new feature (being with her kids) gets added to Angela's list.

Clearly, no one option is going to meet all her desires. She's simply going to have to make some trade-offs.

MICHAEL, A TALENTED college senior, is trying to choose between two jobs. Job A offers a good starting salary, modest opportunities for advancement, excellent security, and a lively, hospitable work atmosphere. Job B offers a modest starting salary, very good opportunities for advancement, decent security, and a rather formal, hierarchical office structure.

While Michael is deliberating between Jobs A and B, Job C becomes available. Job C would take him to an exciting city. All of a sudden, attractiveness of location, something that had not been part of his deliberations, becomes relevant. How do the locations of Jobs A and B stack up against the location of Job C? And how much in salary, security, and so on is he willing to trade to be in this exciting place?

Then the decision gets even more complex. Another job prospect turns up in a location that is close to family and old friends, something Michael had also not considered. How important is that? And then, Michael's girlfriend lands a very good job in the same city as Job A. How much weight should he give to this factor? How serious is this relationship anyway?

In making a job choice, Michael will have to ask himself several hard questions. Is he willing to trade off salary for advancement opportunities? Is he willing to trade off quality of the job for quality of the city in which it is located? Is he willing to trade off both for being near his family? And is he willing to give up all of this to be near his girlfriend?

PART OF THE DOWNSIDE of abundant choice is that each new option adds to the list of trade-offs, and trade-offs have psychological consequences. The necessity of making trade-offs alters how we feel about the decisions we face; more important, it affects the level of satisfaction we experience from the decisions we ultimately make.

Opportunity Costs

CONOMISTS POINT OUT THAT THE QUALITY OF ANY GIVEN OPTION cannot be assessed in isolation from its alternatives. One of the "costs" of any option involves passing up the opportunities that a different option would have afforded. This is referred to as an *opportunity cost*. The opportunity cost of vacationing on the beach in Cape Cod is great restaurants in California. The opportunity cost of taking a job near your romantic partner is that you won't be near your family. Every choice we make has opportunity costs associated with it.

Failing to think about opportunity costs can lead people astray. I often hear people justify their decision to buy a house rather than continue renting by saying that they are tired of letting a landlord build up equity at their expense. Paying a mortgage is investing, whereas paying rent is just throwing money out the window. This line of thinking is fair enough, as far as it goes, but it doesn't go far enough. Here's how far most home buyers take it: "I have to make a down payment of $50,000. My monthly expenses, including mortgage, taxes, insurance, and utilities, will be the same as they would be in a rental. So, in effect, for an investment of $50,000, I get to have my monthly housing costs work for me, building up *my* equity rather than my landlord's. And I'm sure that I'll get more than that $50,000 back when I sell the house."

No doubt about it, owning your own home is usually a smart investment. But what buyers leave out of this line of reasoning is the opportunity cost of putting that $50,000 into the house. What else could you do with it? You could put that $50,000 into stocks or Treasury bills, or you could use it to finish law school and increase your earnings, or you could travel around the world and write that novel that you hope will utterly change your life. Some options are more realistic than others, and the wisdom of each depends on your life goals and your timing. A decade ago, real estate seemed to be a safer choice than stocks (housing prices only go up), but then the housing bubble popped. Two decades ago, in 1996, with the market about to soar, $50,000 in the right tech stocks, with the right exit strategy, might have made a fortune. The point is that even decisions that appear to be no-brainers carry the hidden costs of the options declined. Thinking about opportunity costs may not change the decision you make, but it will give you a more realistic assessment of the full implications of that decision.

According to standard economic assumptions, the only opportunity costs that should figure into a decision are the ones associated with the next-best alternative. So let's say your options for next Saturday night, listed in order of preference, include:

1. Dinner in a nice restaurant
2. A quick, casual dinner and a movie
3. Music at a jazz club
4. Dancing
5. Cooking dinner for a few friends
6. Going to a baseball game.

If you go for the dinner, the "cost" will be whatever you pay for the meal, *plus* the passed-up opportunity to see a movie. According to economists, that's where your "cost accounting" should stop. Which is also excellent advice for managing our own psychological response to choice. Pay attention to what you're giving up in the next-best alternative, but don't waste energy feeling bad about having passed up an option further down the list that you wouldn't have gotten to anyway.

This advice, however, is extremely difficult to follow, and here's why: The options under consideration usually have multiple features. If people think about options in terms of their features rather than as a whole, different options may rank as second best (or even best) with respect to each individual feature. So going to the movies may be the best way to stimulate the intellect. Listening to jazz may be the best way to relax. Dancing may be the most enjoyable way to get some exercise. Going to the ball game may be the best way to blow off some steam. Dinner at home with friends may be the best way to experience intimacy. Even though there may be a single, second-best option overall, each of the options you reject has some very desirable feature on which it beats its competition. So going out to dinner then means giving up opportunities to be intellectually stimulated, to relax, to get exercise, to blow off steam, and to experience intimacy. Psychologically, each alternative you consider may introduce still another opportunity you'll have to pass up if you choose your preferred option.

If we assume that missed opportunities take away from the overall desirability of the most-preferred option and that we will feel the missed-opportunity costs associated with many of the options we reject, then the more alternatives there are from which to choose, the greater our experience of the missed opportunities will be. And the greater our experience of the opportunity costs, the less satisfaction we will derive from our chosen alternative.

Why can't there be a job that offers a good salary, opportunities for advancement, a friendly work environment, an interesting location that has a job for my partner, and proximity to my family? Why can't there be a vacation where I get the beach *and* great restaurants, shops, and tourist attractions? Why can't I have an intellectually stimulating, relaxed, physically active, and intimate night with friends? The existence of multiple alternatives makes it easy for us to imagine alternatives that don't exist—alternatives that combine the

"We found we really missed going to the theatre and eating
in nice restaurants, so we gave our kids away."

**A COUPLE DISCOVERS THE OPPORTUNITY
COSTS OF HAVING CHILDREN**

© *The New Yorker Collection 2000 David Sipress from cartoonbank.com. All Rights Reserved.*

attractive features of the ones that do exist. And to the extent that
we engage our imaginations in this way, we will be even less satisfied
with the alternative we end up choosing. So, once again, a greater
variety of choices actually makes us feel worse.

If there were some way to say, *objectively*, what was the best vacation or the best job or the best way to spend a Saturday night, then adding options could only make people better off. Any new option might turn out to be the best one. But there is no objectively best vacation, job, or Saturday night activity. Ultimately, the quality of choices that matters to people is the *subjective* experience that the choices afford. And if, beyond a certain point, adding options diminishes our subjective experience, we are worse off for it.

The Psychology of Trade-offs

THE PSYCHOLOGY OF TRADE-OFFS HAS BEEN INVESTIGATED IN A series of studies in which participants are asked to make hypothetical decisions about which car to buy or which apartment to rent or which job to take, based on a range of features, including price. The lists of alternatives are constructed so that in choosing one option, the participants will have to make trade-offs. In choosing a car, for example, one option may be more stylish but have fewer safety features than another. In choosing an apartment, one option may offer better space than another but in a less convenient location.

In one study, participants were told that Car A costs $25,000 and ranks high in safety (8 on a 10-point scale). Car B ranks 6 on the safety scale. Participants were then asked how much Car B would have to cost to be as attractive as Car A. Answering this question required making a trade-off, in this case, between safety and price. It required asking how much each extra unit of safety was worth. If someone were to say, for example, that Car B was only worth $10,000, they would clearly be placing great value on the extra safety afforded by Car A. If instead they were to say that Car B was worth $22,000, they would be placing much less value on the extra safety afforded by Car A. Participants performed this task with little apparent difficulty. A little while later, though, they were confronted with a second task. They were presented with a choice between Car A, safety rating 8, and price of $25,000, and Car B, safety rating 6, and the price that they had previously said made the two cars equally attractive. How did they choose between two equivalent alternatives?

Since the alternatives were equivalent, you might expect that about half the people would choose the safer, more expensive car and half would choose the less safe, cheaper car. But that is not what the researchers found. Most participants chose the safer, more expensive car. When forced to choose, most people refused to trade safety for price. They acted as if the importance of safety to their decision was so great that price was essentially irrelevant. This choice was clearly different from the way people reacted to the task in which they had to establish a price that would make the two cars equivalent. If they had thought that safety was of overriding importance, they would have set the price of Car B very low. But they didn't. So it wasn't that people refused to "put a price" on safety. Rather, when the time came to make the choice, they were simply unwilling to live by the price on safety that they had already established.

Even though their decision was purely hypothetical, participants experienced substantial negative emotion when choosing between Cars A and B. And if the experimental procedure gave them the opportunity, they refused to make the decision at all. So the researchers concluded that *being forced to confront trade-offs in making decisions makes people unhappy and indecisive.*

It isn't hard to understand this pattern. Imagine yourself choosing the less safe of two cars to save $5,000, only to have a major car accident later on. Could you live with yourself if it turned out that one of your loved ones would have been spared serious injury if you'd been driving a safer car? Of course you're reluctant to trade off safety for price. Of course safety has overriding importance. But this is a very special case.

Not so, it seems. Participants in these studies showed the pattern of reluctance to make trade-offs whether the stakes were high or low. Confronting any trade-off, it seems, is quite unsettling. And as the available alternatives increase, the extent to which choices will require trade-offs will increase as well.

Avoiding Decisions

WHAT, THEN, DO PEOPLE DO IF VIRTUALLY ALL DECISIONS INVOLVE trade-offs and people resist making them? One option is to postpone or avoid the decision. Imagine being in the market for a new music system and seeing a sign in a store window announcing a one-day clearance sale on CD players. You can get a popular Sony CD player for only $99, well below list price. Do you buy it, or do you continue to research other brands and models? Now imagine that the sign in the window offers both the $99 Sony and a $169 top-of-the-line Aiwa, also well below list price. Do you buy either of them, or do you postpone the decision and do more research?

When researchers asked, they found an interesting result. In the first case, 66 percent of people said they would buy the Sony and 34 percent said they would wait. In the second case, 27 percent said they would buy the Sony, 27 percent said they would buy the Aiwa, and 46 percent said they would wait. Consider what this means. Faced with one attractive option, two-thirds of people are willing to go for it. But faced with two attractive options, only slightly more than half are willing to buy. *Adding the second option creates a conflict, forcing a trade-off between price and quality.* Without a compelling reason to go one way or the other, potential consumers pass up the sale altogether. By creating the conflict, this second option makes it harder, not easier to make a choice.

Consumers need or want reasons to justify choices, as we see in a third hypothetical situation. A similar one-day sale offers the $99 Sony and an inferior Aiwa at the list price of $105. Here, the added option does not create conflict. The Sony is better than the AIWA *and* it's on sale. Not surprisingly, almost no one chooses the Aiwa. Surprisingly, however, 73 percent go with the Sony, as opposed to 66 percent when it was offered by itself. So the presence of a clearly inferior alternative makes it easier for consumers to take the plunge. Perhaps seeing the inferior Aiwa bolsters people's confidence that the Sony is really a good deal, though in a market with dozens of brands and models of CD players available, the presence of this second alternative doesn't really prove much. Even if inferior in every way, the second alternative provides an anchor or comparison that bolsters a buyer's reasons for choosing the first one (see Chapter 3). It helps buyers conclude that the Sony option is of good quality at a good price. Difficult trade-offs make it difficult to justify decisions, so decisions are deferred; easy trade-offs make it easy to justify decisions. And single options lie somewhere in the middle.

Conflict induces people to avoid decisions even when the stakes are trivial. In one study, participants were offered $1.50 for filling out some questionnaires. After the participants had finished, they were offered a fancy metal pen instead of the $1.50 and told that the pen normally costs about $2. Seventy-five percent of people chose the pen. In a second condition, participants were offered the $1.50 or a choice between that same metal pen and two less-expensive felt-tipped pens (also worth about $2). Now fewer than 50 percent chose either of the pens. So the conflict introduced by the added option made it difficult to choose one pen or the other, and the majority of participants ended up choosing neither. It is hard to imagine why adding the pair of cheaper pens to the mix should do anything to alter the value of the good pen in comparison with $1.50. If 75 percent of people think the good pen is a better deal than $1.50 in the first case, then 75 percent ought to think so in the second case as well. And there ought to be some people who think that getting two pens is a better deal. So more people, not fewer, ought to be going with the pens rather than the cash when they have a choice. But the opposite occurs.

There is another, more urgent example of how conflict induces people to avoid decisions. In this study, doctors were presented with a case history of a man suffering from osteoarthritis and asked whether they would prescribe a new medication or refer the patient to a specialist. Almost 75 percent recommended the medication. Other doctors were presented with a choice between *two* new medications or referral to a specialist. Now only 50 percent went with either of the medications, meaning that the percentage of those referring doubled. Referral to a specialist is, of course, a way to avoid a decision.

Similarly, legislators were presented with a case that described a struggling public hospital and asked whether they would recommend closing it. Two-thirds of the legislators recommended shutting it down. Other legislators were presented with a similar case with a new wrinkle, the added possibility of closing a second struggling hospital. When asked which of the two they would prefer to close (they also could choose to make no recommendation), only a quarter of the legislators recommended shutting either of them. Based on these studies, and others like them, researchers concluded that when people are presented with options involving trade-offs that create conflict, all choices begin to look unappealing.

People find decision making that involves trade-offs so unpleasant that they will clutch at almost anything to help them decide. Consider this scenario from another study:

Imagine that you serve on the jury of an only-child, sole-custody case following a relatively messy divorce. The facts of the case are complicated by ambiguous economic, social, and emotional considerations, and you decide to base your decision entirely on the following few observations:

Parent A	Parent B
Average income	*Above-average income*
Average health	*Minor health problems*
Average working hours	*Lots of work-related travel*
Reasonable rapport with child	*Very close relationship with the child*
Relatively stable social life	*Extremely active social life*

To which parent would you award sole custody of the child?

Faced with this scenario, 64 percent of respondents chose to award the child to Parent B. Whereas Parent A was sort of average in every way, Parent B had two very positive features and three negative ones, and for most people, the positives outweighed the negatives.

Or did they? Another group of respondents was given exactly the same information as the first, but asked a slightly different question: Which parent would you *deny* sole custody of the child? With the judgment framed in this negative language, the percentage of those voting for the child to go to B dropped from 64 percent to 55 percent.

Difficult choices like this one set people off on a chase for reasons to justify their decisions. What kinds of reasons are they looking for? In the first instance, they are looking for reasons to *accept* a parent. And Parent B offers them: high income and a close relationship. In the second instance, people are looking for reasons to *reject* a parent. Parent B offers these as well: health problems, work travel, too much socializing. Respondents cling to the form of the question ("award" or "deny") as a guide to the kinds of reasons they will be looking for. It's one way to reduce or avoid conflict. If you're looking only at the negatives, then you don't have to worry about trade-offs with the positives.

Decision conflict is an important ingredient in the examples of decision avoidance that I've just described, but it isn't the only ingredient. Think about trying to decide whether to buy a digital camera with your year-end bonus. A digital camera will allow you to manipulate the images you capture and send them easily to friends and family, both of which attract you. Is it worth the money? You think about it for a while and decide. Now imagine trying to decide whether to buy a mountain bike with your bonus. You love to ride for exercise, especially in the hills outside the town in which you live. Is it worth the money? You think about it for a while and decide. Now imagine trying to decide whether to buy a mountain bike *or* a digital camera. Each option represents a gain (positive features it has that the other doesn't) and a loss (positive features it doesn't have that the other does). We saw in Chapter 3 that people tend to display *loss aversion*. The loss of $100 is more painful than the gain of $100 is pleasurable. What that means is that when the mountain bike and the digital camera are compared, each will suffer from the comparison. If you choose the camera, you'll gain the quality and convenience of digital photography but lose the exercise in lovely surroundings. Because losses have a greater impact than gains, the net result will be that the camera fares less well when compared with the mountain bike than it would have if you were evaluating it on its own. And the same is true of the mountain bike. Once again, this suggests that whenever we are forced to make decisions involving trade-offs, we will feel less good about the option we choose than we would have if the alternatives hadn't been there.

This was confirmed by a study in which people were asked how much they would be willing to pay for subscriptions to popular magazines or to purchase popular movies. Some were asked about individual magazines or videos. Others were asked about these same magazines or videos as part of a group with other magazines or videos. In almost every case, respondents placed a higher value on the magazine or the video when they were evaluating it in isolation than when they were evaluating it as part of a cluster. When magazines are evaluated as part of a group, each of them will both gain *and* lose from the comparisons. And because the losses will loom larger than the gains, the net result of the comparison will be negative. Bottom line—the options we consider usually suffer from comparison with other options.

Trade-offs: Emotional Unpleasantness Makes for Bad Decisions

J UST ABOUT EVERYONE SEEMS TO APPRECIATE THAT THINKING about trade-offs makes for better decisions. We want our doctors to be weighing trade-offs before making treatment recommendations. We want our investment advisers carefully considering trade-offs before making investment recommendations. We want *Consumer Reports* to evaluate trade-offs before making purchasing recommendations. We just don't want to have to evaluate trade-offs ourselves. And we don't want to do it because it is emotionally unpleasant to go through the process of thinking about missed opportunities and the losses they imply.

The emotional cost of potential trade-offs does more than just diminish our sense of satisfaction with a decision. It also interferes with the quality of decisions themselves. There is a great deal of evidence that negative emotional states of mind narrow our focus. Instead of examining all aspects of a decision, we home in on only one or two, perhaps ignoring aspects of the decision that are very important. Negative emotion also distracts us, inducing us to focus on the emotion rather than on the decision itself. As the stakes of decisions involving trade-offs rise, emotions become more powerful, and our decision making can be severely impaired.

Researchers have known for years about the harmful effects of negative emotion on thinking and decision making. More recent evidence has shown that positive emotion has the opposite effect— when we are in a good mood, we think better. We consider more possibilities; we're open to considerations that would otherwise not occur to us; we see subtle connections between pieces of information that we might otherwise miss. Something as trivial as a little gift of candy to medical residents improves the speed and accuracy of their diagnoses. In general, positive emotion enables us to broaden our understanding of what confronts us.

This creates something of a paradox. We seem to do our best thinking when we're feeling good. Complex decisions, involving multiple options with multiple features (like "Which job should I take?"), demand our best thinking. Yet those very decisions seem to induce in us emotional reactions that will impair our ability to do just the kind of thinking that is necessary.

Missed Opportunities, Trade-offs, and Exploding Options

WE'VE SEEN THAT AS THE NUMBER OF OPTIONS UNDER CONSIDERA- tion goes up and the attractive features associated with the rejected alternatives accumulate, the satisfaction derived from the chosen alternative will go down. This is one reason, and a very important one, why adding options can be detrimental to our well-being. Because we don't put rejected options out of our minds, we experience the disappointment of having our satisfaction with decisions diluted by all the options we considered but did not choose.

In light of these cumulative, negative effects of missed opportunities, it is tempting to recommend that in making decisions, we ignore missed opportunities altogether. If missed opportunities complicate the decision and they make us miserable, why think about them? Unfortunately, it is very difficult to judge whether a potential investment is a good one without knowing about the attractiveness of the alternatives. The same is true of a job or a vacation or a medical procedure or almost anything else. And once we start considering alternatives, the matter of missed opportunities is bound to come up. Only rarely is one option clearly better in every way than the rest. Choosing almost always involves giving up something else of value. So thinking about missed opportunities is probably an essential part of wise decision making. The trick is to limit the set of possibilities so that the missed opportunities don't add up to make all the alternatives unattractive.

Appreciating the cumulative burden posed by opportunity costs can help us better understand the findings of the study mentioned in Chapter 1 in which two sets of participants encountered a variety of different flavors of a brand of high-quality jam at a sample table set up in a gourmet food store. Some people were presented with six different samples on the table, while others saw twenty-four. They could taste as many as they wanted, and then were given a coupon for a $1 discount on any jam they purchased. The larger display of samples attracted more shoppers, but these individuals did not sample more different jams. Remarkably, shoppers who saw the larger display were *less* likely actually to buy jam than those who saw the smaller display. *Much* less likely.

In another study, students were offered either six or thirty different topics to choose from for an extra-credit essay. The students offered six topics were more likely to write essays, and wrote better essays, than the students offered thirty topics.

In a third study, students evaluated either six or thirty gourmet chocolates on their visual appeal, then picked one to taste and evaluate, and were then offered a small box of the chocolates in lieu of payment for participating in the study. Students who were exposed to thirty chocolates gave lower ratings to the chocolate they tasted and were less likely to take a box of chocolates rather than money after the experiment than students who were exposed to only six.

This set of results is counterintuitive. Surely, you are more likely to find something you like from a set of twenty-four or thirty options than from a set of six. At worst, the extra options add nothing, but in that case, they should also take away nothing. But when there are twenty-four jams to consider, it is easy to imagine that many of them will have attractive features: novelty, sweetness, texture, color, and who knows what else. As the chooser closes in on a decision, the various attractive features of the jams not chosen can mount up to make the preferred jam seem less exceptional. It may still be the one that wins the competition, but its "attractiveness score" is no longer high enough to warrant a purchase. Similarly, with regard to essay topics, some may be attractive because students already know a lot about them, others because they are provocative, others because they have personal relevance, and still others because they relate to ideas students are discussing in another course. But the potential attractiveness of each will subtract from the attractiveness of all of the others. The net result, after the subtractions, is that none of the topics will be attractive enough to overcome inertia and get the student to sit down at the word processor. And if he does sit down, as he tries to write about the topic he's chosen, he may be further distracted by other appealing but rejected topics. It may prevent him from thinking clearly. Or perhaps the negative emotion aroused by having had to consider trade-offs will narrow his thinking. Either way, the quality of the essay will suffer.

Some years ago, when my wife and I made a trip to Paris for a long weekend, I had an experience that I couldn't understand until I began to write this chapter. We arrived from London on a gorgeous, sunny afternoon. We took a leisurely stroll along one of the city's magnificent boulevards and looked for a place to eat a much-anticipated lunch. At each restaurant we studied the menu posted outside. The first place we saw held out all sorts of enticing possibilities, and I was ready to halt the search right then. But how could we be in Paris and just walk into the first restaurant we encountered? So we kept walking and checked out another. And another. And another. Just about every place we saw seemed wonderful. But after about an hour, and a dozen menus, I found myself losing my appetite. The restaurants we encountered seemed less and less attractive. By the end of an hour, I would have been perfectly happy to skip lunch altogether.

I appeared to have discovered a great new dieting technique—satiation by simulation. You just imagine yourself eating dishes you love, and after you've imagined enough of them, you start to get full. When the time finally comes to sit down and eat, you don't have much appetite. In fact what was happening was the buildup of missed opportunities. As I encountered one attractive alternative after another, each new alternative just reduced the potential pleasure I would feel after I made my choice. By the end of the hour, there was no pleasure left to be had.

Clearly, the cumulative cost of adding options to one's choice set can reduce satisfaction. It may even make a person miserable. But I think there's another reason for this decline, one that I can illustrate with the following example: For almost 30 years, I lived in Swarthmore, Pennsylvania, the beautiful suburban community that houses the college where I teach. This community had a lot going for it. It was densely green, with many old and magnificent trees. It was peaceful and quiet. It was safe. The schools were good. I could walk to work. In short, it was a fine place to live. But one thing it decidedly did not have going for it was a good video store (remember, this was a long time ago, when good video stores mattered). There was only a branch of a national chain, and while it offered about a million copies of the latest box-office smash, there were rather slim pickings among less commercial movies or older movies. And the pickings among movies made in a language other than English were almost nonexistent. This created a problem for me, especially when I had to be the one to choose a movie that my family or friends would watch together.

Choosing a movie for others is not my favorite activity (you'll remember, perhaps, that it's one of the questions on the Maximization Scale that I showed you in Chapter 4). There is pressure to choose a film that will surprise and delight people. And in my circle, it had become something of a parlor game to make fun of a bad selection and the person responsible for it. On the other hand, the critics back home were only kidding. And more important, even if they were serious, they were fully aware that the options at the local video store were profoundly impoverished. So, back in Swarthmore, nobody had high expectations, and nobody seriously faulted the chooser for whatever he came home with.

Then I moved to the heart of downtown Philadelphia. Three blocks from my house was a video store that seemingly had everything. Movies from every era, every genre, every country. So now what was at stake when I went to rent a video for the group? Now whose fault would it be if I brought back something that people regarded as a waste of time? Now it was no longer a reflection of the quality of the store. Now it was a reflection of the quality of my taste. So the availability of many attractive options meant that there was no longer any excuse for failure. The blame for a bad choice would rest squarely with me, and as a result, the stakes involved in my video choice had escalated.

Even decisions as trivial as renting a video become important if we believe that these decisions are revealing something significant about ourselves.

Choices and Reasons

S THE STAKES OF DECISIONS RISE, WE FEEL AN INCREASED NEED to justify them. We feel compelled to articulate—at least to ourselves—why we made a particular choice. This need to search for reasons seems useful; it ought to improve the quality of our choices. But it doesn't necessarily.

It may seem self-evident that every choice requires a reason, but several studies suggest that this simple and straightforward model of decision making isn't always accurate. In one such study, participants were asked to taste and rank five different kinds of jam. One group was given no instructions to follow. A second group was told to think about their reasons as they were determining their rankings. After the tasting, the experimenters compared the participants' rankings to those of experts that had been published in *Consumer Reports*. What the researchers found is that participants who weren't given instructions produced rankings that were closer to those of experts than participants instructed to think about their reasons. While this result doesn't necessarily show that thinking about reasons for decisions makes the decisions worse, it does show that thinking about reasons can alter the decisions. This implies that people are not always thinking first and deciding second.

In another study, college students were asked to evaluate five posters of the sort that often decorate dorm rooms. Two represented works of fine art: a Monet and a van Gogh. The other three featured captioned cartoons or photos of animals. Pretesting with other students had determined that most people preferred the van Gogh and the Monet to the kitschy posters of cartoons and animals. In this particular study, half of the people were asked to write a brief essay explaining why they liked or disliked each of the five. They were assured that no one would read what they wrote. The others weren't given this instruction. The students then rated each of the posters. In addition, when the session was over, the experimenter told them that they could take one of the posters home. Copies of each poster were sitting rolled up in bins, blank side facing out, so that the students didn't have to worry about their taste being judged by others. Several weeks later, each participant received a phone call. Each was asked how satisfied he or she was with the poster. Did they still have it? Was it hanging on the wall? Were they planning to take it home with them for the summer? Could they be talked into selling it?

The first interesting result of this study was that people asked to write down their thoughts preferred the funny posters to those featuring fine art. In contrast, those who were not asked to write preferred the fine art. Inducing people to give reasons for their preferences, even if only to themselves, seemed to change their preferences. Consistent with this effect, participants who wrote down reasons were more likely to choose a funny poster to take home than those who did not give reasons. But most important, in the follow-up phone call, participants who had written down their reasons were *less* satisfied with the poster they had chosen than those who did not. They were less likely to have kept the poster, less likely to have it hanging, less likely to want to take it home, and more willing to sell it.

What these studies show is that when people are asked to give reasons for their preferences, they may struggle to find the words. Sometimes aspects of their reaction that are *not* the most important determinants of their overall feeling are nonetheless easiest to verbalize. People may have less trouble expressing why one poster is funnier than another than why the van Gogh print is more beautiful than the Monet. So they grasp at what they can say, and identify *it* as the basis for their preference. But once the words are spoken, they take on added significance to the person who spoke them. At the moment of choice, these explicit, verbalized reasons weigh heavily in the decision. As time passes, the reasons that people verbalized fade into the background, and people are left with their unarticulated preferences, which wouldn't have steered them to the poster they chose. As the salience of the verbalized reasons fades, so, too, does people's satisfaction with the decision they made.

In a final example, college couples were recruited to participate in a study of the effects of romantic relationships on the college experience. After an initial session in the laboratory, participants filled out a questionnaire about their relationship each week, for four weeks. In the laboratory session, half of the people were asked to fill up a page analyzing the reasons why their relationship with their dating partner was the way it was. The other half filled up a page explaining why they had chosen their major. As you can probably guess, writing about their relationship changed people's attitudes about it. For some, attitudes became more positive; for others, they became more negative. But they changed. Again, the likely explanation is that what is most easily put into words is not necessarily what is most important. But once aspects of a relationship are put into words, their importance to the verbalizer takes on added significance.

A more optimistic view of this last result is that the process of analyzing a relationship actually produces insight, so that we better understand the true nature of our relationship. But the evidence suggests otherwise. When students who had been asked to analyze their relationships were compared to students not asked to do so, the researchers found that unanalyzed attitudes about the relationship were a better predictor of whether the relationship would still be intact months later than analyzed attitudes. Those who were asked to supply reasons and expressed positive feelings about their relationship were not necessarily still in the relationship six months later. As in the poster study, being asked to give reasons can make unimportant considerations salient temporarily and produce a less, not a more, accurate assessment of how people really feel.

In discussing these studies, I am not suggesting that we will always, or even frequently, be better off "going with our gut" when making choices. What I am suggesting is there are pitfalls to deciding after analyzing. My concern, given the research on trade-offs and missed opportunities, is that as the number of options goes up, the need to provide justifications for decisions also increases. And though this struggle to find reasons will lead to decisions that seem right at the moment, it will not necessarily lead to decisions that feel right later on.

I'm fortunate to teach at a college that attracts some of the most talented young people in the world. While students at many colleges are happy to discover a subject to study that not only do they enjoy but that will enable them to make a living, many of the students I teach have multiple interests and capabilities. These students face the task of deciding on the one thing that they want to do more than anything else. Unconstrained by limitations of talent, the world is open to them. Do they exult in this opportunity? Not many of the ones I talk to. Instead, they agonize: Between making money and doing something of lasting social value. Between challenging their intellects and exercising their creative impulses. Between work that demands single-mindedness and work that will enable them to live balanced lives. Between work they can do in a beautifully pastoral location and work that brings them to a bustling city. Between any work at all and further study. With a decision as important as this, they struggle to find the reasons that make one choice stand out above all the others.

In addition, because of the flexibility that now characterizes relations among family, friends, and lovers, my students can't even use obligations to other people as a way to limit their possibilities. Where the people they love are located and how close to them they want to be are just more factors to be entered into the decision, to be traded off against various aspects of the jobs themselves. Everything is up for grabs; almost anything is possible. And each possibility they consider has its attractive features, so that the missed opportunities associated with those attractive options keep mounting up, making the whole decision-making process decidedly unattractive. What, they wonder, is the right thing to do? How can they know?

As this chapter has shown, decisions like these arouse discomfort, and they force indecision. Students take time off, take on odd jobs, try out internships, hoping that the right answer to the "What should I be when I grow up?" question will emerge. One quickly learns that "What are you going to do when you graduate?" is not a question many students are eager to hear, let alone answer. It is hard to avoid the conclusion that my students might be better off with a little less talent or with a little more of a sense that they owed it to their families to settle down back home, or even a dose of Depression-era necessity—take the secure job and get on with it! With fewer options and more constraints, many trade-offs would be eliminated, and there would be less self-doubt, less of an effort to justify decisions, more satisfaction, and less second-guessing of the decisions once made.

The anguish and inertia caused by having too many choices was described in the book *Quarterlife Crisis: The Unique Challenges of Life in Your Twenties*. Through interviews, the book captures the doubts and regrets that seem to be overwhelming successful young adults. No stability, no certainty, no predictability. Intense self-doubt. People taking longer to settle down.

National statistics confirm the impressions captured in the book. Both men and women marry years later now than they did a generation ago. What could raise the spectre of missed opportunities more profoundly than choosing one mate and losing the chance to enjoy all the attractive features of other potential mates? People also stay in their jobs less than half as long, on average, as they did a generation ago. Whereas delaying marriage and avoiding commitment to a particular job would seem to promote self-discovery, this freedom and self-exploration seems to leave many people feeling more lost than found. And as one young respondent put it, "What happens when you have too many options is that you are responsible for what happens to you."

How Can It Be So Hard to Choose?

FOR MOST OF HUMAN HISTORY, PEOPLE WERE NOT REALLY FACED with an array of choices and missed opportunities. Instead of "Should I take A or B or C or . . . ?" the question people asked themselves was more like "Should I take it or leave it?" In a world of scarcity, opportunities don't present themselves in bunches, and the decisions people face are between approach and avoidance, acceptance or rejection. We can assume that having a good sense of this—of what's good and what's bad—was essential for survival. But distinguishing between good and bad is a far simpler matter than distinguishing good from better from best. After millions of years of survival based on simple distinctions, it may simply be that we are biologically unprepared for the number of choices we face in the modern world.

As psychologist Susan Sugarman has pointed out, you can see this thumbnail history of our species played out in the early development of children. Babies don't have to choose among options. They simply accept or reject what the world presents to them. The same is true of toddlers. "Do you want some juice?" "Would you like to go to the park?" "Do you want to go down the slide?" Parents ask the questions, and toddlers answer yes or no. Then, all of a sudden, perhaps when children have developed sufficient skill with language to make communication reliable, their parents are asking them, "Do you want apple juice or orange juice?" "Do you want to go to the park or to the swimming pool?" "Do you want to go down the slide or go on the swings?" Now yes or no will no longer do the job. One mother described the dilemma facing her five-year-old this way:

> I have noticed that my son sometimes has difficulty making the sorts of choices that exclude one thing or another. I have the sense that it has to do with a sense of loss. That choosing one thing over another will mean that one thing is lost. Finally making the choice somehow minimizes the pleasure in the thing that is gained, though there also seems to be an accompanying relief in finally making the choice. I have noticed him deliberating, as if he is frozen with indecision. He literally cannot make the decision, unless he is gently prodded. Most recently I noticed him doing this when given a choice between different-colored popsicles.

We all learn as we grow up that living requires making choices and passing up opportunities. But our evolutionary history makes this a difficult lesson. Learning to choose is hard. Learning to choose well is harder. And learning to choose well in a world of unlimited possibilities is harder still, perhaps too hard.

Reversible Decisions:
An Illusory Solution to the Choice Problem

S IT RETURNABLE?" "CAN I GET MY DEPOSIT BACK?" AFFIRMATIVE answers to these questions have soothed many a troubled decision maker, at least temporarily. We think of trade-offs as hurting less and missed opportunities as less troublesome, if we know that we can change our minds when it looks like we've made a mistake. Indeed, many of us would probably be willing to pay a premium to retain the option of being allowed to change our minds. Often we do just that by rejecting sale merchandise ("no return or exchange permitted") and choosing items at full price. Perhaps one of the reasons major decisions are so difficult is that they are largely nonreversible. Marriage doesn't come with a money-back guarantee. Neither does a career. Changes in either involve substantial costs—in time, energy, emotion, and money.

So it might seem like good advice to encourage people to approach their decisions as reversible and their mistakes as fixable. The door stays open. The account stays active. Facing decisions—large or small—with this attitude should mitigate many of the stresses and negative emotions we've been examining.

Yes, but at a price. A series of studies gave some people a choice that was reversible and others a choice that was nonreversible. In one case, participants chose one photograph from a set of eight-by-ten black-and-white prints they had made in a photography course. In another case, they chose one small poster from a set of fine art reproductions. What emerged from the findings was that, while participants valued being able to reverse their choices, almost no one actually did so. However, those who had the option to change their minds were less satisfied with their choices than participants who did not have that option. And, perhaps most important, the participants had no idea that keeping the option open to change their minds would affect their satisfaction with the things they chose.

So keeping options open seems to exact a psychological price. When we can change our minds, apparently we do less psychological work to justify the decision we've made, reinforcing the chosen alternative and disparaging the rejected ones. Perhaps we do less work putting missed opportunities embodied by the rejected alternatives out of our minds.

After all, if you put down a nonrefundable deposit for a house on Martha's Vineyard, you focus on the beauty of the beach and the dunes. On the other hand, if your deposit is refundable, if the door is still open, you may continue to weigh that jungle hideaway in Costa Rica you were also considering. The beach and the dunes won't get any better in your mind, and the rain forest won't get any less appealing.

Or, to raise the stakes, consider the possible difference between those who regard marital vows as sacred and unbreakable and those who regard them as agreements that can be reversed or undone by mutual consent. We would expect that those who see marriage as a nonreversible commitment will be more inclined to do psychological work that makes them feel satisfied with their decision than will those whose attitude about marriage is more relaxed. As a result, individuals with "nonreversible" marriages might be more satisfied than individuals with "reversible" ones. As we see reversible marriages come apart, we may think to ourselves, how fortunate the couple was to have a flexible attitude toward marital commitment, given that it didn't work out. It might not occur to us that the flexible attitude might have played a causal role in the marriage's failure.

Choices, Missed Opportunities, and Maximizers

NOBODY LIKES TO MAKE TRADE-OFFS. NOBODY LIKES TO WATCH missed opportunities mount. But the problem of trade-offs and missed opportunities will be dramatically attenuated for a satisficer. Recall that satisficers are looking for something that's "good enough," not something that's best. "Good enough" can survive thinking about missed opportunities. In addition, the "good enough" standard likely will entail much less searching and inspection of alternatives than the maximizer's "best" standard. With fewer alternatives under consideration, there will be fewer missed opportunities to be subtracted. Finally, a satisficer is not likely to be thinking about the hypothetical perfect world, in which options exist that contain all the things they value, and trade-offs are unnecessary.

For all these reasons, the pain of making trade-offs will be especially acute for maximizers. Indeed, I believe that one of the reasons that maximizers are less happy, less satisfied with their lives, and more depressed than satisficers is precisely that the taint of trade-offs and missed opportunities washes out much that should be satisfying about the decisions they make.

CHAPTER SEVEN

"If Only . . .": The Problem of Regret

A NYTIME YOU MAKE A DECISION AND IT DOESN'T TURN OUT WELL or you find an alternative that would have turned out better, you're a candidate for regret.

Some years ago my wife and I ordered a high-tech, great-for-the-back desk chair in an online auction on eBay. The chair never appeared, the seller was a fraud, and we (along with several others) lost a tidy sum of money. "How could we have been so stupid?" my wife and I took turns saying to each other. Do we regret having been taken? Indeed we do.

This is *postdecision regret*, regret that occurs after we've experienced the results of a decision. But there is also something called *anticipated regret*, which rears its head even before a decision is made. How will it feel to buy this sweater only to find a nicer, cheaper one in the next store? How will it feel if I take this job only to have a better opportunity appear next week?

Postdecision regret is sometimes referred to as "buyer's remorse." After a purchasing decision, we start to have second thoughts, convincing ourselves that rejected alternatives were actually better than the one we chose, or imagining that there are better alternatives out there that we haven't yet explored. The bitter taste of regret detracts from the satisfaction we get, whether or not the regret is justified. Anticipated regret is in many ways worse, because it will produce not just dissatisfaction but paralysis. If someone asks herself how it would feel to buy this house only to discover a better one next week, she probably won't buy this house.

Both types of regret—anticipated and postdecision—will raise the emotional stakes of decisions. Anticipated regret will make decisions harder to make, and postdecision regret will make them harder to enjoy.

Individuals are not all equally susceptible to regret. Recall that when my colleagues and I measured individual differences in regret, we found that people with high regret scores are less happy, less satisfied with life, less optimistic, and more depressed than those with low regret scores. We also found that people with high regret scores tend to be maximizers. Indeed, we think that concern about regret is a major reason *why* individuals are maximizers. The only way to be sure that you won't regret a decision is by making the best possible decision. So regret doesn't seem to serve people well psychologically. And once again, the more options you have, the more likely it is that you will experience regret, either in anticipation of decisions or after them. Which may be a major reason why adding choices to our lives doesn't always make us better off.

Even though there are differences among individuals in sensitivity to regret, some circumstances are more likely to trigger regret than others.

Omission Bias

ONE STUDY OF REGRET HAD PARTICIPANTS READ THE FOLLOWING:

Mr. Paul owns shares in Company A. During the past year he considered switching to stock in Company B, but he decided against it. He now finds out that he would have been better off by $1,200 if he had switched to the stock of Company B. Mr. George owned shares in Company B. During the past year he switched to stock in Company A. He now finds that he would have been better off by $1,200 if he had kept his stock in Company B. Who feels greater regret?

Because both Mr. Paul and Mr. George own shares of Company A and because they would both have been $1,200 richer if they had owned shares in Company B, they seem to be in exactly the same boat. But 92 percent of the respondents think Mr. George will feel worse than Mr. Paul. The key difference between them is that Mr. George regrets something he *did* (switching from Company B to Company A), while Mr. Paul regrets something he *failed to do*. Most of us seem to share the intuition that we regret actions that don't turn out well more than we regret failures to take actions that *would* have turned out well. This is sometimes referred to as an *omission bias*, a bias to downplay omissions (failures to act) when we evaluate the consequences of our decisions.

However, recent evidence indicates that acts of commission are not always more salient than acts of omission. First, imagine that you're the coach of a soccer team that has lost its last two games by wide margins. Should you change your team's lineup for the next game? What do you think you'd regret more, sticking with your current lineup and losing or changing lineups and losing? Regret expert Marcel Zeelenberg and several colleagues did just this study, and found that in the face of past failure, not changing is more salient and blameworthy than changing.

Second, the omission bias undergoes a reversal when we contemplate decisions made in the more distant past. When asked about what they regret most in the last six months, people tend to identify actions that didn't meet expectations. But when asked about what they regret most when they look back on their lives as a whole, people tend to identify failures to act. In the short run, we regret a bad educational choice, whereas in the long run, we regret a missed educational opportunity. In the short run, we regret a broken romance, whereas in the long run, we regret a missed romantic opportunity. So it seems that we don't close the psychological door on the decisions we've made, and as time passes, what we've failed to do looms larger and larger.

Near Misses

A SECOND FACTOR THAT AFFECTS REGRET IS HOW CLOSE WE COME TO achieving our desired result. Consider this:

> Mr. Crane and Mr. Tees were scheduled to leave the airport on different flights, at the same time. They traveled from town in the same limousine, were caught in a traffic jam, and arrived at the airport thirty minutes after the scheduled departure time of their flights. Mr. Crane is told that his flight left on time. Mr. Tees is told that his flight was delayed and left just five minutes ago. Who is more upset?

When presented with this scenario, 96 percent of respondents thought Mr. Tees would be more upset than Mr. Crane. You can almost feel the frustration that Mr. Tees experiences. "If only that other passenger had gotten to the limo on time." "If only we had used Main Street instead of Elm Street." "If only I had been the first passenger dropped off at the airport instead of the third." There are so many ways to imagine a different outcome. When you miss your objective by a lot, it is hard to imagine that small differences would have led to a successful result. But when you miss by a little, ouch.

Related to this "nearness" effect, who do you think is happier, an athlete who wins a silver medal in the Olympics (second place) or an athlete who wins a bronze medal (third place)? It seems obvious that second is better than third, so silver medalists should be happier than bronze medalists. But this turns out, on average, not to be true. Bronze medalists are happier than silver medalists. As the silver medalists stand on the award platform, they're thinking about how close they came to winning the gold. Just a little more of this, and a little less of that, and ultimate glory would have been theirs. As the bronze medalists stand on that platform, however, they're thinking about how close *they* came to getting no medal at all. The near miss of the silver medalists is triumph, whereas the near miss of the bronze medalists is also-ran obscurity.

Responsibility for Results

THE LAST IMPORTANT DETERMINANT OF REGRET IS RESPONSIBILity. If a friend invites you out to dinner at a restaurant of his choosing and you have a bad meal, you might be disappointed. You might be displeased. But will you be regretful? What is it that you'll regret? Contrast that with how you'll feel after a bad meal if *you* picked the restaurant. This is when you'll feel regret. Several studies have shown that bad results make people equally unhappy whether or not they are responsible for them. But bad results make people regretful only if they bear responsibility.

If we put these factors together, we get a picture of the conditions that make regret especially powerful. If we are responsible for an action that turns out badly and if it almost turned out well, then we are prime candidates for regret. What is important about this picture is that the more that our experiences result from our own choices, the more regret we will feel if things don't turn out as we had hoped. So although adding options may make it easier for us to choose something we really like, it will also make it easier for us to regret choices that don't live up to our hopes or expectations.

Regret and the World of Counterfactuals and Hypotheticals

ND WHAT MAKES THE PROBLEM OF REGRET MUCH WORSE IS THAT such thinking is not restricted to objective reality. The power of the human imagination enables people to think about states of affairs that don't exist. When confronted with a choice between a job that offers the possibility of rapid advancement and a job that offers congenial workmates, I can easily imagine finding a job that has both. This ability to conjure up ideal scenarios provides a never-ending supply of raw material for experiencing regret.

Thinking about the world as it isn't, but might be or might have been, is called *counterfactual thinking*. The limo to the airport went on Elm Street. That's a fact. It could have gone on Main Street. That's contrary to fact. "If only it had gone on Main Street, I would have made my plane." The elective course I took was a bore. The one I passed up was interesting. Those are the facts. "If only I had been willing to wake up a little earlier." "If only it had been scheduled a little later." Thoughts like these invoke circumstances that are contrary to fact.

We couldn't make it through the day without counterfactual thinking. Without the ability to imagine a world that is different from our actual world and then to act to bring this imagined world into being, we never would have survived as a species, much less advanced through the millions of stages of speculation and trial and error that is the history of human progress. But the downside of counterfactual thinking is that it fuels regret, both postdecision regret and anticipated regret.

Psychologists who have studied counterfactual thinking extensively find that most individuals do not often engage in this process spontaneously. We don't sit around, sipping our morning coffee, and ask ourselves what our lives would have been like if we'd been born in South Africa rather than the U.S., or if the earth's orbit had been just a few thousand miles closer to the sun. Instead, counterfactual thinking is usually triggered by the occurrence of something unpleasant, something that itself produces a negative emotion. Counterfactual thoughts are generated in response to experiences such as poor exam grades, trouble in romantic relationships, and the illness or death of loved ones. And when the counterfactual thoughts begin to occur, they trigger more negative emotions, like regret, which in turn trigger more counterfactual thinking, which in turn triggers more negative emotion. Though most people can manage to suppress their counterfactual thoughts before they spin too far down this vicious spiral, some—especially those who suffer from clinical depression—may not be able to arrest the downward pull.

When they examine the actual content of counterfactual thinking, researchers find that individuals tend to focus on aspects of a situation that are under their control. When asked to imagine an automobile accident that involves someone who is speeding while driving on a rainy day with poor visibility, respondents are much more likely to "undo" the accident by having the driver be more cautious than by having the day be clear and dry. This focus on individual control conforms with my earlier point that regret and responsibility go hand in hand. Of course, most of the situations we encounter have a mixture of aspects we could have controlled and aspects we couldn't have. When a student who didn't study much does badly on an exam, he could and should take responsibility for not having studied more. But the exam could have been easier, or it could have been more focused on material that the student knew well. The fact that counterfactual thinking seems to home in on the controllable aspects of a situation only increases the chances that a person will experience regret when engaging in counterfactual thinking.

There is also an important distinction to be made between "upward" and "downward" counterfactuals. *Upward counterfactuals* are imagined states that are *better* than what actually happened, and *downward counterfactuals* are imagined states that are *worse*. The Olympic silver medalist who imagines tripping, falling, and not finishing the race at all is engaging in downward counterfactual thinking, and doing so should enhance her feelings about winning the silver. It's only the upward counterfactual—imagining winning the gold—that will diminish her sense of achievement. So generating downward counterfactuals might engender not only a sense of satisfaction, but a sense of gratitude that things didn't turn out worse. What studies have shown, however, is that people rarely produce downward counterfactuals unless asked specifically to do so.

There is an important lesson to be taken from this research on counterfactual thinking, and it's not that we should stop doing it; counterfactual thinking is a powerful intellectual tool. The lesson is that we should try to do more *downward* counterfactual thinking. While upward counterfactual thinking may inspire us to do better the next time, downward counterfactual thinking may induce us to be grateful for how well we did this time. The right balance of upward and downward counterfactual thinking may enable us to avoid spiraling into a state of misery while at the same time inspiring us to improve our performance.

Regret and Satisfaction

A S WE HAVE SEEN, REGRET WILL MAKE US FEEL WORSE AFTER decisions—even ones that work out—than we otherwise would, especially when we take opportunity costs into consideration.

Missed opportunities capture the benefits that would have come as a result of a different choice, and as soon as you return from that seaside vacation, the counterfactual thinking may begin. "That was a great vacation. If only they had better restaurants there, it would have been perfect. If only there had been some interesting shops. What I wouldn't have given for one really good movie theater." And so on. With each of these counterfactual thoughts, another little smidgen of regret insinuates itself into the evaluation of a decision. And as we saw in the last chapter, if the number of candidates from which the choice is made goes up, each having some attractive feature that the chosen candidate does not, the missed opportunities (and the counterfactual thoughts and the smidgens of regret) mount higher and higher.

Counterfactual thoughts tend to be triggered by negative events, and events can be negative in absolute terms. If the beach is dirty, it rains constantly, and the accommodations are dingy, then the seaside vacation is just bad. But an event also can be negative in relative terms—relative either to aspirations or expectations. So if, by engaging in the careful decision-making process and trade-off assessment I discussed in the last chapter, you bring to mind all the wonderful things a seaside vacation might have included but didn't, there will be no shortage of negatives to occupy your mind, even if your vacation was good.

Exactly the same thing applies prior to a decision. By thinking about what you will give up by going to the seaside, by imagining, in

"I was sad because I had no on-board fax until I saw a man who had no mobile phone."

THE BENEFITS OF DOWNWARD COMPARISON

© *The New Yorker Collection 1993 Warren Miller from cartoonbank.com. All Rights Reserved.*

advance, the opportunities you will be missing, it seems inevitable that the anticipated regret induced by these thoughts will make the most attractive option seem less attractive. Sure, you may still decide to go to the beach, but not with quite the same enthusiasm.

Another way of making this point is in terms of *contrast effects*. If a person comes right out of a sauna and jumps into a swimming pool, the water in the pool feels really cold, because of the contrast between the water temperature and the temperature in the sauna.

Jumping into the same pool after having just come indoors on a sub-zero winter day will produce sensations of warmth. *And what counterfactual thinking does is establish a contrast between a person's actual experience and an imagined alternative.* Any actual seaside vacation suffers by contrast with an imagined, perfect alternative, and with that counterfactual contrast comes regret, more acutely for people who are maximizers than for people who are satisficers. It is the maximizers who will have these counterfactual perfect options in mind, which will make any real-world option pale by comparison.

What Regret Makes Us Do

UNLIKE OTHER NEGATIVE EMOTIONS—ANGER, SADNESS, DISAP-pointment, even grief—what is so difficult about regret is the feeling that the regrettable state of affairs could have been avoided and that it could have been avoided by *you*, if only you had chosen differently.

In the last chapter we saw that individuals facing decisions involving trade-offs, and thus opportunities for regret, will avoid making those decisions altogether. Or if they can't avoid the decisions completely, they will construe them so that they no longer seem to involve trade-offs. "When it comes to buying a car, nothing's more important than the safety of my family." "When it comes to taking vacations, nothing compares to the smell of the ocean and the sound of the surf." "The only thing I care about in a house is that I have enough space to spread out." And so on.

Not surprisingly, when confronted with decisions, we often choose the option that minimizes the chances that we will experience regret.

Regret Aversion

A S WE SAW IN CHAPTER 3, MOST PEOPLE TEND TO BE RISK AVERSE when they are contemplating a choice between a certain small gain and an uncertain large one. So, for example, if given the option between a sure $100 and a fifty-fifty chance to gain $200, most of us will take the sure thing, because, subjectively, $200 is not twice as good as $100, and thus not worth the fifty-fifty risk. But another reason for risk aversion is *regret aversion*. Suppose you have the choice between a guaranteed $100 and a risky $200, and suppose you choose the $100. You'll never know what would have happened if instead you had chosen to go for the risky $200. So you'll have no reason to regret your decision to take the sure thing. In contrast, suppose you go for the risk. Now you can't help but know what would have happened if you had taken the sure thing; that's what *makes* it a sure thing. So if you opt for risk and you lose, not only do you wind up with nothing, but you also have to live with the sting that you could have had $100. Taking the sure thing is a way to guarantee that you won't regret your decision—you won't regret it because you'll never know how the alternative would have turned out.

If this thinking is correct, then it should make a difference to tell someone that if they choose the guaranteed $100, you will still flip the coin and let them know whether they would have won or lost on the riskier proposition. Under these conditions, people can no longer avoid the possibility of regret no matter which option they choose. And, indeed, it does make a difference. We show greater willingness to take risks when we know we will find out how the unchosen alternative turned out, so that there is thus no way to protect ourselves from regret.

Studies like this show that not only is regret an important consequence of many decisions, but that the prospect of regret is an important *cause* of many decisions. People will make choices with the anticipation of regret firmly in mind. If you're trying to decide whether to buy a Toyota Camry or a Honda Accord and your closest friend just bought an Accord, you're likely to buy one too, partly because the only way to avoid the information that you made a mistake is to buy what your friend bought and thus avoid potentially painful comparisons. Of course, you can't really avoid that information completely. Lots of people buy Camrys and Accords, there are articles in newspapers and magazines about them, and so on. But this kind of information pales in comparison to the vivid, detailed, day-after-day confirmation that your friend bought a better car than you did.

Another effect that the desire to avoid regret can have is to induce people not to act at all, what is called *inaction inertia*. Imagine being in the market for a sofa and seeing one you like on sale for 30 percent below list price. It's fairly early in your search, and you think that you may be able to do better, so you pass up the sale. Several weeks of shopping fail to turn up anything better, so you go back to buy the one you saw earlier. The trouble is that now it's selling for 10 percent off list price. Do you buy it? For many shoppers, the answer is no. If they buy it, there will be no way to avoid regretting not having bought it earlier. If they don't buy it, they still keep the possibility alive that they'll find something better.

Examples of inaction inertia abound. Having failed to sign up for a frequent-flyer program and then made a 5,000-mile round-trip flight, we are reluctant to sign up when given the opportunity again. If we do sign up, we can no longer tell ourselves that we don't fly enough and it isn't worth the trouble; instead, we can only regret not having signed up earlier. Having declined to join a fitness club located five minutes from our home, then changed our minds only to discover that the club's membership rolls are closed, we refuse to join one located twenty minutes from our house. Again, by not joining, we can tell ourselves that we get enough exercise anyway or that we don't have the time to make proper use of the club. Once we join the distant club, all the reasons for not joining go out the window and we are left regretting our initial failure to act.

Regret and "Sunk Costs"

EMEMBER THOSE EXPENSIVE SHOES THAT KILL YOUR FEET THAT WE left sitting in the back of your closet in Chapter 3? I mentioned them as an example of what are called *sunk costs*. Having bought the shoes, you keep them in the closet even though you know you're never going to put them on again, because to give the shoes away or throw them away would force you to acknowledge a loss. Similarly, people hold on to stocks that have decreased in value because selling them would turn the investment into a loss. What *should* matter in decisions about holding or selling stocks is only your assessment of *future* performance and not (tax considerations aside) the price at which the stocks were purchased.

In a classic demonstration of the power of sunk costs, people were offered season subscriptions to a local theater company. Some were offered the tickets at full price and others at a discount. Then the researchers simply kept track of how often the ticket purchasers actually attended the plays over the course of the season. What they found was that full-price payers were more likely to show up at performances than discount payers. The reason for this, the researchers argued, was that the full-price payers would feel worse about wasting money if they didn't use the tickets than would the discount payers. Because it would constitute a bigger loss for the full-price payers, failure to attend a performance would produce more regret.

From the perspective of a model of decision making that is future oriented, being sensitive to sunk costs is a mistake. The tickets are bought, and the money is spent. That's over. The only question the ticket holders should be asking themselves on the night of the performance is, "Will I get more satisfaction out of a night at the theater or out of a night spent reading and listening to music at home?" But people don't operate this way.

Sunk-cost effects have been demonstrated in a variety of different settings. In one study, respondents were asked to imagine having purchased nonrefundable tickets for two ski trips to different places, only to discover that the trips are on the same day. One ticket cost $50 and the other cost $25, but there is good reason to think that they'll have a better time on the $25 trip. Which one do people choose to go on? For the most part, they choose the $50 trip. According to the same logic of sunk costs, professional coaches give more playing time to players earning higher salaries, independent of their current level of performance. And people who have started their own businesses are more likely to invest in expanding them than people who have purchased their businesses from others. Again, in these cases, what "should" matter are the prospects for future performance—of the business or of the player. But what also seems to matter is the level of previous investment.

What leads me to believe that sunk-cost effects are motivated by the desire to avoid regret rather than just the desire to avoid a loss is that sunk-cost effects are much bigger when a person bears responsibility for the initial decision (to buy the ski tickets or the expensive shoes). If sunk-cost effects are just about hating to lose, then whether the loss is your responsibility or not is irrelevant; it's the same loss.

I, personally, succumb to sunk-cost effects in a variety of settings that I'm aware of, and probably many others that I'm not. I have clothes in my closet and CDs on my rack that I know I'm not going to wear or listen to again. Yet I can't get rid of them. When I eat in a restaurant, I feel compelled to finish what's on my plate, no matter how full I am. When I'm two hundred pages into reading a book, I force myself to finish it, no matter how little I'm enjoying it or learning from it. The list goes on and on.

Many people persist in very troubled relationships not because of love or what they owe the other person or because they feel a moral obligation to honor vows, but because of all the time and effort they've already put in. How many people stick out an arduous course of training, like, say, medical school, even after they discover that they really don't want to be doctors? And arguably, why did the United States persist as long as it did in Vietnam, even long after it was plain to virtually everyone involved that no good outcome could result from continued involvement? "If we get out now," people said, "then all the thousands of soldiers and civilians who have died will have died in vain." This is thinking in terms of the past, not the future. Those who had died were dead and could not be brought back. The questions that should have been asked (all moral and political considerations about the appropriateness of the war aside) concerned the prospects of soldiers and civilians who were still alive.

Regret, Maximizing, and Choice Possibilities

REGRET OBVIOUSLY PLAYS A VERY BIG ROLE IN ALL OUR DECISIONS, but how does choice, particularly an overabundance of choice, affect regret?

We have seen that two of the factors affecting regret are

1. Personal responsibility for the result
2. How easily an individual can imagine a counterfactual, better alternative.

The availability of choice obviously exacerbates both of these factors. When there are no options, what can you do? Disappointment, maybe; regret, no. When you have only a few options, you do the best you can, but the world may simply not allow you to do as well as you would like. When there are many options, the chances increase that there is a really good one out there, and you feel that you ought to be able to find it. When the option you actually settle on proves disappointing, you regret not having chosen more wisely. And as the number of options continues to proliferate, making an exhaustive investigation of the possibilities impossible, concern that there may be a better option out there may induce you to anticipate the regret you will feel later on, when that option is discovered, and thus prevent you from making a decision at all.

When considering a decision involving complex possibilities, the fact that there is no one option that is best in all respects will induce people to consider the missed opportunities associated with choosing the best option. And the more options there are, the more likely it is that there will be some that are better in certain respects than the chosen one. So missed opportunities will mount as the number of options increases, and as missed opportunities mount, so will regret.

There will be anticipatory regret that the overall best car doesn't have the best sound system ("Will I be kicking myself for not having better sound if I buy this car?"), and there will be postdecision regret that the overall best car doesn't have the best sound system ("Why couldn't they have made the stereo better?"). The more options there are, the more *if only*'s you will be able to generate. And with each *if only* you generate will come a little more regret and a little less satisfaction with the choice you actually made. Though it may be annoying to go into a bank and discover that only a single teller's window is open and the line is long, there won't be anything to regret. But what if there are two long lines and you choose the wrong one? Janet Landman, in her excellent book *Regret*, sums it up this way: "Regret may threaten decisions with multiple attractive alternatives more than decisions offering only one or a more limited set of alternatives. . . . Ironically, then, the greater the number of appealing choices, the greater the opportunity for regret."

It should also be clear that the problem of regret will loom larger for maximizers than for satisficers. No matter how good something is, if a maximizer discovers something better, he'll regret having failed to choose it in the first place. Perfection is the only weapon against regret, and endless, exhaustive, paralyzing consideration of the alternatives is the only way to achieve perfection. For a satisficer, the stakes are lower. The possibility of regret doesn't loom as large, and perfection is unnecessary.

Is There an Upside to Regret?

WE ALL KNOW THAT REGRET CAN MAKE PEOPLE MISERABLE, BUT regret also serves several important functions. First, anticipating that we may regret a decision may induce us to take the decision seriously and to imagine the various scenarios that may follow it. This anticipation may help us to see consequences of a decision that would not have been evident otherwise. Second, regret may emphasize the mistakes we made in arriving at a decision, so that, should a similar situation arise in the future, we won't make the same mistakes. Third, regret may mobilize or motivate us to take the actions necessary to undo a decision or ameliorate some of its unfortunate consequences. Fourth, regret is a signal to others that we care about what happened, are sorry that it happened, and will do what we can to make sure that it doesn't happen again. Because so many of the decisions we make have consequences for others, a sign to those others that we feel their pain may induce them to stick with us and trust us in the future.

And even when decisions don't turn out badly, it is often appropriate and important to experience and acknowledge regret. If you decide to take a job 2,500 miles away from your family, it is appropriate to regret having been put in the position of trading off a good job opportunity against family ties, *even if* the decision works out well. The mere fact that such trade-offs have to be made is regrettable. And to acknowledge the fact of tragic choices is merely to give the sacrifices entailed in a choice their due.

Still, for people who are so plagued by regret that they can't let go of decisions in the past and have enormous difficulty making decisions in the present, taking steps to reduce regret could be extremely beneficial to their well-being.

In Chapter 11, we will discuss a general approach to coping with a world of choice, and many of these methods have the direct effect of diminishing our tendency to regret.

CHAPTER EIGHT

Why Decisions Disappoint: The Problem of Adaptation

W HILE REGRET AND MISSED OPPORTUNITIES CAN FOCUS OUR attention on what we've passed up, there is also plenty of room for dissatisfaction with the options that we actually choose.

Because of a ubiquitous feature of human psychology, very little in life turns out quite as good as we expect it will be. After much anguish, you might decide to buy a Lexus, and you try to put all the attractions of other makes out of your mind. But once you're driving your new car, the experience falls just a little bit flat. You're hit with a double whammy—regret about what you didn't choose, and disappointment with what you did.

This ubiquitous feature of human psychology is a process known as *adaptation*. Simply put, we get used to things, and then we start to take them for granted. My first desktop computer had 8K of memory, loaded programs by cassette tape (it took five minutes to load a simple program), and was anything but user-friendly. I loved it and all the things it enabled me to do. Last year I replaced a computer with about a million times that much speed and capacity because it was too clunky to meet my needs. What I do with my computer hasn't changed all that much over the years. But what I expect it to do for me has. When I first got cable TV, I was ecstatic about the reception and excited about all the choices it provided (many fewer than today). Now I moan when the cable goes out and I complain about the paucity of attractive programs. When it first became possible to get a wide variety of fruits and vegetables at all times of year, I thought I'd found heaven. Now I take this year-round bounty for granted and get annoyed if the nectarines from Israel or Peru that I can buy in February aren't sweet and juicy. I got used to—adapted to—each of these sources of pleasure, and they stopped being sources of pleasure.

Because of adaptation, enthusiasm about positive experiences doesn't sustain itself. And what's worse, people seem generally unable to anticipate that this process of adaptation will take place. The waning of pleasure or enjoyment over time always seems to come as an unpleasant surprise.

Researchers have known about and studied adaptation for many years, but for the most part they emphasized *perceptual adaptation*—decreased responsiveness to sights, sounds, odors, and the like as people continue to experience them. The idea is that human beings, like virtually all other animals, respond less and less to any given environmental event as the event persists. A small-town resident who visits Manhattan is overwhelmed by all that is going on. A New Yorker, thoroughly adapted to the city's hyperstimulation, is oblivious to it.

In the same way that we each have our own internal thermometer for registering sensation, we each have a "pleasure thermometer" that runs from negative (unpleasant), through neutral, to pleasant. When we experience something good, our pleasure "temperature" goes up, and when we experience something bad, it goes down. But then we adapt. In this case it is *hedonic adaptation*, or adaptation to pleasure. An experience that boosts our "hedonic" or pleasure temperature by, say, 20 degrees at the first encounter may boost it by only 15 degrees the next time, by 10 degrees the time after that, and eventually it may stop boosting it at all.

Imagine yourself out running errands on a hot, humid summer day. After several hours of sweating in the heat, you return home to your air-conditioned house. The feeling of the cool, dry air enveloping you is spectacular. At first it makes you feel revived, invigorated, almost ecstatic. But as time passes, the intense pleasure wanes, replaced by a feeling of simple comfort. While you don't feel hot, sticky, and tired, you don't feel cool and energized either. In fact, you don't feel much of anything. You've gotten so accustomed to the air-conditioning that you don't even notice it. That is, you don't notice it until you leave it to go back out into the heat a while later. Now the heat hits you like a blast from an open oven, and you notice the air-conditioning that you no longer have.

In 1973, 13 percent of Americans thought of air-conditioning in their cars as a necessity. Today, virtually everyone does. I know the earth is getting warmer, but the climate hasn't changed that much in forty years. What has changed is our standard of comfort.

Even though we don't expect it to happen, such adaptation to pleasure is inevitable, and it may cause more disappointment in a world of many choices than in a world of few.

Changed Response to a Persistent Event and Changed Reference Point

HEDONIC ADAPTATION CAN BE THE SIMPLE "GETTING USED TO" I JUST described, or it can be the result of a change in reference point, owing to a new experience.

Imagine a woman working contentedly at an interesting job for $40,000 a year. A new job opportunity arises that offers her

$60,000. She switches jobs, but, alas, after six months, the new company goes under. The old company is happy to take her back, so happy, in fact, that it raises her salary to $45,000. Is she happy with the "raise"? Will it even feel like a raise? The answer is probably no. The $60,000 salary, however briefly it was available, may establish for this person a new baseline or reference point of hedonic neutrality, so that anything less is taken as a loss. Though six months earlier, a raise from $40,000 to $45,000 would have felt wonderful, now it feels like a cut from $60,000 to $45,000.

We sometimes hear people say things like, "I never knew wine could taste this good," or "I never knew sex could be this exciting," or "I never expected to make this much money." Novelty can change someone's hedonic standards so that what was once good enough, or even better than that, no longer is. And as we'll see, adaptation can be especially disappointing when we've put much time and effort into selecting the items or experiences we end up adapting to.

Hedonic Adaptation and Hedonic Treadmills

IN WHAT IS PERHAPS THE MOST FAMOUS EXAMPLE OF HEDONIC ADAP-tation, respondents were asked to rate their happiness on a 5-point scale. Some of them had won between $50,000 and $1 million in state lotteries within the last year. Others had become paraplegic or quadriplegic as a result of accidents. Not surprisingly, the lottery winners were happier than those who had become paralyzed. What is surprising, though, is that the lottery winners were no happier than people in general. And what is even more surprising is that the accident victims, while somewhat less happy than people in general, still judged themselves to be happy.

There is little doubt that if you had asked lottery winners how happy they were right after their number was drawn, they would have placed themselves somewhere off the charts. And if you had asked accident victims how happy they were right after they suffered their disability, they would have been as low as can be. But as time passes, and the winners and the accident victims get used to their new circumstances, the "hedonic thermometers" in both groups begin to converge, becoming much more like the population at large.

I'm not suggesting here that, as far as subjective experience goes, in the long run there's no difference between winning a lottery and being paralyzed in an accident. But what I am arguing is that the difference is much smaller than you would expect, and much smaller than it appears to be at the moment at which these life-changing events occur.

As I said, there are two reasons why these dramatic hedonic adaptations occur. First, people just get used to good or bad fortune. Second, the new standard of what's a good experience (winning the lottery) may make many of the ordinary pleasures of daily life (the smell of freshly brewed coffee, the new blooms and refreshing breezes of a lovely spring day) rather tame by comparison. And indeed when the lottery winners were asked to rate the hedonic quality of various everyday activities, they rated them as less pleasurable than non–lottery winners did. So there is both a changed response to a persistent event and a changed reference level.

In the case of the accident victims, there is probably still more going on. The immediate aftermath of the accident is crushing, because these accident victims have lived their lives as mobile individuals and they possess none of the skills that enable paraplegics to negotiate in the environment. As time passes, they develop some of these skills and discover that they are not as impaired as they first thought. Beyond this, they may start paying attention to things that can be done and appreciated by people of impaired mobility that they never gave much thought to prior to their accidents.

Twenty-five years ago, economist Tibor Scitovsky explored some of the consequences of the phenomenon of adaptation in his book *The Joyless Economy*. Human beings, Scitovsky said, want to experience pleasure. And when they consume, they do experience pleasure—as long as the things they consume are novel. But as people adapt—as the novelty wears off—pleasure comes to be replaced by comfort. It's a thrill to drive your new car for the first few weeks; after that, it's just comfortable. It certainly beats the old car, but it isn't much of a kick. Comfort is nice enough, but people want pleasure. And comfort isn't pleasure.

The result of having pleasure turn into comfort is disappointment, and the disappointment will be especially severe when the goods we are consuming are "durable" goods, such as cars, houses, sound systems, elegant clothes, jewelry, and computers. When the brief period of real enthusiasm and pleasure wanes, people still have these things around them—as a constant reminder that consumption isn't all it's cracked up to be, that expectations are not matched by reality. And as a society's affluence grows, consumption shifts increasingly to expensive, durable goods, with the result that disappointment with consumption increases.

Faced with this inevitable disappointment, what do people do? Some simply give up the chase and stop valuing pleasure derived from things. Most are driven instead to pursue novelty, to seek out new commodities and experiences whose pleasure potential has not been dissipated by repeated exposure. In time, these new commodities also will lose their intensity, but people still get caught up in the chase, a process that psychologists Philip Brickman and Donald Campbell labeled the *hedonic treadmill*. No matter how fast you run on this kind of machine, you still don't get anywhere. And because of adaptation, no matter how good your choices and how pleasurable the results, you still end up back where you started in terms of subjective experience.

Perhaps even more insidious than the hedonic treadmill is something that Daniel Kahneman calls the *satisfaction treadmill*. Suppose that in addition to adapting to particular objects or experiences, you also adapt to particular levels of satisfaction. In other words, suppose that with great ingenuity and effort in making decisions, you manage to keep your "hedonic temperature" at +20 degrees, so that you feel pretty good about life almost all of the time. Is +20 degrees good enough? Well, it might be good enough at the beginning, but if you adapt to this particular level of happiness, then +20 won't feel so good after a while. Now you'll be striving to get and do things that push you to +30. So even if you manage to defeat or outsmart the inexorable adaptation to commodities and experiences, you still have to defeat adaptation to subjective feelings about these commodities and experiences. It's a difficult task.

Mispredicting Satisfaction

ADAPTATION TO POSITIVE EXPERIENCES WOULD BE DIFFICULT enough if we knew it was coming and prepared ourselves for it. But oddly enough, the evidence indicates that we tend to be surprised by it. In general, human beings are remarkably bad at predicting how various experiences will make them feel. Chances are that if lottery winners knew in advance just how little winning the lottery would improve their subjective well-being, they wouldn't be buying lottery tickets.

Much of the research that has been done to assess the accuracy of people's predictions about their future feelings has taken this form: One group of participants is asked to imagine some event—good or bad—and then to answer questions about how that event would make them feel. A second group consisting of those who have actually experienced the event is asked how that event *has* actually made them feel. Then the predictions of the first group are compared to the experiences of the second group.

In one study of this type, college students in the Midwest were asked how it would feel to live in California. They judged that students who lived in California were happier with the climate and more satisfied with life as a whole than Midwesterners. They were right about the first point, but not about the second. California college students did like the climate, but they were not happier than Midwest college students. Probably what led the Midwestern students astray is that they focused almost entirely on weather. Just because it's sunny and warm in California most of the time doesn't mean that students who live in California don't have problems—boring classes, too much work, not enough money, hassles with family and friends, romantic disappointments, and so on. It may be marginally more pleasant to be stressed and hassled on a warm, sunny day than on a freezing, snowy one, but not enough to make much of a difference in your outlook on life.

In another study, respondents were asked to predict how various personal and environmental changes would affect their well-being over the next decade. Individuals were asked about changes in air pollution, rain-forest destruction, increased numbers of coffee shops and TV channels, decreased risk of nuclear war, increased risk of AIDS, development of chronic health conditions, changes in income, and increases in body weight. Others were asked not to *predict* how these changes would make them feel, but to *describe* how these changes had made them feel over the last decade (to the extent that they applied in each individual case). The pattern of results was clear: those predicting expected each of the hypothetical changes—both good and bad—to have a bigger effect than was reported by those reflecting back on actual experience.

In still another study, young college professors were asked to think about how they would feel after they were either awarded or denied tenure. They were asked to anticipate their feelings immediately after the decision, and their feelings five and ten years later. The participants in the study were somewhat mindful of adaptation effects, and, accordingly, they expected to be extremely happy (or sad) when the decision was made, but that this joy or sadness would dissipate somewhat over time. Nonetheless, they got it wrong. The predictions of these professors were compared to the experiences of faculty who had *actually* experienced positive or negative tenure decisions either very recently, five years before, or ten years before. Amazingly, with the passage of time, there was no difference in reported well-being between professors who had been awarded tenure and those who had been passed over for the lifetime appointment. Even with adaptation in mind, the predictors substantially overestimated how good a positive decision would make them feel and how bad a negative decision would make them feel in the long run.

Admittedly, there is more to the mismatch between prediction and experience than just the failure to anticipate adaptation. We are ingenious at doing psychological repair work and finding silver linings after things go badly. "My colleagues were a bore." "The students were losers." "The job was killing me; I worked all the time and had no life." "It liberated me; I became a consultant and worked decent hours for twice the salary." But failure to anticipate adaptation is surely a part of this mismatch.

People also overestimate how devastated they will be by bad health news, such as a positive HIV test. And they underestimate how they will adjust to severe illness. Elderly patients suffering from a variety of the most common debilitating illnesses of advanced age reliably judge the quality of their lives more positively than do the physicians who are treating them.

It's easy to see how results like these would follow directly from the fact that we adapt to almost everything, but ignore or under-estimate adaptation effects in predicting the future. When asked to imagine being, say, $25,000 per year richer, it's easy to conjure up what it will feel like at the moment you get the raise. The mistake is to assume that the way it feels at that moment is the way it will feel forever.

Almost every decision we make involves a prediction about future emotional responses. When people marry, they are making predic-tions about how they will feel about their spouse. When they have children, they are making predictions about their enduring feelings about family life. When they embark on a long course of graduate or professional training, they are making predictions about how they'll feel about school and how they'll feel about work. When peo-ple move from the city to a suburb, they're making predictions about how it will feel to cut the grass and be tied to their cars. And when they buy a car or a stereo or anything else, they are predicting how it will feel to own and use that product in the months and years ahead.

If people err systematically and substantially in making those predictions, it's likely that they will make some bad decisions—decisions that produce regret, even when events turn out well.

Adaptation and the Choice Problem

THE ABUNDANCE OF CHOICE AVAILABLE TO US EXACERBATES THE problem of adaptation by increasing the costs, in time and effort, of making a decision. Time, effort, missed opportunities, anticipated regret, and the like are fixed costs that we "pay" up front in making a decision, and those costs then get "amortized" over the life of the decision. If the decision provides substantial satisfaction for a long time after it is made, the costs of making it recede into insignificance. But if the decision provides satisfaction for only a short time, those costs loom large. Spending four months deciding what sound system to buy isn't so bad if you really enjoy that system for fifteen years. But if you end up being excited by it for six months and then adapting, you may feel like a fool for having put in all that effort. It just wasn't worth it.

So the more choices we have, the more effort goes into our decisions, and the more we expect to enjoy the benefits of those decisions. Adaptation, by dramatically truncating the duration of those benefits, puts us into a state of mind where the result just wasn't worth the effort. The more we invest in a decision, the more we expect to realize from our investment. And adaptation makes agonizing over decisions a bad investment.

It should also be obvious that the phenomenon of adaptation will have more profound effects on people who set out to maximize than it will on people who are aiming for good enough. It is maximizers for whom expanded opportunities really create a time and effort problem. It is maximizers who make a really big investment in each of their decisions, who agonize most about trade-offs. And so it is maximizers who will be most disappointed when they discover the pleasure they derive from their decisions to be short-lived.

Happiness isn't everything. Subjective experience is not the only reason we have for existing. Careful, well-researched, and labor-intensive decisions may produce better objective results than impulsive decisions. A world with multiple options may make possible better objective choices than a world with few options. But at the same time, happiness doesn't count for nothing, and subjective experience isn't trivial. If adaptation saddles people with a subjective experience of their choices that doesn't justify the effort that went into making those choices, people will begin to see choice not as a liberator but as a burden.

What Is to Be Done?

I F YOU LIVE IN A WORLD IN WHICH YOU EXPERIENCE MISERY MORE often than joy, adaptation is very beneficial. It may be the only thing that gives you the strength and courage to get through the day. But if you live in a world of plenty, in which sources of joy outnumber sources of misery, then adaptation defeats your attempts to enjoy your good fortune. Most modern Americans live in a bountiful world. While we don't get to do and to have everything we want, no other people on earth have ever had such control over their lives, such material abundance, and such freedom of choice. Whereas adaptation does nothing to negate the objective improvements in our lives that all this freedom and abundance bring, it does much to negate the satisfaction we derive from those improvements.

We could go a long way toward improving the experienced well-being of people in our society if we could find a way to stop the process of adaptation. But adaptation is so fundamental and universal a feature of our responses to events in the world—it is so much a "hardwired" property of our nervous systems—that there is very little we can do to mitigate it directly.

However, simply by being aware of the process we can anticipate its effects, and therefore be less disappointed when it comes. This means that when we are making decisions, we should think about how each of the options will feel not just tomorrow, but months or even years later. Factoring in adaptation to the decision-making process may make differences that seem large at the moment of choice feel much smaller. Factoring in adaptation may help us be satisfied with choices that are good enough rather than "the best," and this in turn will reduce the time and effort we devote to making those choices. Finally, we can remind ourselves to be grateful for what we have. This may seem trite, the sort of thing one hears from parents or ministers, and then ignores. But individuals who regularly experience and express gratitude are physically healthier, more optimistic about the future, and feel better about their lives than those who do not. Individuals who experience gratitude are more alert, enthusiastic, and energetic than those who do not, and they are more likely to achieve personal goals.

And unlike adaptation, the experience of gratitude is something we *can* affect directly. Experiencing and expressing gratitude actually get easier with practice. By causing us to focus on how much better our lives are than they could have been, or were before, the disappointment that adaptation brings in its wake can be blunted.

CHAPTER NINE

Why Everything Suffers from Comparison

I THINK IT IS SAFE TO SAY THAT SLAMMING A CAR DOOR ON YOUR hand is unequivocally bad and that reciprocated love is unequivocally good. But most human experiences cannot be evaluated in such absolute terms; they are judged instead against other factors.

When we consider whether we liked a meal, a vacation, or a class, inevitably we are asking ourselves, "Compared to what?" For purposes of making decisions about what to do in the future, the "Was it good or bad?" question is less important than "How good or bad was it?" Very few meals in restaurants are actually "bad"— distasteful enough to induce us to spit out our food and leave. Nonetheless, we describe restaurants to our friends as bad, and they understand us to mean that compared to some standard, this restaurant is on the wrong side of zero. Comparisons are the only meaningful benchmark.

The circumstances of modern life seem to be conspiring to make experiences less satisfying than they could and perhaps *should* be, in part because of the richness against which we are comparing our own experiences. Again, as we'll see, an overload of choice contributes to this dissatisfaction.

Hopes, Expectations, Past Experience, and the Experience of Others

WHEN PEOPLE EVALUATE AN EXPERIENCE, THEY ARE PERFORMING one or more of the following comparisons:

1. Comparing the experience to what they hoped it would be
2. Comparing the experience to what they expected it to be
3. Comparing the experience to other experiences they have had in the recent past
4. Comparing the experience to experiences that others have had.

Each of these comparisons makes the evaluation of an experience relative, and this may diminish the experience or enhance it. If someone is out for a great dinner, and she's just read glowing reviews of the restaurant, her hopes and expectations will be high. If she's recently had a great meal in another restaurant, her standard of comparison with her past experience will be high. And if just before dinner she listened to one of her dining companions describe in ecstatic detail a meal he recently had, her social standard of comparison will be high. Given all this, the chef in this restaurant is going to be challenged to produce a meal that will move this person's hedonic thermometer any higher. If, in contrast, someone stumbles into the first restaurant she sees because she's very hungry, and if the place looks modest and its menu is simple, and if she had an awful dinner out the day before, and if her friend told her about a recent culinary disaster, chances are she won't be too hard to please. The same meal, in the same restaurant, can be judged negatively on the basis of the first set of comparisons and positively on the basis of the second. And by and large, we are unlikely to realize that our evaluations are as much a commentary on what we bring to the meal as they are on the meal itself.

In the same way, getting a B+ on a difficult exam can fall to either side of the hedonic neutral point. Were you hoping for a B or were you hoping for an A? Were you expecting a B or expecting an A? Do you normally get Bs or do you normally get As? And what grades did your classmates get?

Social scientist Alex Michalos, in his discussion of the perceived quality of experience, argued that people establish standards of satisfaction based on the assessment of three gaps: "the gap between what one has and wants, the gap between what one has and thinks others like oneself have, and the gap between what one has and the best one has had in the past." Michalos found that much of the individual variation in life satisfaction could be explained in terms not of differences in objective experience, but in terms of differences in these three perceived gaps. To these three comparisons I have added a fourth: the gap between what one has and what one expects.

As our material and social circumstances improve, our standards of comparison go up. As we have contact with items of high quality, we begin to suffer from "the curse of discernment." The lower quality items that once were perfectly acceptable are no longer good enough. The hedonic zero point keeps rising, and expectations and aspirations rise with it.

In some respects, rising standards of acceptability are an indication of progress. It is only when people demand more that the market provides more. In part because the members of a society develop higher and higher standards for what is good, people live much better material lives today than they ever did before, objectively speaking.

But not subjectively speaking. If your hedonic assessment derives from the relation between the objective quality of an experience and your expectations, then the rising quality of experience is met with rising expectations, and you're just running in place. The "hedonic treadmill" and the "satisfaction treadmill" that I discussed in the last chapter explain to a significant degree how real income can increase by a factor of two (in the U.S.) or five (in Japan) without having a measurable effect on the subjective well-being of the members of society. As long as expectations keep pace with realizations, people may live better, but they won't *feel* better about how they live.

Prospects, Frames, and Evaluation

N CHAPTER 3, I DISCUSSED A VERY IMPORTANT FRAMEWORK FOR understanding how we assess subjective experience. It is called *prospect theory*, and it was developed by Daniel Kahneman and Amos Tversky. What the theory claims is that evaluations are relative to a baseline. A given experience will feel positive if it's an improvement on what came before and negative if it's worse than what came before. To understand how we will judge an experience, it is necessary first to find out where we set our hedonic zero point.

In Chapter 3, I emphasized how language can affect the framing of an experience and thus, the setting of the zero point. A sign at a gas station that says "Discount for Paying Cash" sets the zero point at the credit card price. A sign that says "Surcharge for Using Credit" sets the zero point at the cash price. Though the difference between cash and credit may be the same at both gas stations, people will be annoyed at having to pay a surcharge and delighted at getting a discount.

But the language of description is not the *only* factor that affects the setting of the zero point. Expectations do as well. "How good did

I expect this meal (exam grade, wine, vacation, job, romantic relationship) to be?" people ask themselves. Then they ask themselves, "How good was it?" If the experience was as good as expected, people may be satisfied, but they won't be ecstatic. Real hedonic charge comes when an experience exceeds expectations. And hedonic distress comes when experience fails to live up to expectations. Past experience also affects the setting of the zero point, which is, in part, what adaptation is about. "Was it as good as last time?" we ask. If so, we may again be satisfied, but we will not be enthused.

The Curse of High Expectations

IN THE FALL OF 1999, THE *NEW YORK TIMES* AND CBS NEWS ASKED teenagers to compare their experience with what their parents had experienced growing up. Overall, 43 percent of the respondents said they were having a harder time than their parents did, but 50 percent of children from affluent households said their lives were harder. When probed, the teenagers from affluent households talked about high expectations, both their own and their parents'. They talked about "too-muchness": too many activities, too many consumer choices, too much to learn. Whereas teens from low-income households talked about how much easier it was to get schoolwork done thanks to computers and the Internet, teens from high-income homes talked about how much had to be sifted through because of computers and the Internet. As one commentator put it, "Children feel the pressure . . . to be sure they don't slide back. Everything's about going forward. . . . Falling back is the American nightmare." So if your perch is high, you have much further to fall than if your perch is low. "Fear of falling," as Barbara Ehrenreich put it, is the curse of high expectations.

One part of life where the curse of high expectations is apparent is health and health care. No matter how frustrating it is for people to get prompt and decent health care in the age of managed care, there is no question that the state of American health is better than it's ever been. Not only do people live longer, but they have a better quality of life while they are alive. Nonetheless, as medical historian Roy Porter points out, in this age of unparalleled longevity and control over disease, there is also unparalleled anxiety about health. Americans expect to live even longer still, and to do so without any diminution of capacity. So though modern health practices help extend our lives, they don't seem to provide an appropriate degree of satisfaction.

What contributes to high expectations, above and beyond the quality of past experience, is, I think, the amount of choice and control we now have over most aspects of our lives. When I was away on vacation several years ago in a tiny seaside town on the Oregon coast, I went into the small local grocery store to buy some ingredients for dinner. When it came to buying wine, they had about a dozen options. What I got wasn't very good, but I didn't expect to be able to get something very good, and so I was satisfied with what I got. If instead I'd been shopping in a store that offered hundreds—even thousands—of options, my expectations would have been a good deal higher. Had I ended up choosing a bottle of wine of the same quality as the one that satisfied me in Oregon, I'd have been sorely disappointed.

And to return to the example with which I began the book, back when jeans came in only one variety, I would be satisfied with the fit, whatever it was. But now, confronted with relaxed fit, easy fit, slim fit, tapered leg, boot cut, and who knows what else, my standards have gone up. With all these options available, I now expect my jeans to fit as though they were custom-made. The proliferation of options seems to lead, inexorably, to the raising of expectations.

Which plays into the tendency to be a maximizer. Almost by definition, to be a maximizer is to have high standards, high expectations. Because of this, and because of the role played by expectations in hedonic evaluations, an experience that is on the positive side of the hedonic thermometer for a satisficer may be on the negative side for a maximizer.

The lesson here is that high expectations can be counterproductive. We probably can do more to affect the quality of our lives by controlling our expectations than we can by doing virtually anything else. The blessing of modest expectations is that they leave room for many experiences to be a pleasant surprise, a hedonic plus. The challenge is to find a way to keep expectations modest, even as actual experiences keep getting better.

One way of achieving this goal is by keeping wonderful experiences rare. No matter what you can afford, save great wine for special occasions. No matter what you can afford, make that perfectly cut, elegantly styled, silk blouse a special treat. This may seem like an exercise in self-denial, but I don't think it is. On the contrary, it's a way to make sure that you can continue to experience pleasure. What's the point of great meals, great wines, and great blouses if they don't make you feel great?

The Curse of Social Comparison

OF ALL THE SOURCES WE RELY ON WHEN WE EVALUATE EXPERIENCES, perhaps nothing is more important than comparisons to other people. Our answer to the "How am I doing?" question depends on our own past experiences, aspirations, and expectations, but the question is virtually never asked or answered in a social vacuum. "How am I doing?" almost always carries "compared to others" in parentheses.

Social comparison provides information that helps people evaluate experiences. Many experiences are ambiguous enough that we aren't completely sure what to make of them. Is a B+ a good grade on an exam? Is your marriage going well? Is there reason to worry because your teenage son is into headbanging music? Are you sufficiently valued at work? Although it is possible to derive approximate answers to questions like these without looking around at others, approximate answers aren't good enough. Looking at others permits the fine-tuning of assessments. This fine-tuning, in turn, helps people decide whether some sort of action is called for.

Just as we saw in Chapter 7 that the counterfactuals we construct can be tilted upward (imagining a better result) or downward (imagining a worse one), so too with social comparisons. People can compare themselves with others who have done better (upward social comparison) or worse (downward social comparison). Usually, downward social comparisons nudge people up the hedonic thermometer, and upward social comparisons nudge them down. Indeed, social psychologists have found that upward comparisons produce jealousy, hostility, negative mood, frustration, lowered self-esteem, decreased happiness, and symptoms of stress. By the same token, downward comparisons have been found to boost self-esteem, increase positive mood, and reduce anxiety.

But it needn't be this way. At times, people engaging in social comparison respond positively to upward comparisons and negatively to downward comparisons. Learning that others are worse off can lead you to consider that you yourself can become worse off. When you compare yourself with others who are worse off, you may take pleasure in your superiority, but you may also experience guilt, embarrassment, the need to cope with other people's envy or resentment, and the fear that their fate could happen to you. And when you compare yourself with others who are better off, you may feel envy or resentment, but you may also be motivated or inspired. For example, in one study, encountering information about other cancer patients who were in better shape improved the mood of cancer patients, probably because it gave them hope that their condition also could improve.

In many ways, social comparison parallels the counterfactual thinking process, but there is one very important difference. In principle, we have a great deal of control over both when we will engage in counterfactual thinking and what its content will be. We are limited only by our imaginations. We have less control over social comparison. If you live in a social world, as we all do, you are always being hit with information about how others are doing. The teacher reports the distribution of class grades, placing your B+ in a comparative social context. You and your spouse fight on the way to a party, only to find yourselves surrounded by couples who seem to delight in each other's presence. You were just passed over for a promotion, and you hear from your sister about how well things are going in her job. This kind of information just can't be avoided. The best you can do is keep yourself from brooding about it.

The Race for Status

PEOPLE ARE DRIVEN TO SOCIAL COMPARISON LARGELY BECAUSE they care about status, and status, of course, has social comparison built into it. Part of the satisfaction from achievements and possessions comes from the awareness that not everyone can match them. As others start to catch up, the desires of those who are ahead in the "race" escalate so that they can maintain their privileged position.

In his book *Choosing the Right Pond*, economist Robert Frank exposes just how much of social life is determined by our desire to be big fish in our own ponds. If there were only one pond—if everyone compared his position to the positions of everybody else—virtually all of us would be losers. After all, in the pond containing whales, even sharks are small. So instead of comparing ourselves to everyone, we try to mark off the world in such a way that in *our* pond, in comparison with *our* reference group, we are successful. Better to be the third-highest-paid lawyer in a small firm and make $120,000 a year than to be in the middle of the pack in a large firm and make $150,000. The way to be happy—the way to succeed in the quest for status—is to find the right pond and stay in it.

Just how profound is this concern for status? Some years ago, a study was conducted in which participants were presented with pairs of hypothetical personal circumstances and asked to state their preferences. For example, people were asked to choose between earning $50,000 a year with others earning $25,000 and earning $100,000 a year with others earning $200,000. They were asked to choose between 12 years of education (high school) when others have 8, and 16 years of education (college) when others have 20. They were asked to choose between an IQ of 110 when the IQ of others is 90 and an IQ of 130 when the IQ of others is 150. In most cases, more than half of the respondents chose the options that gave them better *relative* position. Better to be a big fish, earning $50,000, in a small pond than a small fish, earning $100,000, in a big one.

Status, Social Comparison, and Choice

CONCERN FOR STATUS IS NOTHING NEW. NONETHELESS, I BELIEVE that the problem is more acute now than in the past, and once again it comes back to having a plethora of choices. Given Frank's "choosing the right pond" idea, what is the right pond? When we engage in our inevitable social comparisons, to whom do we compare ourselves? In earlier times, such comparisons were necessarily local. We looked around at our neighbors and family members. We didn't have access to information about people outside our immediate social circle. But with the explosion of telecommunications—TV, movies, the Internet—almost everyone has access to information about almost everyone else. A person living in a blue-collar urban neighborhood fifty years ago might have been content with his lower-middle-class income because that brought him a life comparable to what he saw around him. There would have been little to incite his status-enhancing aspirations. But not anymore. Now this person gets to see how the wealthy live countless times every day. We all seem to be swimming in one giant pond nowadays, and anyone's life could be ours. This essentially universal and unrealistically high standard of comparison decreases the satisfaction of those of us who are in the middle or below, even as the actual circumstances of our lives improve.

Social networking sites like Facebook only exacerbate the problem. People don't write about the boring parts of their lives on Facebook. They don't talk about the jobs they didn't get. They don't post photos of their unsatisfying trips. A part of us probably knows that our Facebook friends are presenting the best possible picture of their lives to us. But then we ask whether our everyday lives measure up. And of course, they don't.

Positional Competition

F WE STOPPED THE DISCUSSION HERE, IT WOULD BE TEMPTING TO conclude that the dissatisfaction that comes with social comparison can be fixed by teaching people to care less about status.

"O.K., if you can't see your way to giving me a pay
raise, how about giving Parkerson a pay cut?"

© *The New Yorker Collection 2001 Barbara Smaller from cartoonbank.com. All Rights Reserved.*

Disappointment from social comparison would be understood as a problem that affects society by affecting individuals and that can be fixed by changing individual attitudes, one person at a time.

But even if people *could* be taught to care less about status, they would still not be satisfied with what they have, because they have legitimate reasons for believing that no matter how much a person has, it may not be enough. Our social and economic system, which is based in part on an unequal distribution of scarce and highly desirable goods, inherently propels people into lives of perpetual social comparison and dissatisfaction, so that reforming people without paying attention to the system won't work.

As I mentioned in Chapter 4, economist Fred Hirsch argued in his book *Social Limits to Growth* that while technological development may continue to increase the number of people who can be fed from an acre of farmland or the number of children who can be inoculated against polio for $1,000, there are certain kinds of goods that no amount of technological development will make universally available. For example, not everyone will be able to own a secluded acre of land at the seashore. Not everyone will have the most interesting job. Not everyone can be the boss. Not everyone can go to the best college or belong to the best country club. Not everyone can be treated by the "best" doctor in the "best" hospital. Hirsch calls goods like these *positional goods*, because how likely anyone is to get them depends upon his position in society. No matter how many resources a person has, if everyone else has at least as much, his chances of enjoying these positional goods are slim. Sometimes these kinds of goods are positional simply because the supply can't be increased. Not everyone can have a van Gogh hanging in his living room. At other times, the problem is that as more consumers gain access to these goods, their value decreases due to overcrowding. The New York City area has several lovely beaches, enough to accommodate thousands. But as more and more people use these areas, they become so crowded that there is barely room to lie down, they become so noisy that people can hardly hear themselves think, they become so dirty that it is no longer pleasant even to look at them, and the highways that lead to them turn into parking lots. Under these conditions, the only way to get the kind of beach experience you want is to travel much farther from the city, which is time-consuming, or to own your own beach, which is expensive.

We might all agree that everyone would be better off if there were less positional competition. It's stressful, it's wasteful, and it distorts people's lives. Parents wanting only the best for their child encourage her to study hard so she can get into a good college. But everyone is doing that. So the parents push harder. But so does everybody else. So they send their child to after-school enrichment programs and educational summer camps. And so does everyone else. So now they borrow money to switch to private school. Again, others follow. So they nag at their youngster to become a great musician or athlete or something that will make her distinctive. They hire tutors and trainers. But, of course, so does everyone else, or at least everyone who has not gone broke trying to keep up. The poor child, meanwhile, has been so tortured by parental aspirations for her that she loses interest in all the things they have forced her to do for the sake of her future.

Students work to get good grades even when they have no interest in their studies. People seek job advancement even when they are happy with the jobs they already have. It's like being in a crowded football stadium, watching the crucial play. A spectator several rows in front stands up to get a better view, and a chain reaction follows. Soon everyone is standing, just to be able to see as well as before. Everyone is on their feet rather than sitting, but no one's position has improved. And if someone, unilaterally and resolutely, refuses to stand, he might just as well not be at the game at all. When people pursue goods that are positional, they can't help being in the rat race. To choose not to run is to lose.

Social Comparison: Does Everybody Do It?

THOUGH SOCIAL COMPARISON INFORMATION IS SEEMINGLY all-pervasive, it appears that not everyone pays attention to it, or at least, not everyone is affected by it. Psychologist Sonja Lyubomirsky and her colleagues have done a series of studies that looked for differences among individuals in their responses to social comparison information, and what they have found is that this kind of data has relatively little impact on happy people.

To begin with, Lyubomirsky developed a questionnaire, which you'll find on page 200, designed to measure what might be called people's chronic level of happiness (as opposed to their moods at a particular moment in time) to categorize participants as relatively happy or unhappy.

Then, in one study, each individual was asked to unscramble anagrams while working alongside another individual (actually a confederate working for the experimenter) doing the same task. Sometimes this other person performed much better than the study participant, and sometimes much worse. Lyubomirsky found that happy people were only minimally affected by whether the person working next to them was better or worse at the anagram task than they were. When asked to assess their ability to unscramble anagrams, and how they felt about it, happy people gave higher ratings after doing the task than before it. Their assessment of ability and their mood were slightly better if they had been working beside a slower peer than if they'd been working beside a faster one, but either way, their self-assessments went up. In contrast, unhappy people showed increases in assessed ability and positive feelings after working beside a slower peer, and *decreases* in assessed ability and positive feelings if they'd been working beside a faster peer.

SUBJECTIVE HAPPINESS SCALE

*For each of the following statements
and/or questions, please circle the point on the scale
that you feel is most appropriate in describing you.*

1. In general, I consider myself:

1 2 3 4 5 6 7

not a very   **a very
happy person**   **happy person**

2. Compared to most of my peers, I consider myself:

1 2 3 4 5 6 7

less happy   **more happy**

3. Some people are generally very happy. They enjoy life regardless of what is going on, getting the most out of everything. To what extent does this characterization describe you?

1 2 3 4 5 6 7

not at all   **a great deal**

4. Some people are generally not very happy. Although they are not depressed, they never seem as happy as they might be. To what extent does this characterization describe you?

1 2 3 4 5 6 7

not at all   **a great deal**

(With kind permission of Kluwer Academic Publishers)

In a second study, participants were asked to videotape a lesson for preschool children. An "expert" (again, actually a confederate) gave the participants detailed feedback on their performance. Participants performed alongside a partner who gave the same lesson. The question of interest was how the feedback would affect participants' moods. The moods of happy people improved when they got positive feedback and worsened when they got negative feedback, but whether they heard or didn't hear the feedback given to their partner made no difference. Unhappy people, on the other hand, were very much affected by the feedback their partner received. If a participant got positive feedback, but her partner got *better* feedback, the participant's mood worsened. If a participant got negative feedback, but her partner got *worse* feedback, the participant's mood improved. Thus it seemed as though the only thing that mattered to the unhappy people was how they did in comparison to their partner. Better to be told that you're a pretty bad teacher but that others are even worse than to be told that you're a pretty good teacher but others are better.

In a follow-up to this study, Lyubomirsky tried to determine which factors about happy and unhappy people make them respond so differently to the same situation. What she found was that when happy and unhappy people were induced to distract themselves by thinking about something else after they got some negative feedback about performance on a task, the difference between them in their reaction to the news went away: both groups responded like happy people. And if happy and unhappy people were induced, after getting negative feedback, to think about it, the difference between them again went away: this time, both groups responded like unhappy people. The inference here is that distraction versus rumination is the critical distinction. Happy people have the ability to distract themselves and move on, whereas unhappy people get stuck ruminating and make themselves more and more miserable.

We can't say for sure in this research what is cause and what is effect. Do unhappy people ruminate more than happy ones about social comparison, or does ruminating more about social comparison make someone unhappy? My suspicion is that both are true— that the tendency to ruminate traps unhappy people in a downward psychological spiral that is fed by social comparison. Certainly, it is safe to say that, based on available research, social comparison does nothing to improve one's satisfaction with the choices one makes.

Maximizing, Satisficing, and Social Comparison

Y OUR LEVEL OF HAPPINESS IS NOT THE ONLY FACTOR THAT COLORS your response to social comparison. Once again, being either a maximizer or a satisficer is significant.

In the research I discussed in Chapter 4, we took participants who had filled out our Maximization Scale, and put them in a situation like the one I just described, in which they had to unscramble anagrams alongside another person who was doing the task faster or slower than they were. We found that maximizers were much more affected by the presence of another person than satisficers were. Solving anagrams alongside someone who seemed to be doing it better produced in maximizers both a deterioration of mood and a lowered assessment of their anagram-solving ability. The social comparison information had no such effect on satisficers.

In addition, when maximizers and satisficers were asked questions about how they shop, maximizers reported being much more concerned with social comparison than satisficers did. They were more attentive than satisficers to what other people were buying, and more influenced in judgments of their own satisfaction by the apparent satisfaction of others.

If you think about what maximizing requires of people, this result is not surprising. Maximizers want the best, but how do you know that you have the best, except by comparison? And to the extent that we have more options, determining the "best" can become overwhelmingly difficult. The maximizer becomes a slave in her judgments to the experiences of other people.

Satisficers don't have this problem. Satisficers who are looking for results that are good enough can use the experiences of others to help them determine exactly what "good enough" is, but they don't have to. They can rely on their own internal assessments to develop those standards. A "good enough" salary is one that enables them to afford a decent place to live, some nice clothes, an occasional night out, and so on. It doesn't matter that others may earn more. A good enough sound system is one that satisfies their own concerns about sound fidelity, convenience, appearance, and reliability.

And in these two contrasting approaches we discover something of a paradox. The word "maximizing," implying as it does a desire for the best, suggests standards that are absolute. There is, it would seem, only one "best," no matter how hard it may be to figure out what that is. Presumably, someone with absolute standards would not be especially concerned or affected by what others are doing. Satisficing, in contrast, implying as it does a desire for good enough, suggests relative standards—relative to one's own past experience and the past experience of others. Nonetheless, what we see is just the reverse. It is maximizers who have the relative standards and satisficers who have the absolute ones. While, in theory, "the best" is an ideal that exists independent of what other people have, in practice, determining the best is so difficult that people fall back on comparisons with others. "Good enough" is not an objective standard that exists out there for all to see. It will always be relative to the person doing the judging. But critically, it will not, or need not, be relative to either the standards or the achievements of others. So, once again, satisficing appears the better way to maintain one's autonomy in the face of an overwhelming array of choices.

Choice Options and Social Comparison

WE HAVE ALREADY SEEN HOW THE MORE OPTIONS WE HAVE, THE more difficulty we have gathering the information necessary to make a good decision. The more difficult information gathering is, the more likely it is that you will rely on the decisions of others. Even if you are not after the best wallpaper for your kitchen, when faced with a choice among hundreds or thousands of possibilities, the search for something good enough can be enormously simplified by knowing what others have chosen. So overwhelming choice is going to push you in the direction of looking over your shoulder at what others are doing. But the more social comparison you do, the more likely you are to be affected by it, and the direction of such effects tends to be negative. So by forcing us to look around at what others are doing before we make decisions, the world of bountiful options is encouraging a process that will often, if not always, leave us feeling worse about our decisions than we would if we hadn't engaged in the process to begin with. Here is yet another reason why increasing the available options will decrease our satisfaction with what we choose.

CHAPTER TEN

Whose Fault Is It?
Choice, Disappointment, and Depression

I HAVE SUGGESTED THAT WITH LIMITLESS CHOICE, WE PRODUCE BET-
ter results with our decisions than we would in a more limited
world, but we feel worse about them. However, the stakes involved
are considerably higher than just creating mild disappointment.
Unlimited choice, I believe, can produce genuine suffering. When
the results of decisions—about trivial things or important ones,
about items of consumption or about jobs and relationships—are
disappointing, we ask why. And when we ask why, the answers we
come up with frequently have us blaming ourselves.

The American "happiness quotient" has been going gently but
consistently downhill for more than a generation. While the American gross domestic product, a primary measure of prosperity, more
than doubled in the last forty years, the proportion of the population describing itself as "very happy" declined. The decline is about
5 percent. This might not seem like much, but 5 percent trans-
lates into about 15 million people—people who would have said
in the seventies they were very happy would not say so today. The
same pattern is present when respondents are asked more specific
questions—about how happy they are with their marriages, their
jobs, their financial circumstances, and their places of residence.
It seems that as American society grows wealthier and Americans

become freer to pursue and do whatever they want, Americans get less and less happy.

The most dramatic manifestation of this decrease in societal happiness is in the prevalence of clinical depression, at the opposite end of the "happiness continuum." By some estimates, depression in the year 2000 was about ten times as likely as depression in the year 1900.

The symptoms of depression include

- Loss of interest or pleasure in routine daily activities, including work and family
- Loss of energy, fatigue
- Feelings of worthlessness, guilt, and self-blame
- Indecisiveness
- Inability to concentrate or think clearly
- Recurrent thoughts of death, including thoughts of suicide
- Insomnia
- Loss of interest in sex
- Loss of interest in food
- Sadness: feelings of helplessness, hopelessness
- Low self-esteem.

Aside from the obvious fact that victims of depression are miserably unhappy, depression also takes a major toll on society in general. The friends, coworkers, spouses, and children of depressed people suffer too. Children are less well cared for, friendships are neglected or abused, coworkers must take up the slack from inadequate job performance. In addition, depressed people get sick more. Mildly depressed individuals miss 1.5 times as much work as the nondepressed, and severely depressed individuals miss five times as much. And depressed people die younger, from a variety of causes, including heart disease. Suicide is, of course, the most extreme consequence of depression. Depressed people commit suicide at roughly 25 times the rate of nondepressed people, and it is estimated that more than 80 percent of suicidal people are significantly depressed.

Clinical depression is a complex phenomenon that comes in several varieties and undoubtedly has multiple causes. As our understanding of depression improves, it may turn out that what we now regard as a single disorder will be viewed as a family of disorders, with overlapping manifestations but distinct causes. So you should understand that the discussion of depression that follows will not capture the experience of every person who suffers from it. But certain themes have emerged that increase our overall understanding of the phenomenon.

Learned Helplessness, Control, and Depression

EARLIER WE DISCUSSED SELIGMAN AND HIS COLLEAGUES' DISCOVery of "learned helplessness." They were conducting a series of experiments on basic learning processes in animals. The experiments required animals to jump over small hurdles to escape from or avoid electric shocks to the feet. The animals typically learn this quickly and easily, but a group of animals that were exposed to the task after having experienced a series of unavoidable shocks failed to learn. Indeed, many of them failed even to try. They sat passively and took the shocks, never venturing over the hurdle at all. The explanation for this failure was that when the animals were being exposed to the uncontrollable shocks, they learned that they were helpless. Having learned this helplessness, the animals then transferred the lesson to the new situation, one in which they actually *did* have control.

As the laboratory work on learned helplessness continued, Seligman was struck by a variety of parallels between helpless animals and people who are clinically depressed. Especially striking was the parallel between the passivity of helpless animals and the passivity of depressed people, who sometimes find trivial tasks like deciding what to wear in the morning overwhelming. Seligman speculated that at least some instances of clinical depression were the result of individuals' having experienced one significant loss of control over their lives and then coming to believe that they were helpless, that they could expect this helplessness to persist into the future and to be present across a wide range of different circumstances. According to Seligman's hypothesis, therefore, having control is of crucial importance to psychological well-being.

The fundamental significance of having control was highlighted in a study of three-month-old infants done more than forty years ago. Infants in one group—those who had control—were placed faceup in an ordinary crib with their heads on a pillow. Mounted on the crib was a translucent umbrella, with figures of various animals dangling from springs inside. These figures were not visible to the infants, but if the infants turned their heads on the pillows, a small light would go on behind the umbrella, making the "dancing" figures visible for a little while. Then the light would go off. When the infants did turn their heads, just by chance, and turned on the light and saw the dancing figures, they showed interest, delight, and excitement. They quickly learned to keep the figures visible by turning their heads, and they kept on doing so, again and again. They also continued to show delight at the visual spectacle. Other infants in the study got a "free ride." Whenever a "control" infant turned on the light behind the umbrella in its crib, that action *also* turned on the light behind the umbrella in the crib of another infant. So these other infants got to see the dancing figures just as often and for just as long as their controlling partners did. Initially, these infants showed just as much delight in the dancing figures. But their interest quickly waned. They adapted.

The different reactions of the two groups caused researchers to conclude that it is not dancing toy animals that are an endless source of delight for infants, but rather having control. Infants kept smiling and cooing at the display because they seemed to know that they made it happen. "I did this. Isn't it great. And I can do it again whenever I want." The other infants, those who got the display for "free," did not have this exhilarating experience of control.

Young infants have little control over anything. They can't move their bodies toward things they want or away from things that are unpleasant. They don't have very good control over their hands, so grasping and manipulating objects is not easy. They get poked, prodded, picked up, and put down at unpredictable and inexplicable times. The world is just a set of things that happen to them, leaving them completely at the mercy of others. It is perhaps for just this reason that the occasional bits of evidence that they can control certain things are so salient and so exciting.

The significance of control to well-being was also dramatically demonstrated by a study of people at the opposite end of the life cycle. One group of nursing home residents was given instruction on the importance of being able to take responsibility for themselves in the home, and a second group was given instruction about how important it was for the staff to take good care of them. The first group was also given several mundane choices to make every day and a plant to take care of in their rooms, while members of the second group had no such choices and had their plants cared for by the staff. The nursing home residents given a small measure of control over their daily lives were more active and alert, and reported a greater sense of well-being than the residents without such control. Even more dramatically, the residents who had control lived several years longer, on average, than the residents who did not. Thus, from cradle to grave, having control over one's life matters.

Helplessness, Depression, and Attributional Style

S ELIGMAN'S HELPLESSNESS-BASED THEORY OF DEPRESSION WAS NOT without problems. Chief among them was that not everyone who experiences a significant lack of control becomes depressed. So the theory was modified by Seligman and coworkers in 1978. The revised theory of helplessness and depression suggested that important psychological steps intervene between the experience of helplessness and depression. According to the new theory, when people experience a failure, a lack of control, they ask themselves why. "Why did my partner end the relationship?" "Why didn't I get the job?" "Why did I fail to close the deal?" "Why did I blow the exam?" In other words, people seek to understand the causes of their failures.

What Seligman and his colleagues proposed was that when people are looking for causes for failure, they display a variety of predispositions to accept one type of cause or another, quite apart from what the actual cause of the failure might be. There are three key dimensions to these predispositions, based on whether we view causes as being global or specific, chronic or transient, personal or universal.

Suppose you apply for a job in marketing and customer relations, but fail to get hired. You ask why. Here are some possible answers:

GLOBAL: I don't look good on paper, and I get nervous at interviews. I'd have trouble getting any job.

SPECIFIC: I don't really know enough about the kinds of products they sell. To look good at an interview, I need more of a feel for the business.

CHRONIC: I don't have a dynamic, take-charge kind of personality. It's just not who I am.

TRANSIENT: I had just recovered from the flu and had not been sleeping well. I wasn't at my best.

PERSONAL: The job was there for the taking. *I* just couldn't get it done.

UNIVERSAL: They probably already had an insider picked out; the job search was just for show, and *no* outsider would have gotten the job.

Having failed to get the job, and explained this failure to yourself in a specific, transient, and universal way, what will you expect at the next job interview? Well, if you look for a job in an area that you're more familiar with, if you have been sleeping well and are more energetic and alert, and if the search is really open, you'll do fine. In other words, your failure to get *this* job has almost no implications for how you'll do when you go after the next one.

Imagine instead that you tend to identify global, chronic, and personal causes for your failures. If your résumé is unimpressive and you choke at interviews, if you're a passive kind of person, and if you believe that the last job was really available for the "right" person (not you), then your expectations for the future are pretty bleak. Not only did you not get *this* job, but you're going to have trouble getting *any* job.

The revised theory of helplessness and depression argued that helplessness induced by failure or lack of control leads to depression if a person's causal explanations for that failure are global, chronic, and personal. It is only then, after all, that people will have good reason to expect one failure to be followed by another, and another, and another. What's the point of getting out of bed, getting dressed, and trying again if the results are foreordained.

Tests of this revised theory have yielded impressive results. People *do* differ in the types of predispositions they display. "Optimists" explain successes with chronic, global, and personal causes and failures with transient, specific, and universal ones. "Pessimists" do the reverse. Optimists say things like "I got an A" and "She gave me a C." Pessimists say things like "I got a C" and "He gave me an A." And it is the pessimists who are candidates for depression. When these predispositions are assessed in people who are not depressed, the predispositions predict who will become depressed when failures occur. People who find chronic causes for failure expect failures to persist; those who find transient causes don't. People who find global causes for failure expect failure to follow them into every area of life; those who find specific causes don't. And people who find personal causes for failure suffer large losses in self-esteem; those who find universal causes don't.

I'm not suggesting that taking credit for every success and blaming the world for every failure is the recipe for a successful and happy life. There is much to be gained by arriving at causal explanations that are accurate, whatever the psychological cost, because it is accurate explanations that offer the best chance of producing better results the next time. Nonetheless, I think it is fair to say that for most people, most of the time, excessive self-blame has bad psychological consequences. And as we'll see, it is much easier to blame yourself for disappointing results in a world that provides unlimited choice than in a world in which options are limited.

Helplessness, Depression, and Modern Life

THE AMERICAN MIDDLE CLASS NOW EXPERIENCES CONTROL AND PER-
sonal autonomy to a degree unimaginable to people living in
other times and places. Millions of Americans can live exactly the
lives they choose, barely constrained by material, economic, or
cultural limitations. They, not their parents, get to decide whether,
when, and whom they marry. They, not their religious leaders,
get to decide how they dress. And they, not their government, get
to decide what they watch on television or read in the newspaper.
This autonomy, coupled with the helplessness theory of depression,
might suggest that clinical depression in the United States should be
disappearing.

Instead, we see explosive *growth* in the disease, what Martin
Seligman describes as an epidemic. Roughly 7 percent of American
adults will have a major depressive episode in a given year. Furthermore, depression seems to attack its victims at a younger age now
than in earlier eras. Current estimates are that as many as 5 percent
of Americans have an episode of clinical depression before they are
fourteen. This is twice the rate seen in young people of the previous
generation.

And the most extreme manifestation of depression—suicide—
is also on the rise, and it, too, is happening younger. Suicide is the
second leading cause of death (after accidents) among American
high school and college students. In the past fifty years, the suicide
rate among American college students has more than doubled.
Throughout the developed world suicide among adolescents and
young adults is increasing. In a study comparing rates in 1990 to
rates in the 1970s and 1980s, UNICEF found that the incidence of
suicide tripled in France, more than doubled in Norway, doubled in

Australia, and increased by 50 percent or more in Canada, England, and the United States. Only in Japan and what was then West Germany did youth suicide go down.

In an era of ever greater personal autonomy and control, what could account for this degree of personal misery?

Rising Expectations

FIRST, I THINK INCREASES IN EXPERIENCED CONTROL OVER THE YEARS have been accompanied, stride for stride, by increases in *expectations* about control. The more we are allowed to be the masters of our fates, the more we expect ourselves to be. We should be able to find education that is stimulating *and* useful, work that is exciting, socially valuable, *and* remunerative, spouses who are sexually, emotionally, and intellectually stimulating *and* also loyal and comforting. Our children are supposed to be beautiful, smart, affectionate, obedient, *and* independent. And everything we buy is supposed to be the best of its kind. With all the choice available, we should never have to settle for things that are just "good enough." Emphasis on freedom of choice, together with the proliferation of possibilities that modern life affords, has, I believe, contributed to these unrealistic expectations.

In the last chapter we saw that the amount of pleasure and satisfaction we derive from experience has as much to do with how the experience relates to expectations as it does with the qualities of the experience itself. People on diets evaluate weight loss relative to expectations about weight loss. It feels great to find out you lost ten pounds when you were expecting to lose five, but not when you were expecting to lose fifteen. College students evaluate grades relative to expectations about grades. It feels great to get a B when you were expecting a C, but not when you were expecting an A. If I'm right about the expectations of modern Americans about the quality of their experiences, almost every experience people have nowadays will be perceived as a disappointment, and thus regarded as a failure—a failure that could have been prevented with the right choice.

Contrast this with societies in which marriages are arranged, so people have little control over whom they marry, or societies in which educational opportunities are limited, so people have little control over what they learn. A key fact about psychological life in societies in which you have little control over these aspects of life is that you also have little *expectation* of control. And because of this, I think, lack of control does not lead to feelings of helplessness and depression.

Rising Individualism and Self-Blame

ALONG WITH THE PERVASIVE RISE IN EXPECTATIONS, AMERICAN CULture has also become more individualistic than it was, perhaps as a by-product of the desire to have control over every aspect of life. To be less individualistic—to tie oneself tightly into networks of family, friends, and community—is to be bound, to some degree, by the needs of family, friends, and community. If our attachments to others are serious, we can't just do whatever we want. I think the single most difficult negotiation that faces young people who marry in today's America is the one in which the partners decide where their individual autonomy ends and marital obligation and responsibility take over.

Our heightened individualism means that, not only do we expect perfection in all things, but we expect to produce this perfection ourselves. When we (inevitably) fail, the culture of individualism biases us toward causal explanations that focus on personal rather than universal factors. That is, the culture has established a kind of officially acceptable style of causal explanation, and it is one that encourages the individual to blame himself for failure. And this is just the kind of causal explanation that promotes depression when we are faced with failure.

As a corollary, the modern emphasis on individual autonomy and control may be neutralizing a crucial vaccine against depression: deep commitment and belonging to social groups and institutions—families, civic associations, faith communities, and the like. There is an inherent tension between being your own person, or determining your own "self," and meaningful involvement in social groups. Significant social involvement requires subordinating the self. So the more we focus on ourselves, the more our connections to others weakens. In his book *Bowling Alone*, political scientist Robert Putnam focused attention on the deterioration of social connection in contemporary life. And in this context it is relevant that in studies conducted thirty years ago, the incidence of depression among the Amish of Lancaster County, Pennsylvania, was less than 20 percent of the national rate. The Amish are a tightly knit traditional community, one in which social ties are extremely strong and life choices are rather meager. Do the Amish have less control over their lives than the rest of us? Undoubtedly yes. Do they have less control than the rest of us compared to what they expect? I think not. How much do they suffer psychologically from the constraints imposed by community membership and its attendant responsibilities? My suspicion is that they suffer rather little. Viewed from within Amish society, where expectations about individual control and autonomy are very different than they are in mainstream America, community membership doesn't entail much in the way of personal sacrifice. For the Amish, the unease that the rest of us may feel at the prospect of significant communal obligation is largely absent. It's just the way things are—for everybody. By elevating everyone's expectations about autonomy and control, mainstream American society has made deep community involvement much more costly than it would be otherwise.

The distortions incumbent in the desire for control, autonomy, and perfection are nowhere more apparent than in the American obsession with appearance. The evidence is rather compelling that most of us can do little over the long term about our body shape and body weight. The combination of genes and early experience plays a major role in determining what we look like as adults, and virtually all diets tend to produce only short-term changes. These facts about body weight are directly contradicted by what the culture tells us every day. Media and peer pressure tells us that obesity is a matter of choice, personal control, and personal responsibility, that we should aspire to look perfect, and that if we don't, we have only ourselves to blame. According to the culture, if we had enough discipline and self-control we could combine sensible eating habits and exercise regimes and all look like movie stars. That in a typical year Americans buy more than 50 million diet books and spend more than $50 billion on dieting suggests that most Americans accept the view that what they look like is up to them.

The illusion that each person can have the body that he or she wants is especially painful for women, and especially in societies, like ours, in which the "ideal" body is extremely thin. Cultures that promote the ultrathin ideal for women (for example, Sweden, Great Britain, Czech Republic, and white America) have much higher rates of eating disorders (bulimia and anorexia nervosa) than cultures that do not. Even more significant for the present discussion is that in cultures that adopt the ultrathin ideal, the rate of depression in women is twice that in men. In cultures that adopt a more reasonable ideal, sex differences in rates of depression are smaller.

The (admittedly speculative) connection between thinness and depression is this: body weight is something people are supposed to control, and to look perfect is to be thin. When efforts to be thin fail, people not only have to face the daily disappointment of looking in the mirror, they also must face the causal explanation that this failure to look perfect is their fault.

Depression When Only the Best Will Do

UNATTAINABLE EXPECTATIONS, PLUS A TENDENCY TO TAKE INTENSE personal responsibility for failure, make a lethal combination. And, as we have come by now to expect, this problem is especially acute for maximizers. As they do in regard to missed opportunities, regret, adaptation, and social comparison, maximizers will suffer more from high expectations and self-blame than will satisficers. Maximizers will put the most work into their decisions and have the highest expectations about the results of those decisions, and thus will be the most disappointed.

The research that my colleagues and I have done suggests that, not surprisingly, maximizers are ripe for depression. With group after group of people—varying in age, gender, educational level, geographical location, race, and socioeconomic status—we have found a strong positive relation between maximizing and measures of depression. Among people who score highest on our Maximization Scale, scores on a standard measure of depression are in the borderline clinical depression range. We find the same relation between maximizing and depression among young adolescents. High expectations and taking personal responsibility for failing to meet them can apply to educational decisions, career decisions, and marital decisions, just as they apply to decisions about where to eat. And even the trivial decisions add up. If the experience of disappointment is relentless, if virtually every choice you make fails to live up to expectations and aspirations, and if you consistently take personal responsibility for the disappointments, then the trivial looms larger and larger, and the conclusion that you can't do anything right becomes devastating.

The Psychology of Autonomy and the Ecology of Autonomy

P ARADOXICALLY, EVEN AT A TIME AND PLACE WHEN EXCESSIVE expectations of and aspirations for control are contributing to an epidemic of depression, those who feel that they have control are in better psychological shape than those who don't.

To understand this, we need to make a distinction between what is good for the individual and what is good for the society as a whole, between the *psychology* of personal autonomy and the *ecology* of personal autonomy. In a study focused on twenty developed Western nations and Japan, Richard Eckersley notes that the factors that seem best correlated with national differences in youth suicide rates involve cultural attitudes toward personal freedom and control. Those nations whose citizens value personal freedom and control the most tend to have the highest suicide rates.

Eckersley is quick to point out that these same values allow certain individuals within these cultures to thrive and prosper to an extraordinary degree. The problem is that on the national or "ecological" level, these same values have a pervasive, toxic effect.

The problem also may be exacerbated by what Robert Lane refers to as *hedonic lag*. Lane says that there is "a tendency of every culture to persist in valuing the qualities that made it distinctively great long after they have lost their hedonic yield." This, he says, "explains a lot of the malaise currently afflicting market democracies." The combination of hedonic lag with the mixture of psychological benefits and

"They never should have allowed us to be free-range."

A CONSEQUENCE OF TOO MUCH FREEDOM

© The New Yorker Collection 1999 Benita Epstein from cartoonbank.com. All Rights Reserved.

ecological costs of the culture's emphasis on autonomy and control makes it extremely difficult for a society to get things right.

Clearly, our experience of choice as a burden rather than a privilege is not a simple phenomenon. Rather it is the result of a complex interaction among many psychological processes that permeate our culture, including rising expectations, awareness of opportunities forgone, aversion to trade-offs, adaptation, regret, self-blame, the tendency to engage in social comparisons, and maximizing.

In the next chapter, we will review and amplify the recommendations we've made throughout the book, exploring what individuals can do, despite societal pressure, to overcome the overload of choice.

What We
Can Do

Part IV

CHAPTER ELEVEN

What to Do About Choice

THE NEWS I'VE REPORTED IS NOT GOOD. HERE WE ARE, LIVING AT THE pinnacle of human possibility, awash in material abundance. As a society, we have achieved what our ancestors could, at most, only dream about, but it has come at a price. We get what we say we want, only to discover that what we want doesn't satisfy us to the degree that we expect. We are surrounded by modern, time-saving devices, but we never seem to have enough time. We are free to be the authors of our own lives, but we don't know exactly what kind of lives we want to "write."

The "success" of modernity turns out to be bittersweet, and everywhere we look it appears that a significant contributing factor is the overabundance of choice. Having too many choices produces psychological distress, especially when combined with regret, concern about status, adaptation, social comparison, and perhaps most important, the desire to have the best of everything—to maximize.

I believe there are steps we can take to mitigate—even eliminate—many of these sources of distress, but they aren't easy. They require practice, discipline, and perhaps a new way of thinking. On the other hand, each of these steps will bring its own rewards.

1. Choose When to Choose

A S WE HAVE SEEN, HAVING THE OPPORTUNITY TO CHOOSE IS ESSEN-
tial for well-being, but choice has negative features, and the
negative features escalate as the number of choices increases. The
benefits of having options are apparent with each particular decision we face, but the costs are subtle and cumulative. In other words,
it isn't this or that particular choice that creates the problem; it's all
the choices, taken together.

It isn't easy to pass up opportunities to choose. The key thing to
appreciate, though, is that what is most important to us, most of
the time, is not the objective results of decisions, but the subjective
results. If the ability to choose enables you to get a better car, house,
job, vacation, or coffeemaker, but the process of choice makes you
feel worse about what you've chosen, you really haven't gained anything from the opportunity to choose. And much of the time, better
objective results and worse subjective results are exactly what our
overabundance of options provides.

To manage the problem of excessive choice, we must decide
which choices in our lives really matter and focus our time and
energy there, letting many other opportunities pass us by. But by
restricting our options, we will be able to choose less and feel better.

Try the following:

1. Review some recent decisions that you've made, both
    small and large (a clothing purchase, a new kitchen
    appliance, a vacation destination, a retirement pension
    allocation, a medical procedure, a job or relationship
    change).

2.   Itemize the steps, time, research, and anxiety that went into making those decisions.
3.   Remind yourself how it felt to do that work.
4.   Ask yourself how much your final decision benefited from that work.

This exercise may help you better appreciate the costs associated with the decisions you make, which may lead you to give up some decisions altogether or at least to establish rules of thumb for yourself about how many options to consider, or how much time and energy to invest in choosing. For example, you could make it a rule to visit no more than two stores when shopping for clothing or to consider no more than two locations when planning a vacation.

Restricting yourself in this way may seem both difficult and arbitrary, but actually, this is the kind of discipline we exercise in other aspects of life. You may have a rule of thumb never to have more than two glasses of wine at a sitting. The alcohol tastes good and it makes you feel good and the opportunity for another drink is right at your elbow, yet you stop. And for most people, it isn't that hard to stop. Why?

One reason is that you get insistent instructions from society about the dangers of too much alcohol. A second reason is that you may have had the experience of drinking too much, and discovered that it isn't pretty. There's no guarantee that the third glass of wine will be the one that sends you over the edge, but why risk it? Unfortunately, there are no insistent instructions from society about shopping too much. Nor, perhaps, has it been obvious to you that choice overload gives you a hangover. Until now. But if you've been convinced by the arguments and the evidence in this book, you now know that choice has a downside, an awareness that should make it easier for you to adopt, and live with, a "two options is my limit" rule. It's worth a try.

2. Be a Chooser, Not a Picker

HOOSERS ARE PEOPLE WHO ARE ABLE TO REFLECT ON WHAT MAKES a decision important, on whether, perhaps, none of the options should be chosen, on whether a new option should be created, and on what a particular choice says about the chooser as an individual. It is choosers who create new opportunities for themselves and everyone else. But when faced with overwhelming choice, we are forced to become "pickers," which is to say, relatively passive selectors from whatever is available. Being a chooser is better, but to have the time to choose more and pick less, we must be willing to rely on habits, customs, norms, and rules to make some decisions automatic.

Choosers have the time to modify their goals; pickers do not. Choosers have the time to avoid following the herd; pickers do not. Good decisions take time and attention, and the only way we can find the needed time and attention is by choosing our spots.

As you go through the exercise of reviewing recent choices you've made, not only will you become more aware of associated costs, you'll discover that there are some things you really care about, and others you don't. This will allow you to

1. Shorten or eliminate deliberations about decisions that are unimportant to you;
2. Use some of the time you've freed up to ask yourself what you really want in the areas of your life where decisions matter;

3. And if you discover that none of the options the world presents in those areas meet your needs, start thinking about creating better options that do.

3. Satisfice More and Maximize Less

I T IS MAXIMIZERS WHO SUFFER MOST IN A CULTURE THAT PROVIDES too many choices. It is maximizers who have expectations that can't be met. It is maximizers who worry most about regret, about missed opportunities, and about social comparisons, and it is maximizers who are most disappointed when the results of decisions are not as good as they expected.

Learning to accept "good enough" will simplify decision making and increase satisfaction. Though satisficers may often do less well than maximizers according to certain objective standards, nonetheless, by settling for "good enough" even when the "best" could be just around the corner, satisficers will usually feel better about the decisions they make.

Admittedly, there are often times when it is difficult to embrace "good enough." Seeing that you could have done better may be irritating. In addition, there is a world of marketers out there trying to convince you that "good enough" isn't good enough when "new and improved" is available. Nonetheless, everybody satisfices in at least some areas of life, because even for the most fastidious, it's impossible to be a maximizer about everything. The trick is to learn to *embrace* and *appreciate* satisficing, to cultivate it in more and more aspects of life, rather than merely being resigned to it. Becoming a conscious, intentional satisficer makes comparison with how other people are doing less important. It makes regret less likely. In the complex, choice-saturated world we live in, it makes peace of mind possible.

To become a satisficer, however, requires that you think carefully about your goals and aspirations, and that you develop well-defined standards for what is "good enough" whenever you face a decision. Knowing what's good enough requires knowing yourself and what you care about. So:

1. Think about occasions in life when you settle, comfortably, for "good enough";
2. Scrutinize how you choose in those areas;
3. Then apply that strategy more broadly.

I remember quite vividly going through this process myself many years ago when competitive long-distance phone services first became available. Because I make a fairly large number of long-distance phone calls and because I was being deluged with unsolicited advertisements from various companies, I found it hard to resist the temptation to try to find the absolute best company and plan for my calling habits. Making the various needed comparisons was difficult, time-consuming, and confusing, because different companies organized their services and charges in different ways. Furthermore, as I worked on the problem, new companies and new plans kept on coming. I knew I didn't want to spend all this time solving my telephone problem, but it was like an itch that I couldn't resist scratching. Then, one day I went out to replace a toaster. One store, two brands, two models, done. As I walked home, it occurred to me that I *could*, if I wanted to, pick my long-distance service in the same way. I breathed a sigh of relief, I did it, and I haven't thought about it since.

4. Think About the Costs
of Missed Opportunities

WHEN MAKING A DECISION, IT'S USUALLY A GOOD IDEA TO THINK about the alternatives we will pass up when choosing our most-preferred option. Ignoring these "missed opportunities" can lead us to overestimate how good the best option is. On the other hand, the more we think about missed opportunities, the less satisfaction we'll derive from whatever we choose. So we should make an effort to limit how much we think about the attractive features of options we reject.

Given that thinking about the attractiveness of unchosen options will always detract from the satisfaction derived from the chosen one, it is tempting to suggest that we forget about comparing options altogether, but often it is difficult or impossible to judge how good an option is except in relation to other options. What defines a "good investment," for example, is to a large degree its rate of return in comparison with other investments. There is no obvious absolute standard that we can appeal to, so some amount of reflection on what else is possible is probably essential.

But not too much. Second-order decisions can help here. When we decide to opt out of deciding in some area of life, we don't have to think about missed opportunities. And being a satisficer can help too. Because satisficers have their own standards for what is "good enough," they are less dependent than maximizers on comparison among alternatives. A "good investment" for a satisficer may be one that returns more than inflation. Period. No need to worry about other options. No need to experience the diminution of satisfaction that comes from contemplating all the other things you might have done with your money. Will the satisficer earn less from investments than the maximizer? Perhaps. Will she be less satisfied with the results? Probably not. Will she have more time available to devote to other decisions that matter to her? Absolutely.

There are some strategies you can use to help you avoid the disappointment that comes from thinking about missed opportunities:

1. Unless you're truly dissatisfied, stick with what you always buy.
2. Don't be tempted by "new and improved."
3. Don't "scratch" unless there's an "itch."
4. And don't worry that if you do this, you'll miss out on all the new things the world has to offer.

You'll encounter plenty of new things anyway. Your friends and coworkers will tell you about products they've bought or vacations they've taken. So you'll stumble onto improvements on your habitual choices without going looking for them. If you sit back and let "new and improved" find you, you'll spend a lot less time choosing and experience a lot less frustration over the fact that you can't find an alternative that combines all the things you like into one neat package.

5. Make Your Decisions Nonreversible

LMOST EVERYBODY WOULD RATHER BUY IN A STORE THAT PERMITS returns than in one that does not. What we don't realize is that the very option of being allowed to change our minds seems to increase the chances that we *will* change our minds. When we can change our minds about decisions, we are less satisfied with them. When a decision is final, we engage in a variety of psychological processes that enhance our feelings about the choice we made relative to the alternatives. If a decision is reversible, we don't engage these processes to the same degree.

I think the power of nonreversible decisions comes through most clearly when we think about our most important choices. A friend once told me how his minister had shocked the congregation with a sermon on marriage in which he said flatly that, yes, the grass *is* always greener. What he meant was that, inevitably, you will encounter people who are younger, better looking, funnier, smarter, or seemingly more understanding and empathetic than your wife or husband. But finding a life partner is not a matter of comparison shopping and "trading up." The only way to find happiness and stability in the presence of seemingly attractive and tempting options is to say, "I'm simply not going there. I've made my decision about a life partner, so this person's empathy or that person's looks really have nothing to do with me. I'm not in the market—end of story." Agonizing over whether your love is "the real thing" or your sexual relationship above or below par, and wondering whether you could have done better is a prescription for misery. Knowing that you've made a choice that you will not reverse allows you to pour your energy into improving the relationship that you have rather than constantly second-guessing it.

6. Practice an "Attitude of Gratitude"

OUR EVALUATION OF OUR CHOICES IS PROFOUNDLY AFFECTED BY what we compare them with, including comparisons with alternatives that exist only in our imaginations. The same experience can have both delightful and disappointing aspects. Which of these we focus on may determine whether we judge the experience to be satisfactory or not. When we imagine better alternatives, the one we chose can seem worse. When we imagine worse alternatives, the one we chose can seem better.

We can vastly improve our subjective experience by consciously striving to be grateful more often for what is good about a choice or an experience, and to be disappointed less by what is bad about it.

The research literature suggests that gratitude does not come naturally to most of us most of the time. Usually, thinking about possible alternatives is triggered by dissatisfaction with what was chosen. When life is not too good, we think a lot about how it could be better. When life is going well, we tend not to think much about how it could be worse. But with practice, we can learn to reflect on how much better things are than they might be, which will in turn make the good things in life feel even better.

It may seem demeaning to accept the idea that experiencing gratitude takes practice. Why not just tell yourself that "starting tomorrow, I'm going to pay more attention to what's good in my life," and be done with it? The answer is that habits of thought die hard. Chances are good that if you give yourself that general directive, you won't actually follow it. Instead you might consider adopting a simple routine:

1. Keep a notepad at your bedside.

2. Every morning, when you wake up, or every night, when you go to bed, use the notepad to list a few things that happened the day before that you're grateful for. These objects of gratitude occasionally will be big (a job promotion, a great first date), but most of the time, they will be small (sunlight streaming in through the bedroom window, a kind word from a friend, a piece of swordfish cooked just the way you like it, an informative article in a magazine).

3. You will probably feel a little silly and even self-conscious when you start doing this. But if you keep it up, you will find that

it gets easier and easier, more and more natural. You also may find yourself discovering many things to be grateful for on even the most ordinary of days. Finally, you may find yourself feeling better and better about your life as it is, and less and less driven to find the "new and improved" products and activities that will enhance it.

7. Regret Less

HE STING OF REGRET (EITHER ACTUAL OR POTENTIAL) COLORS many decisions, and sometimes influences us to avoid making decisions at all. Although regret is often appropriate and instructive, when it becomes so pronounced that it poisons or even prevents decisions, we should make an effort to minimize it.

We can mitigate regret by

1. Adopting the standards of a satisficer rather than a maximizer.
2. Reducing the number of options we consider before making a decision.
3. Practicing gratitude for what is good in a decision rather than focusing on our disappointments with what is bad.

It also pays to remember just how complex life is and to realize how rare it is that any single decision, in and of itself, has the life-transforming power we sometimes think it might. I have a friend, frustrated over his achievements in life, who has wasted countless hours over the past forty years regretting that he passed up the chance to go to a certain Ivy League college. "Everything would have been so different," he often mutters, "if only I had gone." The simple fact is that he might have gone away to the school of his dreams and been hit by a bus. He might have flunked out or had a nervous breakdown or simply felt out of place and hated it. But what I've always wanted to point out to him is that he made the decision he made for a variety of complex reasons inherent in who he was as a young man. Changing the one decision—going to the more prestigious college—would not have altered his basic character or erased the other problems that he faced, so there really is nothing to say that his life or career would have turned out any better. But one thing I do know is that his experience of them would be infinitely happier if he could let go of regret.

8. Anticipate Adaptation

W E ADAPT TO ALMOST EVERYTHING WE EXPERIENCE WITH ANY regularity. When life is hard, adaptation enables us to avoid the full brunt of the hardship. But when life is good, adaptation puts us on a "hedonic treadmill," robbing us of the full measure of satisfaction we expect from each positive experience. We can't prevent adaptation. What we *can* do is develop realistic expectations about how experiences change with time. Our challenge is to remember that the high-quality sound system, the luxury car, and the ten-thousand-square-foot house won't keep providing the pleasure they give when we first experience them. Learning to be satisfied as pleasures turn into mere comforts will ease disappointment with adaptation when it occurs. We can also reduce disappointment from adaptation by following the satisficer's strategy of spending less time and energy researching and agonizing over decisions.

In addition to being aware of the hedonic treadmill, we should also be wary of the "satisfaction treadmill." This is the "double whammy" of adaptation. Not only do we adapt to a given experience so that it feels less good over time, but we can also adapt to a given level of feeling good so that it stops feeling good enough. Here the habit of gratitude can be helpful too. Imagining all the ways in which we could be feeling worse might prevent us from taking for granted (adapting to) how good we actually feel.

So, to be better prepared for, and less disappointed by adaptation:

1. As you buy your new car, acknowledge that the thrill won't be quite the same two months after you own it.
2. Spend less time looking for the perfect thing (maximizing), so that you won't have huge search costs to be "amortized" against the satisfaction you derive from what you actually choose.
3. Remind yourself of how good things actually are instead of focusing on how they're less good than they were at first.

9. Control Expectations

OUR EVALUATION OF EXPERIENCE IS SUBSTANTIALLY INFLUENCED by how it compares with our expectations. So what may be the easiest route to increasing satisfaction with the results of decisions is to remove excessively high expectations about them. This is easier said than done, especially in a world that encourages high expectations and offers so many choices that it seems only reasonable to believe that some option out there will be perfect. So to make the task of lowering expectations easier:

1. Reduce the number of options you consider.
2. Be a satisficer rather than a maximizer.
3. Allow for serendipity.

How often have you checked into your long-awaited vacation spot only to experience that dreaded "underwhelmed" feeling? The thrill of unexpected pleasure stumbled upon by accident often can make the perfect little diner or country inn far more enjoyable than a fancy French restaurant or four-star hotel.

10. Curtail Social Comparison

WE EVALUATE THE QUALITY OF OUR EXPERIENCES BY COMPARING ourselves to others. Though social comparison can provide useful information, it often reduces our satisfaction. So by comparing ourselves to others less, we will be satisfied more. "Stop paying so much attention to how others around you are doing" is easy advice to give, but hard advice to follow, because the evidence of how others are doing is pervasive, because most of us seem to care a great deal about status, and finally, because access to some of the most important things in life (for example, the best colleges, the best jobs, the best houses in the best neighborhoods) is granted only to those who do better than their peers. Nonetheless, social comparison seems sufficiently destructive to our sense of well-being that it is worthwhile to remind ourselves to do it less. Because it is easier for a satisficer to avoid social comparison than for a maximizer, learning that "good enough" is good enough may automatically reduce concern with how others are doing.

Following the other suggestions I've made may sometimes mean that when judged by an absolute standard, the results of decisions will be less good than they might otherwise have been—all the more reason to fight the tendency to make social comparisons.

So:

1. Remember that "He who dies with the most toys wins" is a bumper sticker, not wisdom.

2. Focus on what makes *you* happy, and what gives meaning to *your* life.

11. Learn to Embrace Constraints

As the number of choices we face increases, freedom of choice eventually becomes a tyranny of choice. Routine decisions take so much time and attention that it becomes difficult to get through the day. In circumstances like this, we should learn to view limits on the possibilities we face as liberating not constraining. Society provides rules, standards, and norms for making choices, and individual experience creates habits. By deciding to follow a rule (for example, always wear a seat belt; never drink more than two glasses of wine in one evening), we avoid having to make a deliberate decision again and again. This kind of rule-following frees up time and attention that can be devoted to thinking about choices and decisions to which rules don't apply.

In the short run, thinking about these second-order decisions—decisions about when in life we will deliberate and when we will follow predetermined paths—adds a layer of complexity to life. But in the long run, many of the daily hassles will vanish, and we will find ourselves with time, energy, and attention for the decisions we have chosen to retain.

Take a look at the cartoon on page 240. "You can be anything you want to be—no limits," says the myopic parent fish to its offspring, not realizing how limited an existence the fishbowl allows. But is the parent really myopic? Living in the constrained, protective world of the fishbowl enables this young fish to experiment, to explore, to create, to write its life story without worrying about starving or being eaten. Without the fishbowl, there truly would be

"You can be anything you want to be—no limits."

© *The New Yorker Collection 2001 Peter Steiner from cartoonbank.com. All Rights Reserved.*

no limits. But the fish would have to spend all its time just struggling to stay alive. Choice within constraints, freedom within limits, is what enables the little fish to imagine a host of marvelous possibilities.

Notes

Prologue

3   *Many years ago* I. Berlin, *Four Essays on Liberty* (London: Oxford University Press, 1969). See especially the essay "Two Concepts of Liberty."

3   *Nobel Prize–winning economist and philosopher* A. Sen, *Development as Freedom* (New York: Knopf, 2000).

Chapter 1

12   *A typical supermarket* See G. Cross, *An All-Consuming Century: Why Commercialism Won in Modern America* (New York: Columbia University Press, 2000) for data on the number of items available in supermarkets. Cross points out that the number of different items available in supermarkets has doubled every ten years or so since the 1970s.

19   *Americans spend more time* Studies on time spent shopping and attitudes toward shopping are reviewed by R. E. Lane in *The Loss of Happiness in Market Democracies* (New Haven, CT: Yale University Press, 2000), pp. 176–179.

20   *A series of revolutionary studies* S. Iyengar and M. Lepper, "When Choice Is Demotivating: Can One Desire Too Much of a Good Thing?" *Journal of Personality and Social Psychology*, 2000, *79*, 995–1006. Iyengar has been the leading investigator of the "too-much-choice effect," demonstrating it in many different domains of decision making. For a very readable summary of her research, see *The Art of Choosing* (New York: Twelve, 2010). Since this initial demonstration, the too-much-choice effect has been shown repeatedly, in a wide variety of different domains, including

automobiles, outfitting of new houses, prescription drug plans, medical procedures, and even selection of romantic partners. But it has not always been shown. In a widely cited review of existing research, the authors concluded that on average, the effects of choice set size on choice were tiny (B. Scheibehenne, R. Greifeneder, and P. M. Todd, "Can There Ever Be Too Many Options?" *Journal of Consumer Research*, 2010, *37*, 409–425). However, the tiny average effect masked the fact that there were often quite large effects, but the large effects went in both directions: sometimes large choice sets inhibited choice and sometimes they promoted it. A more recent review of existing studies strongly suggests that the too-much-choice-effect is real, and even identifies factors that may determine when large choice sets will enhance choice and when they will suppress it (A. Chernev, U. Bockenholt, and J. Goodman, "Choice Overload: A Conceptual Review and Meta-Analysis." *Journal of Consumer Psychology*, 2015, *25*, 333–358).

21   *Third, we may suffer* F. Hirsch, *Social Limits to Growth* (Cambridge, MA: Harvard University Press, 1976).

22   *There are now several* Two very influential examples from this movement are J. Dominquez and V. Robin, *Your Money or Your Life* (New York: Viking, 1992), and S. B. Breathnach, *Simple Abundance: A Daybook of Comfort and Joy* (New York: Warner Books, 1995).

Chapter 2

24   *In discussing the introduction* The Smeloff quote and the Yankelovich survey appear in an article by K. Johnson ("Feeling Powerless in a World of Greater Choice") in the *New York Times* (August 27, 2000, p. 29).

25   *And in Philadelphia* The information on phone- and electric-service shopping comes from an article by J. Gelles ("Few Bother to Search for Best Utility Deals") in the *Philadelphia Inquirer* (June 20, 2000, p. A1).

27   *The variety of pension plans* On how increased retirement options decrease retirement participation, see S. S. Iyengar, G. Huberman, and W. Jiang, "How Much Choice Is Too Much? Contributions to 401(k) Retirement Plans. In O. S. Mitchell and S. Utkus (eds.), *Pension Design and Structure: New Lessons from Behavioral Finance* (pp. 83–95) (Oxford: Oxford University Press, 2004).

28   *Just how well do people* See W. Samuelson and R. Zeckhauser, "Status Quo

Bias in Decision Making," *Journal of Risk and Uncertainty*, 1988, *1*, 7–59. On retirement investment decisions, see S. Benartzi and R. Thaler, "Naïve Diversification Strategies in Defined Contribution Savings Plans," 1998 working paper (Anderson School at UCLA).

31   *The attitude was well described* A. Gawande, "Whose Body Is It Anyway?" *New Yorker*, October 4, 1999, p. 84.

31   *According to Gawande* J. Katz, *The Silent World of Doctor and Patient* (New York: Free Press, 1984); on patient autonomy, see also F. H. Marsh and M. Yarborough, *Medicine and Money: A Study of the Role of Beneficence in Health Care Cost Containment* (New York: Greenwood Press, 1990). For a brilliant discussion of the complexities that surround issues of patient autonomy, see C. E. Schneider, *The Practice of Autonomy: Patients, Doctors, and Medical Decisions* (New York: Oxford University Press, 1998).

31   *But he also suggests* Gawande, "Whose Body Is It Anyway," p. 90.

33   *When it comes to* See S. G. Stolberg, "The Big Decisions? They're All Yours," *New York Times*, June 25, 2000, Section 15, p. 1.

33   *And beyond the sources* Statistics on the use of nontraditional treatments appear in M. Specter's "The Outlaw Doctor," *New Yorker*, February 5, 2001, pp. 46–61.

33   *The combination* Perhaps realizing that leaving all decisions in patients' hands is not good medicine and not what patients want, a new model of "shared decision making" has been developing. For a very thoughtful and perceptive account of the problems with doctor paternalism and patient autonomy and a model of a shared alternative, see P. Ubel, *Critical Decisions* (New York: HarperOne, 2012).

33   *The latest indication* On advertising of prescription drugs, see M. Siegel, "Fighting the Drug (Ad) Wars," *The Nation*, June 17, 2002, pp. 21–24.

34   *What do you want to* W. Kaminer, "American Beauty," *American Prospect*, February 26, 2001, p. 34. See also M. Cottle, "Bodywork," *New Republic*, March 25, 2002, pp. 16–19; and S. Dominus, "The Seductress of Vanity," *New York Times Magazine*, May 5, 2002, pp. 48–51.

36   *The average American* See K. Clark, "Why It Pays to Quit," *U.S. News & World Report*, November 1, 1999, p. 74.

36   *Even how we dress* J. Seabrook, "The Invisible Designer," *New Yorker*, September 18, 2000, p. 114.

39   *Comedian Aziz Ansari* A. Ansari, *Modern Romance* (New York: Penguin, 2015).

40   *According to a decades-old* The statistics on religious belief are taken from
      D. Myers, *The American Paradox* (New Haven, CT: Yale University Press,
      2000). Recent evidence, reported in May 2015 by the Pew Foundation,
      suggests a decrease in religiosity among Americans, with about 22
      percent identifying as "unaffiliated," in contrast to 16 percent a decade
      ago. Unaffiliated does not mean unreligious, of course, but the two
      attitudes are probably correlated.

41   *Sociologist Alan Wolfe* A. Wolfe, *Moral Freedom: The Search for Virtue in a
      World of Choice* (New York: W. W. Norton, 2001). The quote comes from
      his article "The Final Freedom," *New York Times Magazine*, March 18,
      2001, pp. 48–51.

41   *We have another kind* On choice of who to be, see B. Schwartz, "Be
      Careful What You Wish For: The Dark Side of Freedom." In R. M. Arkin,
      K. C. Oleson, and P. J. Carroll (eds.), *Handbook of the Uncertain Self* (pp.
      62–77) (New York: Psychology Press, 2010). Also, for evidence that
      people think that the choices they make—even trivial ones—reflect
      who they are, see N. Olson and K. Vohs, "Thinking that Choices Reflect
      the Self Leads to Maximizing Behavior." Paper presented at the annual
      conference for the Association for Consumer Research, Chicago, IL,
      2013.

43   *Amartya Sen has* A. Sen, "Other People," *New Republic*, December 18,
      2000, p. 23; and A. Sen, "Civilizational Imprisonments," *New Republic*,
      June 10, 2002, pp. 28–33.

43   *Every second of every day* There are interesting cultural differences in
      people's perceptions of what counts as a choice. When groups of North
      Americans and South Asians watch a video of someone engaging in a
      series of mundane activities, or engage in such a series of such activities
      themselves, the North Americans identify many more choices being
      made than do the South Asians. See K. Savani, H. R. Markus, and A.
      Connor, "Let Your Preferences Be Your Guide? Preferences and Choices
      Are More Tightly Linked for North Americans than for Indians," *Journal
      of Personality and Social Psychology*, 2008, 95, 861–876.

45   *we are trapped* F. Hirsch, *Social Limits to Growth* (Cambridge, MA:
      Harvard University Press, 1976). See also T. Schelling, *Micromotives and
      Macrobehavior* (New York: W. W. Norton, 1978).

Chapter 3

49 *Choosing well* Two wonderful recent books meant for popular audiences, both written by giants in the field of decision making, provide much more detail about the kinds of findings discussed in this chapter. See D. Kahneman, *Thinking Fast and Slow* (New York: Farrar, Straus, & Giroux, 2011) and R. Thaler, *Misbehaving* (New York: W. W. Norton, 2015).

50 *being able to anticipate accurately* Psychologists Daniel Gilbert and Timothy Wilson, together with many collaborators, have amassed a great deal of evidence showing how bad people are at predicting the satisfaction they will get from their experiences. See D. Gilbert, *Stumbling on Happiness* (New York: Knopf, 2006) and T. Wilson, *Strangers to Ourselves* (Cambridge, MA: Belknap, 2002).

51 *Noble Prize–winning* See D. Kahneman, "Objective Happiness," in D. Kahneman, E. Diener, and N. Schwarz (eds.), *Well-Being: The Foundations of Hedonic Psychology* (New York: Russell Sage, 1999), pp. 3–25.

52 *Men undergoing* The colonoscopy study can be found in D. Redelmeier and D. Kahneman, "Patients' Memories of Painful Medical Treatments: Real-Time and Retrospective Evaluations of Two Minimally Invasive Procedures," *Pain*, 1996, *116*, 3–8. Note that whereas there was a trend for patients who had the less unpleasant exam to be more compliant about follow-up exams, the difference between groups did not reach conventional levels of statistical significance.

52 *In the same way* For evidence on how much our assessments of vacations are determined by what we expect and what we remember instead of what we actually experience, see D. Wirtz, J. Kruger, C. N. Scollon, and E. Diener, "What to Do on Spring Break? The Role of Predicted, On-line, and Remembered Experience on Future Choice," *Psychological Science*, 2003, *14*, 520–524.

53 *Another illustration of* See I. Simonson, "The Effect of Purchase Quantity and Time on Variety-Seeking Behavior," *Journal of Marketing Research*, 1990, *27*, 150–162; D. Read and G. Loewenstein, "Diversification Bias: Explaining the Discrepancy in Variety-Seeking between Combined and Separate Choices," *Journal of Experimental Psychology: Applied*, 1995, *1*, 34–49. There are many other demonstrations of our inability to predict

accurately how some event or other will make us feel. Some of them will be discussed in Chapter 8, on adaptation. For a review of these demonstrations and a discussion of the processes that underlie them, see G. Loewenstein and D. Schkade, "Wouldn't It Be Nice? Predicting Future Feelings," in D. Kahneman, E. Diener, and N. Schwarz (eds.), *Well-Being: The Foundations of Hedonic Psychology* (New York: Russell Sage, 1999), pp. 85–108.

55 *And increasingly, we use* For an interesting discussion of the potential (and pitfalls) of "e-commerce" to help us make wise choices, see M. S. Nadel, "The Consumer Product Selection Process in an Internet Age: Obstacles to Maximum Effectiveness and Policy Options," *Harvard Journal of Law and Technology*, 2000, *14*, 185–266. The numbers on catalog distribution come from this article.

55 *As advertising professor* J. Twitchell, *Lead Us into Temptation: The Triumph of American Materialism* (New York: Columbia University Press, 1999). The quote is on p. 53.

56 *Yet several studies* R. B. Zajonc, "Attitudinal Effects of Mere Exposure," *Journal of Personality and Social Psychology*, 1968, 9 (part 2), 1–27.

57 *The Internet can* On rating the raters one finds on the Internet, see the Nadel article.

57 *The avalanche of electronic information* For a thorough discussion of strategies for information seeking and decision making in the modern, information-laden world, see J. W. Payne, J. R. Bettman, and E. J. Johnson, *The Adaptive Decision Maker* (New York: Cambridge University Press, 1993).

57 *The RAND Corporation* On the accuracy of medical websites, see T. Pugh, "Low Marks for Medical Web Sites," *Philadelphia Inquirer*, May 23, 2001, p. A3.

58 *Even if we can* There are several very useful compendia of research on how we make decisions. See D. Kahneman, P. Slovic, and A. Tversky (eds.), *Judgment Under Uncertainty: Heuristics and Biases* (New York: Cambridge University Press, 1982); D. Kahneman and A. Tversky (eds.), *Choices, Values, and Frames* (New York: Cambridge University Press, 2000); and T. Gilovich, D. Griffin, and D. Kahneman (eds.), *Heuristics and Biases: The Psychology of Intuitive Judgment* (New York: Cambridge University Press, 2002). For a systematic overview of this area of research, see J. Baron, *Thinking and Deciding* (New York: Cambridge University Press, 2000).

59   *Kahneman and Tversky discovered* See A. Tversky and D. Kahneman, "Judgment Under Uncertainty: Heuristics and Biases," *Science*, 1974, *185*, 1124–1131.

60   *There are many examples* For a detailed discussion of many examples of human susceptibility to the availability heuristic, especially in social situations, see R. Nisbett and L. Ross, *Human Inference: Strategies and Shortcomings of Social Judgment* (Englewood Cliffs, NJ: Prentice-Hall, 1980).

61   *How we assess risk* P. Slovic, B. Fischoff, and S. Lichtenstein, "Facts Versus Fears: Understanding Perceived Risk," in D. Kahneman, P. Slovic, and A. Tversky (eds.), *Judgment Under Uncertainty: Heuristics and Biases* (New York: Cambridge University Press, 1982), pp. 463–489.

62   *The benefits of* For a discussion of bandwagon effects in financial decision making and group wisdom in picking Academy Award winners, see J. Surowieski, "Manic Monday (and Other Popular Delusions)," *New Yorker*, March 26, 2001, p. 38.

63   *But while diversity* On "bandwagon effects" see T. Kuran and C. Sunstein, "Controlling Availability Cascades," in C. Sunstein (ed.), *Behavioral Law and Economics* (New York: Cambridge University Press, 2000), pp. 374–397. See also T. Kuran, *Private Truths, Public Lies: The Social Consequences of Preference Falsification* (Cambridge, MA: Harvard University Press, 1995); and M. Gladwell, *The Tipping Point* (Boston: Little Brown, 2000), for vivid examples of how small errors can turn into big ones.

64   *One high-end catalog* The bread-maker example is discussed in E. Shafir, I. Simenson, and A. Tversky, "Reason-Based Choice," *Cognition*, 1993, *49*, 11–36.

64   *A more finely tuned* J. E. Russo, "The Value of Unit Price Information," *Journal of Marketing Research*, 1977, *14*, 193–201.

66   *Call this effect* framing The classic paper on framing is D. Kahneman and A. Tversky, "Choices, Values, and Frames," *American Psychologist*, 1984, *39*, 341–350. Many other examples are collected in D. Kahneman and A. Tversky (eds.), *Choices, Values, and Frames* (New York: Cambridge University Press, 2000).

69   *In sum, just how well* The relation between framing and subjective experience is well discussed by D. Frisch, "Reasons for Framing Effects," *Organizational Behavior and Human Decision Processes*, 1993, *54*, 399–429.

73   *we give disproportionate weight* A. J. Sanford, N. Fay, A. Stewart, and

L. Moxey, "Perspective in Statements of Quantity, with Implications for Consumer Psychology," *Psychological Science*, 2002, *13*, 130–134.

73   *Or suppose you are* Many examples of phenomena discussed in this section can be found in articles collected in D. Kahneman and A. Tversky (eds.), *Choices, Values, and Frames* (New York: Cambridge University Press, 2000). On the endowment effect, see D. Kahneman, J. Knetsch, and R. Thaler, "Anomalies: The Endowment Effect, Loss Aversion, and Status Quo Bias." On decisions to sell stock, see T. Odean, "Are Investors Reluctant to Realize Their Losses?" On sunk costs, see R. Thaler, "Mental Accounting Matters," and R. Thaler, "Toward a Positive Theory of Consumer Choice." On health insurance decisions, see E. Johnson, J. Hershey, J. Mezaros, and H. Kunreuther, "Framing, Probability Distortions, and Insurance Decisions." On health plans and pension plans, see C. Camerer, "Prospect Theory in the Wild: Evidence from the Field" [the original research on this is in W. Samuelson and R. Zeckhauser, "Status Quo Bias in Decision Making," *Journal of Risk and Uncertainty*, 1988, *1*, 7–59]. The car-buying example is found in C. W. Park, S. Y. Jun, and D. J. MacInnis, "Choosing What I Want Versus Rejecting What I Don't Want: An Application of Decision Framing to Product Option Choice Decisions," *Journal of Marketing Research*, 2000, *37*, 187–202.

76   *Is there anyone* See J. Baron, *Thinking and Deciding* (New York: Cambridge University Press, 2000) for a systematic and thorough discussion of the psychology of decision making.

Chapter 4

80   *The alternative to maximizing* The distinction between maximizers and satisficers originated with Herbert Simon in the 1950s. See his "Rational Choice and the Structure of the Environment," *Psychological Review*, 1956, *63*, 129–138; and *Models of Man, Social and Rational* (New York: Wiley, 1957).

81   *We came up with a* This research on maximizers and satisficers is described in detail in B. Schwartz, A. Ward, J. Monterosso, S. Lyubomirsky, K. White, and D. R. Lehman, "Maximizing versus Satisficing: Happiness Is a Matter of Choice," *Journal of Personality and Social Psychology*, 2002, *83*, 1178–1197.

82   *Maximization Scale* The research my colleagues and I did on maximizing

generated a good deal of interest, including a fair amount of criticism of our scale, with suggested alternatives. Our scale seems to consist of three distinct factors—high standards, difficulty making decisions, and tendency to seek alternatives. Critics of the scale pointed out that these three separate factors were not all related to such things as unhappiness and lack of optimism. Some critics offered alternative scales that seemed to measure just a single factor. Debate about this topic continues. The interested reader should consult some of the relevant papers. But be warned. The debate is very much an "academic debate," full of subtle distinctions and statistical quarrels. And at the moment, there is no agreement about either what *does* the Maximization Scale measure or what *should* a Maximization Scale measure. A few representative articles: D. L. Diab, M. A. Gillespie, and S. Highhouse, "Are Maximizers Really Unhappy? The Measurement of Maximizing Tendency," *Judgment and Decision Making*, 2008, *3*, 364–370; L. Lai, "Maximizing without Difficulty: A Modified Maximization Scale and Its Correlates," *Judgment and Decision Making*, 2010, *5*, 164–175; G. Y. Nenkov, M. Morrin, A. Ward, B. Schwartz, and J. Hulland, "A Short Form of the Maximization Scale: Factor Structure, Reliability and Validity Studies, "*Judgment and Decision Making*, 2008, *3*, 371–388; B. R. Turner, H. B. Rim, N. E. Betz, and T. E. Nygren, "The Maximization Inventory," *Judgment and Decision Making*, 2012, *7*, 48–60; S. Iyengar, R. E. Wells, and B. Schwartz, "Doing Better but Feeling Worse: Looking for the 'Best' Job Undermines Satisfaction," *Psychological Science*, 2006, *17*, 143–150.

84 *Lori Gottleib* L. Gottleib, *Marry Him: The Case for Settling for Mr. Good Enough* (New York: Dutton, 2010).

90 W. H. Huang and M. Zeelenberg, "Investor Regret: The Role of Expectation in Comparing What Is to What Might Have Been." *Judgment and Decision Making*, 2012, *7*, 441–451.

98 *There's another dimension* See R. Frank, *Choosing the Right Pond* (New York: Oxford University Press, 1985); F. Hirsch, *Social Limits to Growth* (Cambridge, MA: Harvard University Press, 1976); and R. Frank and P. Cook, *The Winner-Take-All Society* (New York, Free Press, 1985).

Chapter 5

104 *Over two centuries ago* Adam Smith's *The Wealth of Nations* was published in 1776. For a more recent, impassioned defense of freedom of choice in the market, see M. Friedman and R. Friedman, *Free to Choose* (New York: Harcourt Brace, 1980). For more critical views of the market and its miracles, see my *The Battle for Human Nature* (New York: W. W. Norton, 1986) and *The Costs of Living* (Philadelphia: XLibris, 2001).

105 *An illustration of* The story about the political scientists appears in R. Kuttner, *Everything for Sale* (New York: Knopf, 1996).

105 *Every choice we make* On choice and autonomy, see R. E. Lane, *The Loss of Happiness in Market Democracies* (New Haven, CT: Yale University Press, 2000), pp. 231–234. See also Gerald Dworkin, *The Theory and Practice of Autonomy* (New York: Cambridge University Press, 1988).

106 *In the 1960s* The research literature on learned helplessness is vast. For excellent summary discussions of the phenomenon and its consequences, see M. E. P. Seligman, *Helplessness: On Depression, Development, and Death* (San Francisco: W. H. Freeman, 1975), and C. Peterson, S. F. Maier, and M. E. P. Seligman, *Learned Helplessness: A Theory for the Age of Personal Control* (New York: Oxford University Press, 1993).

107 *however, pollster Louis Harris* L. Harris, *Inside America* (New York: Random House, 1987). This work is discussed in Lane, p. 29.

109 *In one study* The study of pen purchasing is A. M. Shah and G. Wolford, "Buying Behavior as a Parametric Variation of Number of Choices," *Psychological Science*, 2007, *18*, 369–370. The relation between choice set size and purchase has the shape that psychologists call an "inverted-U." Purchase goes up as options increase until it reaches a maximum, and then it goes down. Adam Grant and I published a paper that suggests this inverted-U may be a commonplace in psychological research and not a rarity. See A. Grant and B. Schwartz, "Too Much of a Good Thing: The Challenge and Opportunity of the Inverted-U," *Perspectives on Psychological Science*, 2011, *6*, 61–76.

109 *In addition, there is evidence* For evidence that when people know what they want, more choice is better than less, see A. Chernev, "Product Assortment and Individual Decision Processes," *Journal of Personality and Social Psychology*, 2003, *85*, 151–162.

109 *Researchers* A central figure in the study of happiness is psychologist

Ed Diener. For a sample of Diener's work on the topic, see E. Diener, "Subjective Well-Being: The Science of Happiness and a Proposal for a National Index," *American Psychologist*, 2000, *55*, 34–43; E. Diener, M. Diener, and C. Diener, "Factors Predicting the Subjective Well-Being of Nations," *Journal of Personality and Social Psychology*, 1995, *69*, 851–864; E. Diener and E. M. Suh (eds.), *Subjective Well-Being Across Cultures* (Cambridge, MA: MIT Press, 2001); E. Diener, E. M. Suh, R. E. Lucas, and H. L. Smith, "Subjective Well-Being: Three Decades of Progress." *Psychological Bulletin*, 1999, *125*, 276–302; E. Diener and R. Biswas-Diener, *Happiness* (New York: Blackwell, 2008). See also S. Lyubomirsky, "Why Are Some People Happier Than Others?" *American Psychologist*, 2001, *56*, 239–249; S. Lyubomirsky, *The How of Happiness* (New York: Penguin, 2007); M. E. P. Seligman, *Flourish* (New York: Free Press, 2011).

109   *Here is an example* E. Diener, R. A. Emmons, R. J. Larson, and S. Griffin, "The Satisfaction with Life Scale," *Journal of Personality Assessment*, 1985, *49*, 71–75.

111   *And one of the things* The relation between wealth and happiness continues to be a topic of hot debate, with researchers disagreeing about what to measure and how to measure it and thus coming to different conclusions. Though the story I tell in the book, that wealth makes a big difference to happiness below subsistence but a small one thereafter, was the accepted view for many years, a recent analysis by D. Kahneman and A. Deaton, using data from many thousands of respondents, suggests that whereas what they call emotional well-being grows with income but levels off at incomes of about $75,000 in the U.S., positive life evaluation continues to rise as incomes rise. See D. Kahneman and A. Deaton, "High Income Improves Evaluation of Life but Not Emotional Well-Being," *Proceedings of the National Academy of Sciences*, 2010, *107*, 16489–16493.

111   *You find as many* For a wealth of information on differences in happiness across nations and across time, see R. Inglehart, *Modernization and Postmodernization: Cultural, Economic, and Political Changes in Societies* (Princeton, NJ: Princeton University Press, 1997); R. E. Lane, *The Loss of Happiness in Market Democracies* (New Haven, CT: Yale University Press, 2000); and D. G. Myers, *The American Paradox* (New Haven, CT: Yale University Press, 2000).

114 *But, as Lane* R. E. Lane, *The Loss of Happiness in Market Democracies,* Chapter 9. The quote is from p. 165.

114 *but we spend less time* See also R. D. Putnam, *Bowling Alone* (New York: Simon & Schuster, 2000) for a detailed account of the decreased social connectedness of modern American life along with some efforts to figure out its causes.

115 *As Lane writes* R. E. Lane (*The Loss of Happiness in Market Democracies*) reviews the evidence for the importance of close social relations in Chapters 5 and 6. The quote is from p. 108.

115 *Who has this kind of time?* I write about the time problem in *The Costs of Living: How Market Freedom Erodes the Best Things in Life* (Philadelphia: Xlibris, 2001). Sociologist Arlie Hochschild writes brilliantly about it in *The Time Bind: When Work Becomes Home and Home Becomes Work* (New York: Metropolitan, 1997).

116 *Economist and historian* A. O. Hirschman, *Exit, Voice, and Loyalty* (Cambridge, MA: Harvard University Press, 1970).

118 *These are what Cass Sunstein* C. R. Sunstein and E. Ullmann-Margalit, "Second-Order Decisions," in C. R. Sunstein (ed.), *Behavioral Law and Economics* (New York: Cambridge University Press, 2000), pp. 187–208.

119 *At the turn of* J. von Uexkull, "A Stroll Through the Worlds of Animals and Men," in C. H. Schiller (ed.), *Instinctive behavior* (New York: International Universities Press, 1954), pp. 3–59. The quote is on page 26.

120 *But powerful evidence* K. Berridge, "Pleasure, Pain, Desire, and Dread: Hidden Core Processes of Emotion," in D. Kahneman, E. Diener, and N. Schwarz (eds.), *Well-Being: The Foundations of Hedonic Psychology* (New York: Russell Sage Foundation, 1999), pp. 525–557.

Chapter 6

128 *The psychology of trade-offs* M. F. Luce, J. R. Bettman, and J. W. Payne, *Emotional Decisions: Tradeoff Difficulty and Coping in Consumer Choice* (Chicago: University of Chicago Press, 2001).

129 being forced to confront For illuminating discussions of how people handle trade-offs when they make choices, see A. Tversky, "Elimination by Aspects: A Theory of Choice," *Psychological Review,* 1972, *79,* 281–299; and J. W. Payne, J. R. Bettman, and E. J. Johnson, *The Adaptive Decision Maker* (Cambridge, England: Cambridge University Press, 1993).

130   *When researchers asked* A. Tversky and E. Shafir, "Choice under Conflict: The Dynamics of Deferred Decision," *Psychological Science*, 1992, *3*, 358–361.

132   *doctors were presented* D. A. Redelmeier and E. Shafir, "Medical Decision Making in Situations that Offer Multiple Alternatives," *Journal of the American Medical Association*, 1995, *273*, 302–305.

132   *Consider this scenario* E. Shafir, I. Simenson, and A. Tversky, "Reason-Based Choice," *Cognition*, 1993, *49*, 11–36.

134   *This was confirmed by* L. Brenner, Y. Rottenstreich, and S. Sood, "Comparison, Grouping, and Preference," *Psychological Science*, 1999, *10*, 225–229.

135   *We just don't want to* B. E. Kahn and J. Baron, "An Exploratory Study of Choice Rules Favored for High-Stakes Decisions," *Journal of Consumer Psychology*, 1995, *4*, 305–328.

135   *The emotional cost* For a discussion of how negative emotion affects thinking, see M. F. Luce, J. R. Bettman, and J. W. Payne, *Emotional Decisions: Tradeoff Difficulty and Coping in Consumer Choice* (Chicago: University of Chicago Press, 2001). For evidence on the role of positive emotion in medical decision making, see A. M. Isen, A. S. Rosenzweig, and M. J. Young, "The Influence of Positive Affect on Clinical Problem Solving," *Medical Decision Making*, 1991, *11*, 221–227. For evidence of the positive contribution to decision making in general made by positive emotion, see A. M. Isen, "Positive Affect and Decision Making." In M. Lewis and J. Haviland (Eds.), *Handbook of Emotion* (New York: Guilford Press, 1993, pp. 261–277), and B. E. Fredrickson, "What Good Are Positive Emotions?" *Review of General Psychology*, 1998, *2*, 300–319.

137   *in which two sets of participants* S. Iyengar and M. Lepper, "When Choice Is Demotivating: Can One Desire Too Much of a Good Thing?" *Journal of Personality and Social Psychology*, 2000, *79*, 995–1006.

141   *Even decisions as trivial* For a discussion of self-blame and self-esteem, see B. Weiner, "An Attributional Theory of Achievement Motivation and Emotion," *Psychological Review*, 1985, *92*, 548–573.

143   *their importance to the verbalizer* The jam study is from T. D. Wilson and J. S. Schooler, "Thinking Too Much: Introspection Can Reduce the Quality of Preferences and Decisions," *Journal of Personality and Social Psychology*, 1991, *60*, 181–192. The art poster study is from T. D. Wilson, D. J. Lisle, J. S. Schooler, S. D. Hodges, K. J. Klaren, and S. J. LaFleur, "Introspecting

About Reasons Can Reduce Post-Choice Satisfaction," *Personality and Social Psychology Bulletin*, 1993, *19*, 331–339. The dating study is from T. D. Wilson and D. Kraft, "Why Do I Love Thee? Effects of Repeated Introspections About a Dating Relationship on Attitudes Toward the Relationship," *Personality and Social Psychology Bulletin*, 1993, *19*, 409–418. Also see T. D. Wilson, D. S. Dunn, J. A. Bybee, D. B. Hyman, and J. A. Rotundo, "Effects of Analyzing Reasons on Attitude-Behavior Consistency," *Journal of Personality and Social Psychology*, 1984, *47*, 5–16. Also see J. McMackin and P. Slovic, "When Does Explicit Justification Impair Decision Making?" *Applied Cognitive Psychology*, 2000, *14*, 527–541. In this paper, the authors try to distinguish the kinds of decisions that are improved by giving reasons from the kinds of decisions that are impaired by giving reasons.

146 *The anguish and inertia* A. Robbins and A. Wilner, *Quarterlife Crisis: The Unique Challenges of Life in Your Twenties* (New York: Jeremy P. Tarcher/Putnam, 2001).

146 *as one young respondent* M. Daum, *My Misspent Youth* (New York: Grove/Atlantic, 2001). The quote appears in R. Marin, "Is This the Face of a Midlife Crisis?" *New York Times*, June 24, 2001, Section 9, pp. 1–2.

146 *acceptance or rejection* For some interesting evidence and discussion suggesting that basic "accept-reject," judgments have deep evolutionary and biological roots, see A. Damasio, *Descartes' Error: Emotion, Reason, and the Human Brain* (New York: G. P. Putnam, 1994); and R. B. Zajonc, "On the Primacy of Affect," *American Psychologist*, 1984, *39*, 117–123.

147 *As psychologist Susan Sugarman* S. Sugarman, "Choice and Freedom: Reflections and Observations Based Upon Human Development," [unpublished manuscript, 1999].

148 *Yes, but at a price* D. T. Gilbert and J. E. Ebert, "Decisions and Revisions: The Affective Forecasting of Changeable Outcomes," *Journal of Personality and Social Psychology*, 2002, *82*, 503–514.

Chapter 7

152 *Recall that when* B. Schwartz, A. Ward, J. Monterosso, S. Lyubomirsky, K. White, and D. R. Lehman, "Maximizing Versus Satisficing: Happiness Is a Matter of Choice," *Journal of Personality and Social Psychology*, 2002, *83*, 1178–1197.

152   *some circumstances are more likely* D. Kahneman and A. Tversky, "The Simulation Heuristic," in D. Kahneman, P. Slovic, and A. Tversky (eds.), *Judgment Under Uncertainty: Heuristics and Biases* (New York: Cambridge University Press, 1982).

153   *However, recent evidence* T. Gilovich and V. H. Medvec, "The Experience of Regret: What, When, and Why," *Psychological Review*, 1995, *102*, 379–395.

153   *Regret expert Marcel Zeelenberg* M. Zeelenberg, K. van den Bos, E. van Dijk, and R. Pieters, "The Inaction Effect in the Psychology of Regret," *Journal of Personality and Social Psychology*, 2002, *82*, 314–327.

154   *A second factor* D. Kahneman and A. Tversky, "The Simulation Heuristic," in D. Kahneman, P. Slovic, and A. Tversky (eds.), *Judgment Under Uncertainty: Heuristics and Biases* (New York: Cambridge University Press, 1982).

155   *Related to this "nearness"* V. H. Medvec, S. F. Madley, and T. Gilovich, "When Less Is More: Counterfactual Thinking and Satisfaction Among Olympic Athletes," *Journal of Personality and Social Psychology*, 1995, *69*, 603–610.

155   *But bad results make* T. Gilovich and V. H. Medvec, "The Temporal Pattern to the Experience of Regret," *Journal of Personality and Social Psychology*, 1994, *67*, 357–365; and M. Zeelenberg, W. W. van Dijk, and A. S. R. Manstead, "Reconsidering the Relation Between Regret and Responsibility," *Organizational Behavior and Human Decision Processes*, 1998, *74*, 254–272.

156   *Thinking about the world as it isn't* See N. J. Roese, "Counterfactual Thinking," *Psychological Bulletin*, 1997, *21*, 133–148.

157   *may not be able to arrest* For evidence in support of a relation between regret and depression, see L. Lecci, M. A. Okun, and P. Karoly, "Life Regrets and Current Goals as Predictors of Psychological Adjustment," *Journal of Personality and Social Psychology*, 1994, *66*, 731–741.

158   *There is an important* On upward and downward counterfactuals, see N. J. Roese, "Counterfactual Thinking," *Psychological Bulletin*, 1997, *21*, 133–148. Roese is perhaps the world's leading expert on the psychological effects of counterfactual thinking. See N. J. Roese and A. Summerville, "What We Regret Most . . . And Why," *Personality and Social Psychology Bulletin*, 2005, *31*, 1273–1285 and K. Epstein and N. J. Roese, "The Functional Theory of Counterfactual Thinking," *Personality and Social Psychology Review*, 2008, *12*, 168–192.

162 *But another reason for* M. Zeelenberg and J. Beattie, "Consequences of Regret Aversion 2: Additional Evidence for Effects of Feedback on Decision Making," *Organizational Behavior and Human Decision Processes,* 1997, *72,* 63–78. There are other studies reporting similar results. See M. Zeelenberg, J. Beattie, J. van der Pligt, and N. K. de Vries, "Consequences of Regret Aversion: Effects of Feedback on Risky Decision Making," *Organizational Behavior and Human Decision Processes,* 1996, *65,* 148–158; I. Ritov, "Probability of Regret: Anticipation of Uncertainty Resolution in Choice," *Organizational Behavior and Human Decision Processes,* 1996, *66,* 228–236; and R. P. Larrick and T. L. Boles, "Avoiding Regret in Decisions with Feedback: A Negotiation Example," *Organizational Behavior and Human Decision Processes,* 1995, *63,* 87–97.

163 *what is called* inaction inertia O. E. Tykocinski and T .S. Pittman, "The Consequences of Doing Nothing: Inaction Inertia as Avoidance of Anticipated Counterfactual Regret, *Journal of Personality and Social Psychology,* 1998, *75,* 607–616.

164 *what are called* sunk costs H. R. Arkes and C. Blumer, "The Psychology of Sunk Cost," *Organizational Behavior and Human Decision Processes,* 1985, *35,* 124–140.

165 *of the business or of the player* On basketball players, see B. M. Staw and H. Hoang, "Sunk Costs in the NBA: Why Draft Order Affects Playing Time and Survival in Professional Basketball," *Administrative Science Quarterly,* 1995, *40,* 474–493. For business expansion, see A. M. McCarthy, F. D. Schoorman, and A. C. Cooper, "Reinvestment Decisions by Entrepreneurs: Rational Decision-Making or Escalation of Commitment?" *Decision Sciences,* 1993, *8,* 9–24.

166 *why did the United States* B. M. Staw, "Knee Deep in the Big Muddy: A Study of Escalating Commitment to a Chosen Course of Action," *Organizational Behavior and Human Performance,* 1976, *16,* 27–44.

168 *sums it up this way* J. Landman, *Regret: The Persistence of the Possible* (New York: Oxford University Press, 1993, p. 184.) For more on this point, see also I. Janis and L. Mann, *Decision Making: A Psychological Analysis of Conflict, Choice, and Commitment* (New York: Free Press, 1977), pp. 219–242; and D. Bell, "Regret in Decision Making Under Uncertainty," *Operations Research,* 1982, *30,* 961–981.

169 *And to acknowledge the fact* My discussion of the benefits of regret borrows

substantially from J. Landman, *Regret: The Persistence of the Possible* (New York: Oxford University Press, 1993).

Chapter 8

173   *In 1973* The data about car air conditioners are in D. G. Myers, *The American Paradox* (New Haven, CT: Yale University Press, 2000).

173   *Hedonic adaptation can be* For a discussion of the two different types of adaptation, and of adaptation in general, see S. Frederick and G. Loewenstein, "Hedonic Adaptation," in D. Kahneman, E. Diener, and N. Schwarz (eds.), *Well-Being: The Foundations of Hedonic Psychology* (New York: Russell Sage, 1999), pp. 302–329. Two of the classic theoretical accounts of adaptation are H. Helson, *Adaptation-Level Theory: An Experimental and Systematic Approach to Behavior* (New York: Harper and Row, 1964), and A. Parducci, *Happiness, Pleasure, and Judgment: The Contextual Theory and Its Applications* (Hove, England: Erlbaum, 1995).

174   *In what is perhaps* P. Brickman, D. Coates, and R. Janoff-Bulman, "Lottery Winners and Accident Victims: Is Happiness Relative?" *Journal of Personality and Social Psychology*, 1978, *36*, 917–927.

176   *Twenty-five years ago* T. Scitovsky, *The Joyless Economy* (New York: Oxford University Press, 1976). For an account of how pleasure becomes comfort, see R. Solomon, "The Opponent Process Theory of Motivation," *American Psychologist*, 1980, *35*, 691–712.

176   *disappointment with consumption increases* On adaptation and durable goods, see A. O. Hirschman, *Shifting Involvements* (Princeton, NJ: Princeton University Press, 1982).

176   *the* hedonic treadmill P. Brickman and D. Campbell, "Hedonic Relativism and Planning the Good Society," in M. H. Appley (ed.), *Adaptation Level Theory: A Symposium* (New York: Academic Press, 1971), pp. 287–302.

177   *the* satisfaction treadmill D. Kahneman, "Objective Happiness," in D. Kahneman, E. Diener, and N. Schwarz (eds.), *Well-Being: The Foundations of Hedonic Psychology* (New York: Russell Sage, 1999), pp. 3–25.

177   *human beings are remarkably bad* For a general review of how inaccurate people are at predicting future feelings, see G. Loewenstein and D. Schkade,

"Wouldn't It Be Nice? Predicting Future Feelings," in D. Kahneman, E. Diener, and N. Schwarz (eds.), *Well-Being: The Foundations of Hedonic Psychology* (New York: Russell Sage, 1999), pp. 85–105.

178   *college students in the Midwest* D. Schkade and D. Kahneman, "Does Living in California Make People Happy? A Focusing Illusion in Judgments of Life Satisfaction," *Psychological Science*, 1998, *9*, 340–346.

178   *respondents were asked to predict* G. Loewenstein and S. Frederick, "Predicting Reactions to Environmental Change," in M. Bazerman, D. Messick, A. Tenbrunsel, and K. Wade-Benzoni (eds.), *Environment, Ethics, and Behavior* (San Francisco: New Lexington Press, 1997), pp. 52–72. Psychologists Dan Gilbert and Timothy Wilson discuss people's failures to anticipate adaptation as failures of "affective forecasting," and they have done many impressive studies of this phenomenon. It is important to realize that every decision we make is a prediction—about how satisfying the results of that decision will be. And if we fail to anticipate adaptation, we will consistently mispredict satisfaction. See D. Gilbert, *Stumbling on Happiness* (New York: Knopf, 2006).

179   *young college professors* D. T. Gilbert, E. C. Pinel, T. D. Wilson, S. J. Blumberg, and T. P. Whatley, "Immune Neglect: A Source of Durability Bias in Affective Forecasting," *Journal of Personality and Social Psychology*, 1998, *75*, 617–638.

180   *Elderly patients suffering* On the elderly, see R. A. Pearlman and R. F. Uhlmann, "Quality of Life in Chronic Diseases: Perceptions of Elderly Patients," *Journal of Gerontology*, 1988, *43*, M25–30. For a discussion of the importance of predicting future feelings, see J. March, "Bounded Rationality, Ambiguity, and the Engineering of Choice," *Bell Journal of Economics*, 1978, *9*, 587–608.

183   *experience and express gratitude* The person most responsible for recent research on gratitude is psychologist Robert Emmons. See M. E. McCullough, S. D. Kilpatrick, R. A. Emmons, and D. B. Larson, "Is Gratitude a Moral Affect?" *Psychological Bulletin*, 2001, *127*, 249–266; R. A. Emmons and C. A. Crumpler, "Gratitude as a Human Strength: Appraising the Evidence," *Journal of Social and Clinical Psychology*, 2000, *19*, 56–69; and R. A. Emmons and M. E. McCullough, "Counting Blessings Versus Burdens: An Experimental Investigation of Gratitude and Subjective Well-Being," *Journal of Personality and Social Psychology*, 2003, *84*, 377–389.

Chapter 9

185 *Comparisons are* R. E. Lane discusses the relative nature of evaluation in *The Loss of Happiness in Market Democracies* (New Haven, CT: Yale University Press, 2000).

187 *Michalos found that* A. Michalos, "Job Satisfaction, Marital Satisfaction, and the Quality of Life," in F. M. Andrews (ed.), *Research on the Quality of Life* (Ann Arbor, MI: Institute for Social Research, 1986), p. 75.

188 *What the theory claims* The classic paper on framing is D. Kahneman and A. Tversky, "Choices, Values, and Frames," *American Psychologist*, 1984, *39*, 341–350. Many other examples are collected in D. Kahneman and A. Tversky (eds.), *Choices, Values, and Frames* (New York: Cambridge University Press, 2000).

189 *In the fall of 1999* For the poll, see T. Lewin, "It's a Hard Life (or Not)," *New York Times*, November 11, 1999, p. A32. On fear of falling, see B. Ehrenreich, *Fear of Falling* (New York: HarperCollins, 1990).

189 *Affluent households* Psychologist Suniya Luthar has spent years studying what might be called the "pathology of affluence" among American teenagers. She finds that upper-middle-class teenagers are at least as high a risk for substance abuse and various forms of psychological disturbance (depression, anxiety, eating disorders) as lower-class youth. To a large degree, Luthar traces the problem to high expectations, by parents, teachers, and the kids themselves, that every aspect of their lives will be perfect. For a recent review of her work, see S. Luthar, S. H. Barkin, and E. J. Crossman, " 'I Can, Therefore I Must': Fragility in the Upper-Middle Class," *Development and Psychopathology*, 2013, *25*, 1529–1549.

190 *anxiety about health* R. Porter, *The Greatest Benefit to Mankind: A Medical History of Humanity* (New York: W. W. Norton, 1998).

192 *Social comparison provides* Two useful compendia of research on social comparison are B. Buunk and F. Gibbons (eds.), *Health, Coping, and Well-Being: Perspectives from Social Comparison Theory* (Mahwah, NJ: Erlbaum, 1997); and J. M. Suls and T. A. Willis (eds.), *Social Comparison: Contemporary Theory and Research* (Mahwah, NJ: Erlbaum, 1991). In addition to these compendia, see L. G. Aspinwall and S. E. Taylor, "Effects of Social Comparison Direction, Threat, and Self-Esteem on Affect, Self-Evaluation, and Expected Success," *Journal of Personality and*

Social Psychology, 1993, *64*, 708–722; F. X. Gibbons and M. Gerrard, "Effects of Upward and Downward Social Comparison on Mood States," *Journal of Social and Clinical Psychology*, 1993, *8*, 14–31; S. Lyubomirsky, K. L. Tucker, and F. Kasri, "Responses to Hedonically-Conflicting Social Comparisons: Comparing Happy and Unhappy People," *European Journal of Social Psychology*, 2001, *31*, 1–25; and S. E. Taylor, "Adjustment to Threatening Events," *American Psychologist*, 1983, *38*, 1161–1173.

192 *But it needn't be this way* B. P. Buunk, R. L. Collins, G. A. Dakof, S. E. Taylor, and N. W. Van Yperen, "The Affective Consequences of Social Comparison: Either Direction Has Its Ups and Downs," *Journal of Personality and Social Psychology*, 1992, *59*, 1238–1249.

194 *big fish in our own ponds* R. Frank, *Choosing the Right Pond* (New York: Oxford University Press, 1985). See also his more recent *Luxury Fever* (New York: Free Press, 1999), in which he argues that much of the modern American taste for excess is driven by social comparison.

194 *better* relative *position* S. J. Solnick and D. Hemenway, "Is More Always Better? A Survey on Positional Concerns," *Journal of Economic Behavior and Organization*, 1998, *37*, 373–383.

195 *explosion of telecommunications* For a discussion of how modern telecommunications as well as advertising has changed the relevant comparison group for most people, see M. L. Richins, "Social Comparison, Advertising, and Consumer Discontent," *American Behavioral Scientist*, 1995, *38*, 593–607; and S. J. Hoch and G. F. Loewenstein, "Time-Inconsistent Preferences and Consumer Self-Control," *Journal of Consumer Research*, 1991, *17*, 492–507.

197 *economist Fred Hirsch* F. Hirsch, *Social Limits to Growth* (Cambridge, MA: Harvard University Press, 1976).

198 *We might all agree* On what positional competition does to adolescents, see the Luthar, Barkin, and Crossman article mentioned above. For a way out of the positional competition problem when it comes to admission to selective colleges and universities, see B. Schwartz, "Top Colleges Should Select Randomly from a Pool of 'Good Enough,'" *Chronicle of Higher Education*, February 25, 2005, B20–B25.

198 *crowded football stadium* The football stadium analogy comes from T. C. Schelling, *Micromotives and Macrobehavior* (New York: W. W. Norton, 1978).

198 *To choose not to run* See R. E. Lane, *The Loss of Happiness in Market*

Democracies (New Haven, CT: Yale University Press, 2000), Chapter 17, for a discussion of the social welfare implications of social comparison processes.

199   *developed a questionnaire* For the Subjective Happiness Scale, see S. Lyubomirsky and H. S. Lepper, "A Measure of Subjective Happiness: Preliminary Reliability and Construct Validation," *Social Indicators Research*, 1999, *46*, 137–155. For the studies of social comparison, see S. Lyubomirsky and L. Ross, "Hedonic Consequences of Social Comparison: A Contrast of Happy and Unhappy People," *Journal of Personality and Social Psychology*, 1997, *73*, 1141–1157; S. Lyubomirsky and L. Ross, "Changes in Attractiveness of Elected, Rejected, and Precluded Alternatives: A Comparison of Happy and Unhappy Individuals," *Journal of Personality and Social Psychology*, 1999, *76*, 988–1007; and S. Lyubomirsky, K. L. Tucker, and F. Kasri, "Responses to Hedonically-Conflicting Social Comparisons: Comparing Happy and Unhappy People," *European Journal of Social Psychology*, 2001, *31*, 1–25.

202   *we took participants* This research on maximizers and satisficers is described in detail in B. Schwartz, A. Ward, J. Monterosso, S. Lyubomirsky, K. White, and D. R. Lehman, "Maximizing versus Satisficing: When Happiness Is a Matter of Choice," *Journal of Personality and Social Psychology*, 2002, *83*, 1178–1197.

Chapter 10

205   *The American "happiness quotient"* See the references in Chapter 5, and for summaries, R. E. Lane, *The Loss of Happiness in Market Democracies* (New Haven, CT: Yale University Press, 2000), and D. Myers, *The American Paradox* (New Haven, CT: Yale University Press, 2000).

206   *prevalence of clinical depression* M. E. P. Seligman, *Learned Helplessness: On Depression, Development, and Death* (San Francisco: W. H. Freeman, 1975). See also his *Learned Optimism: The Skill to Conquer Life's Obstacles, Large and Small* (New York: Random House, 1991), and D. L. Rosenhan and M. E. P. Seligman, *Abnormal Psychology* (New York: W. W. Norton, 1995).

207   *are significantly depressed* The statistics on the consequences of depression are from Lane, p. 329.

207   *discovery of "learned helplessness"* See J. B. Overmier and M. E. P. Seligman, "Effects of Inescapable Shock upon Subsequent Escape and Avoidance

Behavior, *Journal of Comparative and Physiological Psychology*, 1967, *63*, 23–33; M. E. P. Seligman and S. F. Maier, "Failure to Escape Traumatic Shock," *Journal of Experimental Psychology*, 1967, *74*, 1–9; and S. F. Maier and M. E. P. Seligman, "Learned Helplessness: Theory and Evidence," *Journal of Experimental Psychology: General*, 1976, *105*, 3–46.

208 *more than forty years ago* J. S. Watson, "Memory and 'Contingency Analysis' in Infant Learning," *Merrill-Palmer Quarterly*, 1967, *12*, 139–152; J. S. Watson, "Cognitive-Perceptual Development in Infancy: Setting for the Seventies," *Merrill-Palmer Quarterly*, 1971, *17*, 139–152.

209 *opposite end of the life cycle* E. Langer and J. Rodin, "The Effects of Choice and Enhanced Personal Responsibility for the Aged: A Field Experiment in an Institutional Setting," *Journal of Personality and Social Psychology*, 1976, *34*, 191–198; and J. Rodin and E. Langer, "Long-Term Effects of a Control-Relevant Intervention with the Institutionalized Aged," *Journal of Personality and Social Psychology*, 1977, *35*, 897–902.

210 *control over one's life matters* R. E. Lane provides a detailed discussion of the prominence given to personal control, or self-determination, in the history of Western philosophy and democratic theory. See *The Loss of Happiness in Market Democracies*, Chapter 13. As should be clear both from the title of Lane's book and from the title of that chapter ("The Pain of Self-Determination in Democracy"), the general thrust of his argument is that excessive aspiration to self-determination brings suffering in its wake.

210 *revised theory of helplessness* L. Y. Abramson, M. E. P. Seligman, and J. Teasdale, "Learned Helplessness in Humans: Critique and Reformulation," *Journal of Abnormal Psychology*, 1978, *87*, 32–48.

212 *yielded impressive results* For a review of tests of the role of attributional style in helplessness-induced depression, see C. Peterson and M. E. P. Seligman, "Causal Explanations as a Risk Factor for Depression: Theory and Evidence," *Psychological Review*, 1984, *91*, 347–374. For another very influential theory of depression related to helplessness theory, see A. T. Beck, *Depression: Clinical, Experimental, and Theoretical Aspects* (New York: Hoeber, 1967); A. T. Beck, *The Diagnosis and Management of Depression* (Philadelphia, University of Pennsylvania Press, 1971); and A. T. Beck, *Cognitive Therapy and Emotional Disorders* (New York: International Universities Press, 1976).

212 *causal explanations that are accurate* There are studies that suggest that

taking responsibility for bad events can be helpful psychologically, at least under some circumstances. See R. Janoff-Bulman and C. Wortman, "Attributions of Blame and Coping in the 'Real World': Severe Accident Victims React to Their Lot," *Journal of Personality and Social Psychology*, 1977, *35*, 351–363; H. Tennen and G. Affleck, "Blaming Others for Threatening Events," *Psychological Bulletin*, 1990, *107*, 209–232.

213 *Instead, we see explosive* For current statistics on the incidence of depression and other mood disorders, see statistics compiled by the National Institute of Mental Health [http://www.nimh.nih.gov/health/statistics/index.shtml]

213 *is also on the rise* For statistical information on depression and on suicide see D. L. Rosenhan and M. E. P. Seligman, *Abnormal Psychology* (New York: W. W. Norton, 1995); R. E. Lane, *The Loss of Happiness in Market Democracies* (New Haven, CT: Yale University Press, 2000); American Psychiatric Association, *Diagnostic and Statistical Manual of Mental Disorders*, 4th ed. (Washington, DC: American Psychiatric Association, 1994); J. Angst, "The Epidemiology of Depressive Disorders," *European Neuropsychopharmacology*, 1995, *5*, 95–98; G. L. Klerman, P. W. Lavori, J. Rice, T. Reich, J. Endicott, N. C. Andreasen, M. Keller, and R. M. A. Hirschfeld, "Birth Cohort Trends in Rates of Major Depressive Disorder: A Study of Relatives of Patients with Affective Disorder," *Archives of General Psychiatry*, 1985, *42*, 689–693; and G. L. Klerman and M. M. Weissman, "Increasing Rates of Depression," *Journal of the American Medical Association*, 1989, *261*, 2229–2235; and UNICEF, *The Progress of Nations* (New York: United Nations, 1993).

214 *to these unrealistic expectations* On the importance of expectations to assessments of success and failure, see B. A. Mellars, A. Schwartz, K. Ho, and I. Ritov, "Decision Affect Theory: Emotional Reactions to the Outcomes of Risky Actions," *Psychological Science*, 1997, *8*, 423–429; B. Mellars and A. P. McGraw, "Anticipated Emotions as Guides to Choice," *Current Directions in Psychological Science*, 2001, *10*, 210–214; and J. A. Shepperd and J. K. McNulty, "The Affective Consequences of Expected and Unexpected Outcomes," *Psychological Science*, 2002, *13*, 85–88.

216 *social connection in contemporary life* R. D. Putnam, *Bowling Alone* (New York: Simon and Schuster, 2000). For data on rates of depression and other psychopathology among the Amish, see J. A. Egeland and

A. M. Hostetter, "Amish Study, I: Affective Disorders Among the Amish, 1976–1980," *American Journal of Psychiatry*, 1983, *140*, 56–61.

217 *body shape and body weight* M. E. P. Seligman, *What You Can Change and What You Can't* (New York: Knopf, 1993). See also D. L. Rosenhan and M. E. P. Seligman, *Abnormal Psychology* (New York: W. W. Norton, 1995) for a discussion of culture, ideal weight, and depression.

218 *ripe for depression* B. Schwartz, A. Ward, J. Monterosso, S. Lyubomirsky, K. White, and D. R. Lehman, "Maximizing versus Satisficing: Happiness Is a Matter of Choice," *Journal of Personality and Social Psychology*, 2002, *83*, 1178–1197; and J. A. Gillham, A. Ward, and B. Schwartz, "Maximizing and Depressed Mood in College Students and Young Adolescents," manuscript in preparation.

219 *highest suicide rates* See R. Eckersley and K. Dear, "Cultural Correlates of Youth Suicide," *Social Science and Medicine*, 2002, *55*, 1891–1904; and R. Eckersley, "Culture, Health, and Well-Being," in R. Eckersley, J. Dixon, and B. Douglas (eds.), *The Social Origins of Health and Well-Being* (Cambridge, England: Cambridge University Press, 2002), pp. 51–70. Eckersley's approach to the determinants of suicide may be seen as a modern development of the classic ideas of sociologist Emile Durkheim. See E. Durkheim, *Suicide: A Study in Sociology* (London: Routledge and Kegan Paul, 1970; originally published in 1897).

219 *refers to as* hedonic lag R. E. Lane, *The Loss of Happiness in Market Democracies* (New Haven, CT: Yale University Press, 2000). The quote is from p. 131.

Index

Page numbers in *italics* refer to illustrations.

Permissions

Pp. 82–83. The *Maximization Scale* is adapted from "Maximizing versus Satisficing: Happiness Is a Matter of Choice" by B. Schwartz, A. Ward, J. Monterosso, S. Lyubomirsky, K. White, and D. R. Lehman, *Journal of Personality and Social Psychology*, 2002, *83*, 1178–1197. Copyright 2002 by the American Psychological Association. Adapted with permission.

P. 90. The *Regret Scale* is adapted from "Maximizing versus Satisficing: Happiness Is a Matter of Choice" by B. Schwartz, A. Ward, J. Monterosso, S. Lyubomirsky, K. White, and D. R. Lehman, *Journal of Personality and Social Psychology*, 2002, *83*, 1178–1197. Copyright 2002 by the American Psychological Association. Adapted with permission.

P. 110. The *Satisfaction with Life Scale:* E. Diener, R. A. Emmons, R. J. Larson, and S. Griffin. *Journal of Personality Assessment,* 1985, *49*, 71–75. Reprinted with permission from Lawrence Erlbaum Associates.

P. 200. The *Subjective Happiness Scale.* S. Lyubomirsky and H. S. Lepper, "A Measure of Subjective Happiness: Preliminary Reliability and Construct Validation." *Social Indicators Research,* 1999, *46*, 137–155. Reprinted with kind permission of Kluwer Academic Publishers.